HODDEL STREET

The Ambush and the Tragedy

Peter Haddow

Published by Strategic Australia Pty Ltd
Melbourne Victoria Australia

© Peter Haddow

This publication is copyright. Apart from any use as permitted under the Copyright Act 1968, no part may be reproduced by any process without prior written permission from the publisher.
Requests and inquiries concerning reproduction should be addressed to
Mr Denis Moriarty
Managing Director
Strategic Australia Pty Ltd
PO Box 2444
Fitzroy Business Centre
Fitzroy 3065 Victoria Australia.

Haddow, Peter
 Hoddle Street : the ambush and the tragedy

ISBN 0 9586092 0 9

1. Hoddle Street Massacre, Melbourne 1987. 2. Mass murder
 -   Victoria. 1. Title.

364.1523099451

Cover Design, Andrew Bond

First published December 1998

Contents

	Page
All the Nuffies	15
The Killing Zone	33
Closing In	119
The Investigation	147
The Aftermath	193
Julian Knight	253

ACKNOWLEDGEMENTS

This book could not have been written without the assistance and encouragement of a large number of people. It is impossible to list everyone who has assisted me over the past five years but I would generally like to thank members of the Victoria Police, the Victorian Ambulance Service, the Office of Corrections, the State Forensic Science Laboratory, and the Office of the State Coroner; former and serving members of the Australian Army including the Army Reserve; various school teachers, the State Library and *The Age* library. I would particularly like to thank those survivors and their families who gave so much of their time and without whose cooperation the book would not have been written.

There are also the many people who spoke to me on a confidential basis whose names I cannot include but whose input was invaluable.

I would also like to thank each of the following people for their help and encouragement. Stavros, Richard Tonkin, Ric Burtan, Steve James, Merrianne Sinclair, Gerard Wright, David Neale, Glenda James, Robert Lang, Colleen Sweet, Janine Fellowes, John Powers, Steve Judd, Sally Webster, Judith Rodriquez, John Curran, Jane Munday, Fred Johansen, Greg Roberts, Margaret Schafferius, Lisa McCune, Harry Stevens, Kathy Stevens, Lorraine Coleman, Bill and Hannelore Cook, Alan Brown, Freda Rowe, Serge Zarconi, Ria McMahon, Megan Billington, Bruce Piper, Gary Thompson, Mary Toohey, Simon Brown-Greaves, Doug Trapnell, Liesl Trapnell, Piers Hobson, Rod Chandler and Ysabelle Hobson.

I would particularly like to thank my family for their unswerving belief, and, most of all, my wife for her support and understanding.
Special thanks to Louis De Vries

The photographic credits relate to the numbered photos in this book.

1. Val Corrigan; 2. *The Age*; 3. Freda Rowe; 4. Susan Rodaughan; 5. Mary Toohey; 6. Christos Papaioannou; 7. Bill and June Stanton; 8. Herald Sun; 10. Victoria Police; 11. Victoria Police; 12. Victoria Police; 15. Victoria Police; 16. Victoria Police; 17. Victoria Police; 18. Herald Sun; 19. Dianne Fitzpatrick; 20. Herald Sun; 22. Victoria Police; 23. Victoria Police; 26. Victoria Police; 28. Victoria Police; 30. Victoria Police; 31. Victoria Police; 36. Victoria Police; 37. Victoria Police; 40. Victoria Police; 41. Victoria Police; 49. Victoria Police.

FOREWORD

It is less than three years since the mass murders in Dunblane in Scotland and Port Arthur in Tasmania. These incidents caused shock, dismay and the worldwide question "Why?" While the 1987 mass murder in Hoddle Street, Clifton Hill, preceded those at Dunblane and Port Arthur by almost ten years, the effects were, and continue to be, the same.

About a year after Hoddle Street I was walking with another police officer in a Fitzroy street when a car backfired. The police officer threw himself up against the locked door of a hotel, and as I helped him back to his feet, I saw that his face and shirt were saturated with sweat. Seeing his reactions, and believing that the real story of the Hoddle Street ambush and the tragedy that followed had not been told, I decided to tell it.

As a serving police officer at the time of the Hoddle Street mass murders I knew many of the police who were involved in the incident. I saw a change in them and I saw the effects of the incident on police in general. Officers became less blasé; they carried extra bullets; those who usually did not wear firearms now carried them. Some even carried a knife at their ankle. No call was treated as a likely hoax. Even children playing with toy guns with their dad along the Merri Creek were investigated.

Among the police who had been at Hoddle Street were some who had previously been critical of others who had been involved in major traumatic incidents such as the Russell Street bombing on 27 March 1986. There was a perception that it was a sign of weakness to continue to be affected by the trauma of being involved in a violent incident; that if you sought psychological or psychiatric help you were weak. There was a change of attitude from some towards those who had been in such incidents; a more compassionate and understanding change.

At the same time, however, there was a lack of understanding from other police, including those who had a lot of operational experience (and should have known better). It was not unusual to hear someone remark that, "He/she should be over it by now." This seems to be the general feeling towards the victims as well. Like characters from some action film, they should be back to normal the next day. In an attempt to make clear that this does not happen, either physically or psychologically, I have described the victims' injuries in some detail. Hopefully, the families of the deceased will understand. While people remain ignorant of their plight they will continue to be thought of as having experienced something minor in their lives.

In 1992 I contacted John Delahunty, Ralph Lockman and Graham Kent and discussed my intention. It was never my plan to make the book Julian Knight's story, however I was interested in getting his perspective. Initially I corresponded with him, holding back my police background, believing I should reveal it in person. The opportunity to do so never arrived as he declined to speak to me when I visited him at Pentridge. Someone else had told him before I had the chance. However, I was not concerned, as he was not to be the main focus, and there were documents on public record and people who knew him who were prepared to speak about him.

After gathering as much factual information as possible, I contacted people who were directly or indirectly involved. I spoke to more than 300 people, some for several lengthy sessions. This was the most harrowing part of the whole process. To witness men and women break down and cry is something that will always haunt me. At one point the book was put away and no work was done on it for over six months while I wondered whether it was worth continuing. I was particularly affected when one interview resulted in a person having a breakdown and being unable to return to work. I had brought to the surface repressed feelings where a time bomb was waiting to explode.

However, after a break, I returned to the book when I realised that by not completing it I would have let down everyone who had given me their time and who believed in the project. It was a difficult book to research with many interviewees' emotions being exposed again after so long. There were people who had refused other approaches but had agreed to co–operate with me; these people could not be let down. I had witnessed their tears and their grief, and their story had to be told. With encouragement from these and other people I persevered.

The book contains three key sections. The first section, All The Nuffies, and others following are a reconstruction of the incident through interviews, transcripts, police statements and newspaper articles. Then comes The Aftermath, which explores the feelings of many who were involved in some way and who have never really recovered. There is a constant thread in these stories. Everyone tells of the difficulty of coming to terms with what happened; trying to go on while dealing with sleeplessness and nightmares and anxiety attacks and depression. Of journalists waiting outside their homes all hours of the day and night. Of constant telephone calls. Of funerals being photographed and filmed, their private expressions of grief being shown at length. Of having their feelings trivialised in sensationalist prose. Of having to leave their homes to escape the man or woman with a microphone or a pen or a camera. Of an hour–long interview reduced on television to a ten-second 'grab'.

Most of the victims and their families abhor reading anything about Julian Knight, particularly his opinions on matters ranging from firearms to how life had been unkind to him. His sentence was felt to be inadequate by most and the thought that he will be free again produces a great deal of anger, and a lack of faith in the criminal justice system. This was particularly evident in those who lost a member of their family or came close to losing their own life. It is tragic that, ten years later, many survivors of Hoddle Street live in fortresses they call home. They trust few people, and their lives have been altered forever.

Not a day passes without some reflection on 9 August 1987.

The victims and their families and friends see Knight as a person who craves publicity and wants to be noticed. Most of them expressed the view that he should have no voice at all.

The third section of this book looks at Julian Knight: his background; the court case concerning Hoddle Street; and his experience in jail. A number of his friends and acquaintances declined to assist because they did not have his permission to speak to me. However there was a significant number of friends, acquaintances and others who did not seek his permission and have assisted greatly. Members of his family were not approached although it was my original intention to do so. They are just as much victims of Julian Knight as those he murdered and attempted to murder.

Among the police who were at the incident there seems to be universal disappointment that their employer, the Victoria Police, has not recognised everyone who put their lives at risk for the safety of others. Apart from John Delahunty and Ralph Lockman, no police officers received any official recognition from the police department for their actions in Hoddle Street. The Victoria Police sent congratulatory letters to the recipients of awards given by the Royal Humane Society of Australasia.

Over the years there have been changes in the way major traumatic incidents have been addressed by the police and the ambulance service. There is also less resistance towards their members seeking specialist help to cope with these incidents.

Transcripts, statements, interviews and newspapers have been sourced to write this book. Where there have been conflicting viewpoints in relation to certain incidents, court documents and personal interviews have been given priority. I have endeavoured to portray, as accurately as possible, what occurred during the Hoddle Street incident. I have given priority to the stories of the victims, police, railway personnel and ambulance officers. It may seem to some that Knight would be the expert, but even he has conceded, during his police interviews, that he did not remember everything.

There have been many mass murders since Hoddle Street throughout the world and after each one I have reflected on the problems each of the survivors and their network of family and friends would experience. Each succeeding incident brings back memories of what happened at Hoddle Street. Hopefully, readers of this book will come to understand the trauma and life–long baggage that these people carry.

At the request of some people who were involved in Hoddle Street, their names have reluctantly been changed.

This book is dedicated to the victims.

A brief history of the area

Clifton Hill is an inner suburb of Melbourne, covering just 4 square kilometres with a population of 14,870 residents. Four major roads cut through Clifton Hill – from the east, the Eastern Freeway; from the north-east, Heidelberg Road; and from the north, Queens Parade and Hoddle Street. All roads lead to the central business area of Melbourne, an area of 6,129 square kilometres with a diverse population of more than 2.8 million.

Sixty-seven per cent of those living in Clifton Hill were born in Australia. While less than half a per cent of the residents are Aboriginal, 3.6 per cent are of British origin, 5 per cent from Greece and 7 per cent from Italy. While 18 per cent of the population has a tertiary qualification, 5 per cent has a trade and 51 per cent has no qualifications. 72.5 per cent earn no more than $22,000 a year and most people are employed in community service, finance and business, power services and retail. The majority of residents travel by car to work despite being well serviced with public transport.

The Clifton Hill Railway Station carries large volumes of commuters over Queens Parade along a viaduct bridge following the course of the Merri Creek to Rushall and terminating at Epping. A second line from Clifton Hill carries trains north-east over the Urquhart Street bridge servicing those living as far away as Hurstbridge.

In 1835 John Batman signed a treaty – later declared void by the Governor of New South Wales – alongside the Merri Creek in Northcote with the Dutigalla, a branch of the Wurundjeri tribe of Aborigines whose land extended from Werribee to Kinglake to the Dandenong Ranges. The treaty gave Batman 243,000 hectares in exchange for twenty pair of blankets, thirty tomahawks, flour, knives and shirts. Batman wrote that the Merri Creek, an area of red gums, rocks, reeds and bush so thick that settlers could easily get lost, was "a beautiful stream of water which exceeds anything I ever saw."

In 1836 it was estimated that 350 Aboriginals lived in the area. During 1837 Robert Hoddle surveyed the Merri Creek from near where High Street and Queens Parade stand, to the junction with the Yarra River between the Eastern Freeway and Dight's Falls. A grassy track running north from Clifton Hill to Richmond in the south became known as Hoddle Street.

In December 1841, Aboriginals lived on the Clifton Hill side of the Merri Creek, a situation tolerated by the settlers because the land at that stage had not yet been sold for private use. Inevitably, the settlers took over and, eventually, the Aboriginals moved camp, 64 km further north along the Yarra River, after unsuccessful attempts to re-educate them.

Beside the Merri Creek is a native graveyard. Corroborees were held near where Victoria Park is today. In 1973 descendants of these people laid claim to 27 acres of Clifton Hill.

By 1850 bluestone metal replaced the grassy track of Hoddle Street. One of the first roads built extended from Melbourne to the then country area of Heidelberg. Initially the boulder-strewn flats of the Merri were built up to form a ford but, in 1850, a bridge was erected. In 1854 a toll gate was erected on the Clifton Hill side of the Merri Creek bridge to pay for road works along the Upper Plenty Road.

In 1855 East Collingwood became the first suburb to gain local self-government and one of its first objectives was to include Clifton Hill within its area. Named after the suburb in Bristol, England, by JH Knipe, Clifton Hill was chiefly Crown Land, apart from a quarry at the Yarra end of Roseneath Street. There was also a small area bounded by Hoddle, Ramsden, Roseneath and Field Streets, which had been subdivided and settled in 1851. Many of the families living near the quarry objected to being included in East Collingwood where the working class and factories were, as it would devalue their own land.

In 1883 a railway line, described by one journalist as the "nowhere to nowhere line", was opened from Clifton Hill to Alphington to give the appearance that the Government was doing something. The original plan for a direct route from Melbourne to Heidelberg was considered too expensive. At one point trains from Melbourne, taking a roundabout journey, took one and a half hours to reach Heidelberg. In October 1901, the first direct train line linking the two was established via Jolimont, Collingwood and Clifton Hill. Two years later a rail link from Clifton Hill to Northcote was completed.

From 1890 a cable tram service, which often did not run for months or years, operated from Queens Parade, crossing the Merri and north along High Street. In 1954 land was reserved for the Eastern Freeway, from Doncaster to Collingwood, but it was not until 1969 that plans were announced. Work began in November 1971 but, due to demonstrations, it was not completed until December 1976.

*Ambush/**n.1.** the act of lying concealed so as to attack by surprise. 2. The act of attacking unexpectedly from a concealed position. 3. A secret or concealed position where men lie in wait to attack unawares. 4. A person or body of men lying in wait. – v.t 5. To attack from ambush.*

– The Macquarie Dictionary

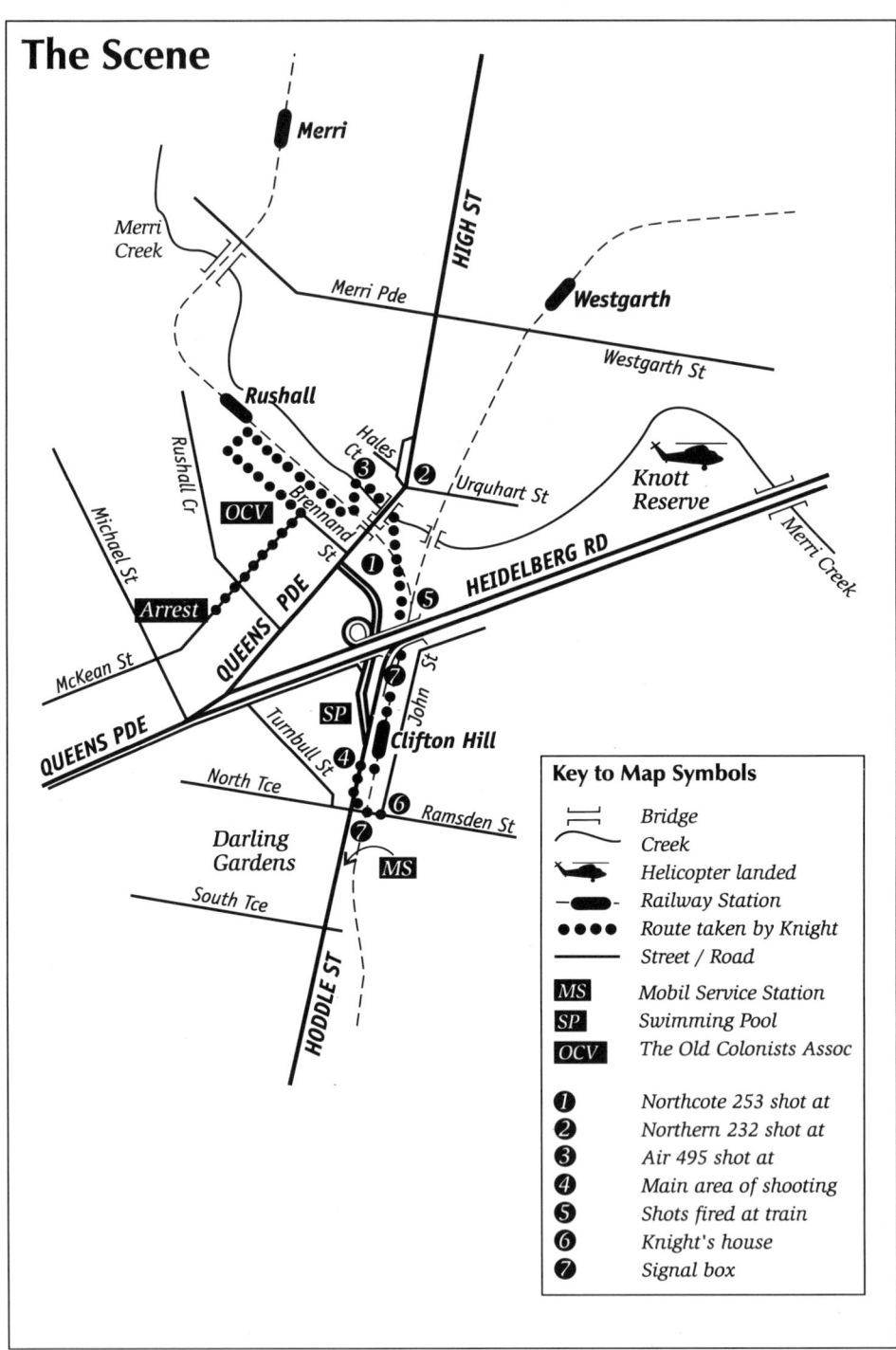

For the victims

ALL THE NUFFIES

1

Quiet nights brought with them the opportunity to catch up on paperwork.

On busier nights, the watchhouse keeper was constantly answering telephones, checking prisoners, bailing prisoners and handling counter inquiries. Most officers preferred to be busy. Generally it was an effort to type, an effort to complete briefs of evidence. Some police read magazines or books that demanded little concentration rather than do paperwork. Experience had taught them that whatever paperwork they did at night was usually returned by a sergeant to be done again, as points were missed or omitted.

Jenenne Stiles, 23, had given up trying to complete a report. She was never satisfied with her efforts and decided to put it away until she returned to dayshift. She looked at her watch and saw that it was almost time for the van to come in for a meal break. She set the door alarm and went upstairs to the kitchen of the Collingwood Police Station where she lit the top of the oven and put the water on to boil. As the watchhouse keeper for the last night shift of the week, it was her turn to provide the meal for that shift. She adjusted the flame on the stove, believing that her partners would not be long, then returned downstairs to the watchhouse.

She tidied the office area for the next shift and went through a stack of newspapers. The week's headlines were not remarkably different from any other week.

Saturday 1 August 1987: talks between transport union and government officials had averted a threatened shutdown of the rail system, however trams would not be running during the week. Six killed in separate car accidents the previous day. Andrew Mark Norrie, who murdered a couple in a shooting spree on the New South Wales coast in 1986, was given a life sentence. Tension in the Persian Gulf increased when 402 people, mainly Iranian pilgrims, were killed in a demonstration outside Mecca's Grand Mosque. The Crimes Confiscation of Profits Act *became law so that the courts now had the power to seize the profits and property accumulated by people involved in serious criminal activity. The assets of suspects could be frozen. In football, Sydney had thrashed another club for the third week in a row.*

The Government was intending to scrap the six hour limit on voluntary questioning of suspects after a committee found that it hindered police investigations, particularly in complex crimes. Interviews for indictable offences were to be recorded on audiotape, *after a pilot program had been successfully tried at some suburban police stations. The Government would consider giving police the power to fingerprint suspects and take body samples of suspects and offenders, and require offenders to take part in identification parades. Muhammad Ali admitted to having Parkinson's Syndrome. Phillip 'The Iceman' Wilson, an alleged standover man, murderer and drug runner, was found murdered in South Yarra. There had been a record $37 million invested in Tattslotto for an $11 million first prize, which was shared by eleven people. Police were hunting for a gang dubbed the "Eastern Gang" which had been responsible for several armed robberies, netting it half-a-million dollars. The Homicide Squad investigated four murders, three caused by knife attacks and one by shotgun. Irex Tawfik became the first person outside the police force to receive a Certificate of Bravery from the Chief Commissioner, Sinclair 'Mick' Miller. Tawfik had raced to within metres of the blazing car that had exploded outside Russell Street Police Station on 27 March 1986, and had shut off the main gas supply, despite being blown off his feet by a second explosion. The month before, Tawfik had told police from California who were on a study tour, "We don't have that sort of madness over here," when asked about safeguards to police premises and bomb attacks. St Kilda football coach, Darrel Baldock had suffered a stroke and was unable to continue coaching for the remainder of the season. Aubrey Maurice Broughill, 62, was sentenced in the Melbourne County Court to twelve years imprisonment for nine armed robberies which netted him over $50,000. Turbulence during a Sydney-Tokyo flight resulted in twenty-six passengers being injured.*

As Jenenne tossed the newspapers into a bin she thought about local news that did not make the newspapers. It had been Fitzroy Police Station's week for crime, while at Collingwood it had been relatively quiet, just a few drunks. The Fitzroy night shift crew had arrested several burglars and a car thief. When it rained the homeless came to the watch house and asked to spend the night in the cells, so they were given a swig of port and then charged with being drunk and disorderly. It was better than finding them dead from exposure.

Midweek, a youth, who would not take no for an answer from his former girlfriend, was arrested outside her home after police lost patience. The struggle created a minor brawl with a number of police units from Carlton, Collingwood and Russell Street coming along as back-up. In response to criticism from the Fitzroy van, that D24 ignored their calls for assistance, Sergeant Mick Hogan, from D24, explained that operators answered the strongest signals. Sometimes you just could not be heard above other police making inquiries at the same time.

There were calls of "shots being fired" which were actually marbles or ball bearings being fired by youths armed with sling shots or shanghais at pedestrians, cars and shop windows. This had been an on-going problem for several months, particularly in Fitzroy, Carlton, Collingwood and Clifton Hill. Some youths had been arrested but the incidents continued to occur.

Jenenne decided it must be Fitzroy's big week as it had even won the annual grudge match against Carlton the Sunday they started night shift. She laughed at the memory of the Fitzroy players wearing black arm bands, which was usually a mark of respect when someone had died. After the game it was revealed that a Fitzroy police officer, the day before, had had cosmetic surgery on his nose. It was shortened, to make him look less like Cyrano de Bergerac. The arm bands were in memory of his old nose.

Jenenne went back upstairs to the kitchen to check the water. Some of her colleagues did not put much effort into the night shift dinner but others prepared meals that would not be bettered by a qualified chef.

By 5 a.m. Jenenne had removed the veal parmigiana and vegetables from the oven and wrapped each plate in plastic wrap. The Collingwood divisional van crew had arrested a youth, who was on speed, in Wellington Street. He had threatened Shane Keogh and Glen Sheluchin with a roadside guard rail but had dropped it when Shane pulled out his revolver. While Glen removed handcuffs from the offender in the interview room, Belinda Bourchier, who had been part of the back up, criticised Shane for being gun happy. Shane handed Jenenne the keys to the gun safe after placing his and Glen Sheluchin's revolvers inside.

At 7 a.m. Jenenne put the plates in the refrigerator. Her night shift partners had gone home, wanting to get as much sleep as possible before returning in eight hours for the afternoon quick-change-over shift. Jenenne was rostered to work the divisional van but swapped with Belinda Bourchier so that she could again present her meal.

2

Kevin Farmer, 27, his wife, Tracey, 23, and their 18-month-old son, Adrian, were driving in their red Datsun sedan along Victoria Street, Richmond. They were running late getting to his mother's house in Northcote to celebrate Kevin's and his brother Craig's birthdays. Their birthdays were a day apart so their mother arranged for the party on the in-between day, Sunday 9 August. Tracey had not wanted to go as Adrian had been restless during the night and she had not slept for long.

Kevin checked the intersection and, on the green light, accelerated right, into Hoddle Street. Tracey turned in her seat to return a dropped toy to Adrian. Kevin checked the mirrors then moved across to the centre lane, one of four that carried north-bound traffic towards the Eastern Freeway. As they changed lanes Tracey adjusted the heater control and rubbed her hands together. It was cold. Before getting into the car Adrian had been fascinated at the little puffs of cloud that came from Tracey's mouth as she spoke.

Earlier that day Tracey and Adrian had walked the hundred and twenty metres from their flat to the house in Vesper Street, Richmond that belonged to Tracey's mother, Val Corrigan. Kevin was working at the carpark where he was an attendant, and would be home after lunch. Tracey and Val were more like sisters than mother and daughter and saw each other almost every day. Val had worked with Tracey in various jobs and was with her when she met her husband for the first time. They were working at the Australia Hotel, Val a cook and Tracey a waitress. Kevin, at 179 cm and strongly built, was at the bar and could not take his eyes off Tracey, a petite 155 cm. Six weeks later, during Easter of 1985, they married in the Fitzroy Gardens. Kevin continued playing football for a Hawthorn district side but at the start of the 1987 season gave away the game to earn more money working overtime. They were saving for their own house and looking forward to not paying rent. They were also trying for a second child and did not want their children to go without.

They were very close and enjoyed each other's company. Tracey wanted everything to be perfect and, before Adrian was born, painted his bedroom while Kevin worked. Her own parents had separated when she was six weeks old and she had only seen her father once, when she was two. It had been a struggle for her mother to work and raise two girls under five. Tracey was determined that she and Kevin were going to be together forever. They were both determined that their own children would have a better life than they had had.

In the distance, as they travelled along Hoddle Street, Kevin and Tracey could see the Clifton Hill shot tower which had been built in the 1890s. It looked like a chimney and, until the end of the second world war, was one of the tallest structures in Melbourne and had been an air navigation aid.

As they passed over the Eastern Freeway, Adrian sang quietly to himself. Tracey played with the engagement and wedding rings on her left hand, and the gold and diamond ring on her right hand. Hoddle Street narrowed from eight to four lanes and at Ramsden Street their car was only one of twenty-nine thousand that passed through that intersection every Sunday.

3

The red Datsun coupe continued on past the Clifton Hill Railway Station and the Collingwood Leisure Centre, then followed the left-hand bend in the road, stopping at the lights, then turning right into Queens Parade. It crossed the Merri Creek and continued on to High Street, stopping outside a house in Charles Street, Northcote. He and Tracey went inside carrying a present, Adrian, and a small supply of nappies, clothes and change bag. Tracey commented on how much more they would have to bring when they had another child.

When Belinda Bourchier arrived for duty at the Collingwood Police Station that same afternoon after a week of night shift, her eyes adjusted to the daylight better than she had anticipated. There was a lot of cloud cover and for the whole day there would be just twenty-four minutes of sunshine. Twenty-four minutes when a shadow could be formed. That Sunday, 9 August 1987, had, so far, been the coldest day of the month. At 10.9 degrees it was four degrees colder than Saturday, the day of her twenty-third birthday.

Belinda went upstairs and changed into her uniform, then returned to the watchhouse to check the equipment in the battered, brown briefcase which would sit between her, the observer, and the divisional van driver, Glen Sheluchin, 25. Together they checked the portable radio, the Melway street directory, torches, parking and traffic infringement books, and traffic-light key. They each took a revolver from the safe and holstered them. Everyone talked about meeting in the park beside the Yarra River under Hawthorn Bridge where they would gather later with Richmond police to celebrate Belinda's birthday and the end of night shift.

As Belinda and Glen were about to leave the Police Station, Belinda was called to the telephone. Minutes later, Fitzroy detective, Senior Constable Tony Doherty, met her outside the station, while Jenenne Stiles took her place in the divisional van. You had to be flexible in the police force. Jenenne would work the van until Belinda returned, hopefully in enough time to allow Jenenne to reheat the Saturday night meal. A trainee, Byron Sedgewick, would work the watchhouse on his own.

Tony Doherty drove with Belinda in the CIB car to Ascot Vale to pick up a suspect who Belinda wanted to interview for fraud. He wasn't there. They then went to another address in Brunswick where they were told that he had already left the country. Returning to the Collingwood Police Station they travelled east along Johnston Street towards Hoddle Street. Belinda studied the bright orange moon as it hung over the horizon. It was the most enormous, full moon she had ever seen.

"All the nuffies will be out tonight," she said, giggling.

Nuffies, police jargon for the mentally unstable, seemed to make their presence known during a full moon. For the police it usually meant more violence and more accidents to attend. People were more aggressive. Workers in such service industries as ambulance, prisons, police and medical believed a full moon brought out the worst in many people.

Dianne Fitzpatrick shared a pot of tea with the other nurses working the morning shift at the Macleod Repatriation Hospital. Dianne liked to read the tea leaves and was the only one who did not strain the tea as it was poured into her cup. A nurse for thirty years, she and the other nurses chatted about the unusual behaviour of their patients, who were all former armed servicemen. They were restless and tried to open a locked door. Those outside in the garden tried to climb over the cyclone fence. The incontinent were wetting themselves more often and the normally placid had become aggressive.

Dianne felt a shiver down her spine as she looked into her empty cup. She walked to the sink, concerned about what the tea leaves had revealed. For the third day in a row there had been a car in the tea leaves and she tried to understand the meaning. She felt there was going to be an accident or perhaps a windscreen was to be shattered. She washed her cup and tried to forget about what she had seen. Another nurse asked if she was all right, curious about what she had seen.

"I hope something isn't going to happen," Dianne said.

Constable Phil Bradley, 31, was happy to fault the green, Parks and Gardens van. It was difficult to drive and even more difficult to stop. He filled in the vehicle log book and wrote that the van was 'faulted – no brakes'. He and Gary Maddern, his partner for the shift, put their equipment into a white, marked sedan then turned right into Russell Street. Gary took the radio handset and advised the D24 operator, Sergeant Mick Hogan, that "Russell 2-1-3" was "code one" – on patrol.

Noel Shiels loved sport and activity. He had spent eight years training in the martial arts of karate and taekwondo and liked to be fit. It helped him cope with the stresses of his job as a trainee mobile intensive care ambulance officer, a position he had wanted since 1979 when he joined the ambulance service in response to a newspaper advertisement. In early 1987 he transferred to the MICA (Mobile Intensive Care Ambulance) unit, where the entry examinations alone were of a very high standard. To qualify, one required a minimum of five years ambulance service experience, an entrance examination with a minimum mark of 80 per cent, and 100 per cent success in several practical examinations. Once qualified, the eleven week course was intense and required a lot of study. Noel was looking forward to it coming to an end as the year had been a difficult one. His wife had been ill, and between them they had only one car, which was inconvenient. He would be a 'frog' after he had successfully appeared for questioning before an examination board of doctors. If he passed that component he would then be further assessed by an anaesthetist during theatre and if that went well he would be in. He could hardly wait.

On the weekends when he was not working, Noel played the bass guitar in a cover band. That weekend he was rostered to work two fourteen-hour shifts on MICA One, the busiest MICA in the Melbourne metropolitan area. He and his trainer, clinical instructor, Peter Collins, would be the first to be called to life-and-death situations.

Peter Collins had been a frog for four years, frog being the nickname given to qualified MICA officers because they attended jobs where patients died (croaked). For the moment Noel was a 'tadpole'. To be a frog meant you had reached the highest level in the ambulance service.

When Noel Shiels reached his home in Elsternwick that Sunday morning, his two children, Bridie, 5 and Becky, 3, were in the lounge room watching cartoons. He talked to his wife, Sally, about the work he had done overnight, then cuddled his daughters and went to bed. By midday he was working out on a skipping rope to shake the fatigue out of his body. He and his wife then worked together on the renovations to their home and before he knew it he was on the bus to the ambulance depot in La Trobe Street, Melbourne, just around the corner from the Russell Street Police Station.

John Delahunty, 24, went to the safe in the Fitzroy Police Station watchhouse. He looked along the row of revolvers and took out the one with the serial number 909. It felt comfortable in his hand and he checked that it was clean, then inserted six rounds into the barrel chamber and placed it in the holster on his right hip. He pressed the studs together, ensuring the revolver was secure, then signed for the pistol in the watchhouse keeper's book. He gave the safe keys back to the watchhouse keeper, Margaret Kidd, 34, who was typing at the desk. John ran up the stairs to the files office, directly above the watchhouse and picked up the phone. He had some calls to make before going out in the police car. He was one of three police assigned the task of working on files. It was not what he considered real police work. He preferred to work the divisional van and be among all the action because, ultimately, he wanted to be a detective. However, everyone at Fitzroy had to work files for at least four months and John had another two months left.

John was responsible for the North Fitzroy area and his daily duties involved executing warrants, taking statements, serving summonses and collecting fines. He came to Fitzroy in January after two years at Russell Street.

Despite several renovations and coats of paint, Fitzroy was 128 years old and was a building in decay. As you walked up the steps to the front entrance, you were immediately taken back in time despite the two-way mirrored glass, the buzzer and the security door which led you into one of the State's oldest police stations. To some citizens the Station was depressing – they often asked how anyone could work there in the dark lighting and primitive conditions – but John, like most who worked there, loved the Station and its atmosphere. Occasionally, he would touch the walls and comment, "If only these walls could talk."

Detective Tony Doherty let Belinda Bourchier out at the Collingwood Police Station then returned to Fitzroy where he handed his revolver in to Margaret Kidd. He locked up the CIB office and drove back to Collingwood in his private car. To a bachelor the offer of a free meal was too good to refuse.

Inspector Adrian Fyfe, 41, slept poorly that Sunday morning. He was anxious not to sleep through the alarm. At midday he got up and readied himself for the quick-change-over shift and waited for his driver to pick him up. In the car he spoke briefly to the dayshift inspector who was on his way home in another police car and was told there was no carry over. That was good news as it meant he had no work to follow through that had occurred during the dayshift. He then visited each station in the district, including the City Watchhouse, and spoke to every prisoner. The prisoners seemed satisfied with their lot and he crossed over Russell Street and up the stairs to the first floor where his office was located. He adjusted the volume of the police radio on the office wall and, momentarily, tilted back his head and closed his eyes.

Adrian had been promoted to inspector rank two months earlier, after twenty-two years' service. It had been a long haul but he enjoyed the police force. It was better than being a bank teller where the biggest adventure in his time with the National Bank at Goroke was ensuring that the figures were right at the end of each day. In the police it seemed to be non-stop adventure seeing life as it really was. He enjoyed being able to help people. He wondered where he would be today if a friend had not persuaded him to leave the bank and join the police.

He had worked at Wodonga and Warrnambool Police Stations, with the Stolen Motor Vehicle Squad, Crime Cars, Licensing, Gaming and Vice, D24, and at Fitzroy and Carlton, and had been commended several times for good work in the course of duty. He had had several close calls.

When he was at Warrnambool, an offender in a stolen car had shot at him when cornered in a carpark following a 25-kilometre car chase. Then at North Melbourne, a shotgun was held to his head during a hostage siege. He had genuinely believed that at any moment he would be killed. However, another police officer pressed a revolver against the head of the offender who then lowered his shotgun.

In February 1983, during the Ash Wednesday bushfires, Adrian risked his life to save farmers and their families while knowing his own property was under threat. At the first opportunity, he returned home to learn that his family had escaped the advancing fire. But he later discovered the charred remains of his neighbour's wife and child in a nearby paddock. They had been trying to save their cattle and sheep.

Adrian opened his eyes and told himself that he was going to have a good shift. It was usually a good omen if the prisoners were not complaining. He opened his briefcase and looked for a file that he wanted to complete that day. He looked at the file and picked up the telephone. He felt like shit but there was work to do.

Belinda Bourchier wrote the log or running sheet, and operated the radio. In times of an emergency she would operate the blue, flashing lights and the siren while the driver, Glen Sheluchin, concentrated on getting quickly and safely through the traffic.

Many police referred to the divisional van as the truck because it drove like one. It was basically a standard panel van with a number of cosmetic changes including the wire grills across the back door and rear windows. Prisoners sat on a short, narrow bench behind the front cabin area and two padlocks secured the back door. The aerial, blue lights and siren were mounted on a rack on the roof, and were activated from the dashboard instrument panel.

Separating Belinda from Glen was the battered, brown briefcase. It embarrassed Belinda that Glen, a probationary constable, could drive the van. She had yet to pass the divisional-van driving test. It was galling to her that she was a confirmed Constable in the Victoria Police and he was still a trainee. He could drive the van while she could not. She reassured herself that, at least, he was a mature-age trainee. It wasn't as if he had just left school, and was covered in pimples.

As Glen drove the van through the streets of Collingwood, Belinda thought about how her previous job, as a public servant, had had its advantages. There were regular hours and no night shift, and you never missed family or other important occasions. Or birthdays. Saturday was the first time she had missed being with her family on her birthday. It would have to wait. If she had remained in the public service Belinda would already have seen her family, but the down side of being a public servant was the lack of action or adventure. As a police officer, every day was different and you never knew what was going to happen next.

MICA One left the depot early that afternoon for the Carlton high-rise flats where another ambulance crew was trying to revive an elderly woman. Peter Collins looked forward to another busy shift, he felt it was good training for his tadpole. Peter had slept for four hours during the day; it was the most he could expect with three children under the age of seven. When they arrived at the flat, Peter and Noel Shiels took over from the original crew. The woman was clinically dead. Her pupils were dilated and her heart had stopped beating but they revived her and took her to the Royal Melbourne Hospital, knowing that it was only a matter of time before she would die.

At 8.30 p.m. MICA One parked outside a Chinese take-away in Russell Street. Noel was feeling the effects of little sleep and the cold air. He looked to the sky and saw the full moon. He pointed to it and said to Peter, "It's Sunday night and we're going to be okay." Then to the moon he said, "I don't care."

They drove back to the ambulance depot with their take-away food and went into the "cupboard", a small room with two lounge couches, and watched television while they ate. Peter quizzed Noel on various scenarios that he might encounter as a MICA officer. It was part of the on-the-job training and assessment.

"You've got a call to attend a man who is diabetic. His wife can't revive him and he is in a coma. You find him lying on the kitchen floor covered in sweat. What do you do to help the patient?"

Noel answered and Peter continued his questioning. Noel knew he could relax when Peter asked him about a man found on a train with a bite to his body – a dragon bite! They sat back and watched the movie, *Risky Business*.

Graham Kent held the hand of his 18-month-old son and looked to the eastern sky where the orange yolk hung over the Dandenong Ranges. From his home in St Kilda it looked large and non-threatening, yet there was something about it which disturbed him. He knew the chances of being called out to a job were great; 20 per cent of murders occurred on a Sunday; but with a full moon he felt the chances were even greater.

"I bet Dad won't be here tomorrow morning," he said to his son.

With the rubbish bin in place on the nature strip Graham tightened the cord on his son's dressing gown and hugged him tightly. He carried the boy inside and tucked him into bed. Graham's wife, also a detective, was working afternoon shift and would not be home until after eleven. Graham went to the lounge room and picked up a book he had been trying to finish since June, when he transferred to Homicide from the Armed Robbery Squad. Since then he had taken few rest days, or days off, as the Squad was under-staffed.

Graham worked in a team of six but he was the only one available, due to holidays, trials, sickness or involvement in other murder investigations. In the past two months Graham had taken charge of two murder inquiries and had assisted other teams in several complicated investigations.

Graham's partner, Senior Sergeant Brian McCarthy, set the pager on the bedside table, next to the light and hoped not to be disturbed by it during the night. He had a long and complicated trial commencing on Tuesday, and on Monday he was required to go through some of the brief with the prosecutor. Despite being involved in ninety murder inquiries as the chief investigator since joining Homicide in 1978, he had yet to get used to the pager. He disliked the noise it made, but it was part of the job and the police force was the only job he had ever loved.

He had had about fifty different jobs prior to joining the police force. It was something that concerned the then Chief Commissioner, Selwyn Porter, who took part in the intake selection process. He asked Brian how they could be confident that he was going to stay in the police force with such a poor work record. Brian countered that, after fifty jobs, he knew that the police force was right for him.

As a country boy he imagined that police spent a lot of time directing traffic. It was a job he never did although he pounded the beat at Bourke Street West and, at Russell Street on night shift, rode a bicycle. Then he worked at Footscray, Williamstown, and the Gaming Squad. From there he went to Yarraville and worked the Special Patrol where he was groomed for entry into the CIB. Then it was Russell Street CIB, Footscray CIB, the Wireless Patrol, Ascot Vale Crime Cars and Ferntree Gully CIB.

He had only one period of non-operational duty and that was while attached to the Transport Branch. The hours were regular and he could work on the house he was building, before and after work; and he always got to take his rest days. Not like in the Homicide Squad where, at the age of fifty-six, he regularly worked seven days straight and had accumulated sixty-nine hours overtime in the previous month alone.

Brian turned off the light and again thought about the trial that was starting on Tuesday. It had been the longest murder investigation he had been involved in and he had invested a lot of himself in the case. For seven weeks he had lived in Mildura investigating the crime, seeing his wife twice in that time, and always working sixteen hour days.

Still, he loved the work and enjoyed the consideration given to him and other members by the public and the police administration. While money dictated what you could do in all areas of policing, in the Homicide Squad you generally got whatever you needed to complete an enquiry. As a senior sergeant in the Homicide Squad you were not just an administrator. You were actually involved in the day-to-day investigations, not stuck behind a desk shifting paper from one tray to the next and initialing the mark left by a rubber stamp. He also appreciated working with younger people, they made him feel young despite how they teased him.

He was often joshed for being the oldest man in the Squad – for being the oldest man alive. When relating something he had personally experienced he would often be told, "I wasn't even born then."

He would be teased about how dreadful he looked, yet he felt marvellous. In seven months he had lost 35 kilograms on the Pritikin diet. He no longer ate fast food, smoked cigarettes or drank too much beer. He could never give up a beer as it made him relax but he found going for a walk every day was more beneficial. In the past he would have a drink to help him sleep but now he didn't need to. He would not rest properly tonight though because he and Graham Kent were on call. It was important not to sleep through the pager or the ringing of the telephone.

4

Sergeant Mick Hogan, 36, went in to the D24 mess room and made himself a cup of coffee. Another fourteen months to serve at D24 and he would be free to transfer. He had not intended to go back after working there as a constable. He had seen enough of the place after three years of double shifts and cancelled rest days, but it had served a purpose, as it did now. The first time around it enabled him to save for a home for Sharon, his wife, and their three children. This time he chose D24 as a means of getting promoted as quickly as possible. Almost everyone wanted to work at a station, but not everyone was prepared to transfer to D24 where you were virtually chained to a desk answering telephones and working the radio.

Mick sipped his coffee and yawned. He had just finished night shift and during the eight-hour break between the night and afternoon shifts, he had managed just three hours sleep. It was the same for nearly everyone who had finished night shift that morning so he could not complain. At home Sharon was taking their elder daughter to debutante practice. He hoped he would not miss the actual debutante ball. Mick took another drag from his cigarette and looked at the clock. It was almost time to relieve the dayshift.

"Quiet tonight, Mick?" asked Constable Greg Splatt, who was drying his cup.

"Dunno Greg. Always expect the unexpected."

Since May, Pat Murtagh, 39, had been upgraded to Acting Chief Inspector and worked from a former police station in North Carlton where he could supervise the Carlton, Royal Park and City West Police Stations. He had had a quiet week leading up to night shift and he hoped the trend would continue. The only dampener on his week occurred when he travelled to Kardinia Park on Saturday to watch Essendon play Geelong. Despite being in front by 14 points at halftime, his Bombers lost the match by 27 points. It was a long drive home from Kardinia Park, the only consolation being a warm house and his family waiting for him to join them for dinner. During the afternoon he relaxed at home and tried to make the most of the daylight as his next week would be upside down.

Sergeant Peter Butts, 31, entered the District Support Group office at Prahran Police Station clapping his hands together.

"What's doing? Come on, let's go. Let's go!" he said, stirring his team, of Senior Constables Bruce Lowe and Tim Edgeworth, and Constable Donna Randall, into action.

As the Officer in Charge of the Prahran DSG he was keen to get results on a drug-trafficking operation in St Kilda. They had worked night shift for most of the week, walking along Fitzroy Street trying to get a buy from dealers trafficking in heroin and, in some instances, making themselves known to drug users.

Peter Butts knew an amusement parlour was responsible for much of the heroin being used in the area and he wanted to arrest the main dealers. It was difficult as the deal was made away from the amusement parlour, yet the heroin itself was to be collected from behind or under various pinball machines. Peter knew who was responsible for the trafficking but to get sufficient evidence for a conviction, let alone an arrest, was difficult. The DSG worked in plain clothes, its personnel seconded from various police stations throughout the district as a reward for good work performance. It was seen as a stepping-stone to the CIB.

While Peter and Bruce went to Melbourne's western suburbs to take statements, Donna and Tim went to Fitzroy Street. Donna sat in the unmarked police car keeping surveillance and monitoring the police radio while Tim stood in a doorway waiting for someone to offer him drugs.

Danielle Kissas took her time to get ready. Unpressured in the privacy of her own bedroom she listened to English black soul music. She had only recently been given her own bedroom and she enjoyed not having to share with her sister, Frances, anymore. She had spent the day cleaning and rearranging the room and, when she was not doing that, she was talking to her friends on the phone arranging her very active social life. She often went to nightclubs and disco's and spent a lot of time with her best friends, Monica Vitelli and Alan Jury. There was not a day when they did not talk to or see each other.

Danielle put on a red stocking, and then a black stocking on the other leg. She put on her favourite red dress which gathered around the waist, and teased out her hair. She painted her fingernails and lips red. Monica would soon be picking her up and together with Monica's boyfriend, Alan, they would go to a South Yarra nightclub.

Constable Ralph Lockman, 29, sat at his desk in the muster room of Russell Street Police Station. He had ten briefs to complete and he didn't like being behind in paperwork. He had been told that a copper was no good if his paperwork wasn't done "like having a crap".

It was 7.00 p.m. and he was four hours early to start night shift. He sorted through the briefs and worked the manual typewriter. The Police Force was like the Army, but better. There was less discipline in the police and more personal freedom. For nine years he was in the Australian Army and did his basic training at Kapooka before joining a Signallers Corp. The Army had taken him all over Australia, and acquainted him with all kinds of firearms and explosives. Even though he loved the Army he was glad to be free of it. It was limiting and he left for fresh horizons.

On the advice of a girlfriend, and against the wishes of his stepfather and mother, he applied to join the Victoria Police but was unsuccessful on his first two attempts. He filled in the time working for his stepfather in a catering business and on the third attempt he was accepted into the police academy. He was made a squad leader and felt, at twenty-eight, that he was an old man compared to the rest in his intake. The majority of police recruits were in their late teens or early twenties.

While the others complained about the discipline and rigidity of Academy life, Ralph Lockman felt it was heaven. In the Army he had slept in a dormitory while with the police he had his own room or, at worst, shared it with one other person. In the Army if you were late for Parade you were charged, whereas the police recruit was given a demerit or made to run around the athletic track. His only disappointment with the police was having to leave Reservoir for Russell Street, the senior phase training station, where there was less practical police work. He could not wait to finish his two-year probation period and transfer back to Reservoir or somewhere near there, where there was excitement and plenty of crime. He just wanted to catch crooks and contribute to making the streets safe.

Steve Wight left his brother's birthday party in Reservoir at 5.15 p.m. He was reluctant to go to work at the Collingwood Leisure Centre in Turnbull Street, Clifton Hill and contemplated taking a sickie, as his family and friends had urged him to do. But he was not like that. He believed you went sick when you were genuinely unwell. Right now he felt terrific. There would be other parties in the future where he could stay as long as he liked.

During the day Steve and his family watched football. The Brisbane-Collingwood game was broadcast live on TV. They loved football and were fanatical about Collingwood, particularly since Steve's older brother, Terry, had played 39 games for the club. Once the game was over they resumed the party in the garage.

Steve left his wife, Lucy, and six-year-old stepson, Jesse, at the party. He parked the car in Turnbull Street then walked to the swimming centre situated on the west side of Hoddle Street and almost opposite the Clifton Hill Railway Station. He put down the lanes and tested the microphone in readiness for the district swimming championships. The competitors ranged from six-year-olds to those on the aged pension.

By 9 p.m. the two hundred spectators and competitors filed out of the centre and into their cars in Turnbull Street and in the carpark. Steve then began to clean up the pool, hosing down the concourse and the changing rooms and putting equipment away. He thought about having a sauna but felt tired and decided to go home early. He turned off the sauna and began to lock the external doors and switch off the lights. He hoped to be home before ten.

Alan Jury came off the exit ramp and on to Bell Street, Pascoe Vale. On the eastern horizon sat the full moon; it stood out against the overcast backdrop. He had spent much of that Sunday in bed reading a book he had borrowed on mass murders in the United States. Then he watched the Brisbane-Collingwood game on TV before going out to deliver Herbal Life products and return the book. He wondered what it would be like to be ambushed, not having any chance to defend yourself. He also wondered what it would be like to be rich; filthy rich. He wanted to be a millionaire and had hoped to be one of those who had shared the first division prize of $11 million in Tattslotto. He had sold Herbal Life for the past two years but preferred to party and go to nightclubs, and, on weekends, to the football to watch Carlton. His Tattslotto tickets proved to be worthless. He wound down the drivers-side window and stared at the moon. It was a marvellous and beautiful sight. He put his head out of the window and howled like a wolf.

Belinda Bourchier advised D24 that Collingwood 311 was back on patrol. The operator corrected her, something he would do several times during the course of the shift to several units. As most of the police on duty that Sunday afternoon were on a quick-change over from night shift they continued to use the night shift call signs out of habit. Jenenne Stiles went upstairs with Tony Doherty, a Fitzroy detective, to wash the dishes. While she washed and he dried, some other police went out to buy some beer and wine to celebrate Belinda Bourchier's birthday at the end of the shift.

Giovanni Di Vincenzo looked up from his desk in the portable aluminium building that temporarily served as the Station Master's office and the booking office for the Clifton Hill Railway Station. Situated on the east side of the railway tracks it replaced the original building which, earlier in the year, had been burned down by vandals. Two windows at the northern end of the office gave them restricted vision to anything that was happening outside, and they had a single door which opened out onto the south, Melbourne-bound, platform. As Station Master, Giovanni supervised his assistant, Fernando Myra, and the two signalmen, Wayne Monohan and Peter Harvey, who were in their respective signal boxes.

Fernando came in talking about his passion for Flamenco dancing. During a lull in the conversation Fernando said, "Gee, it's quiet tonight."

"Shush," Giovanni said. "Let's keep it that way."

As part of their duties Sergeant Paul McNicol and his partner, Constable Shane Keogh, 25, delivered internal police mail to the divisional office in Spensley Street, Clifton Hill. It was about 5.00 p.m. when they opened the front door. They checked that the offices were secure, left the mail on the enquiry counter and returned to their car.

As Paul was not familiar with the area Shane guided him through the short cuts to avoid traffic and one-way signs. They turned left into narrow John Street and approached Ramsden Street. On the west side of John Street was the Clifton Hill Railway Station where a few people stood waiting on the Melbourne-bound platform.

Shane brought to Paul's attention a Torana sedan parked close to the intersection. Paul stopped the police car behind the Torana while Shane walked around the vehicle, looking inside the cabin and checking the door handles. When he returned to the police car Paul gave him the running sheet where he had written down the owner details. Shane read that the vehicle belonged to Julian Knight of 6 Ramsden Street, Clifton Hill. This was the two-storey terrace house outside which the Torana was parked. The side of the house overlooked John Street, the Railway Station and Hoddle Street. Shane wrote on his running sheet, "not listed. N.O.D." Paul put the police car into gear and turned right into Ramsden Street crossing the railway tracks and stopping at the Hoddle Street intersection.

Inspector Pat Murtagh read the mail and the running sheets before changing into his uniform. He heard his driver pull up outside and he locked the North Carlton office. At Russell Street he expected to find Inspector Adrian Fyfe, but he was not at his office. Adrian was at the City Watchhouse making a final check of the prisoners. Pat lit up another cigarette, picked up the telephone and dialled D24. He wanted to catch up with Adrian before he went home.

It was almost 9.00 p.m. when Dianne Fitzpatrick decided to leave her daughter's flat and go home. Since finishing her shift at the Macleod Repatriation Hospital she had driven around several suburbs before finding a fruit shop that was open. She then went to the Alfred Hospital in Prahran with apples and pears to visit a sick friend but found that she had been discharged earlier that morning. Dianne then headed to her daughter's flat a few kilometres away in Windsor, for a roast dinner and to meet Christine's boyfriend, Bill, for the first time. After dinner, Dianne decided to leave as she had an early start the next morning. Christine did not want her mother to go so early and made another coffee. She wanted her mother to feel special, they were more like friends. Dianne announced she could drink no more and the three walked to her car, a blue Torana sedan which she had bought new in 1977. Dianne kissed her daughter and future son-in-law and thanked them for the evening. Five minutes later she was driving north along Hoddle Street listening to radio station 3UZ, relaxing to the music.

Belinda Bourchier and Glen Sheluchin had been on patrol for about an hour. In that time it was quiet. They checked a car containing Vietnamese youths in Johnston Street, then, in Mayfield Street, obtained particulars for a theft report.

Sergeant Max Drake had come in to the Richmond Police Station more than two hours before he was due to start night shift. It had been a practice he had developed since 1982 when, as a detective at Doncaster CIB, he was diagnosed with the blood disorder Alpha One Anti Tripsum Deficiency. It made him feel weak and short of breath. His doctor had wanted him to take oxygen at home but Max saw that as the beginning of the end. He was not an invalid and did not want to be thought of as one. To get through a normal eight-hour shift he needed to come in early. Only two people in the police force knew of his debilitating illness and only then after Max had sworn them to secrecy. Having to take oxygen would mean the end of his career and at 35 he did not want to become a 'desk jockey'. To be confined to a desk for the rest of his police career would be like taking poison.

Max had been in the army as a conscript during the Vietnam conflict. When his time was up a friend tried to persuade him to become an army mercenary – the two of them would be soldiers for hire in the world's trouble spots – Max declined. But Max did want a job that enabled him to be outdoors and to experience life. While working for a newspaper in accounts he applied to join both the airforce and the police. Every day in accounts was a grind so when the police replied first he could not wait to start the training.

In the twelve years since, he had always been a street policeman, working at Mordialloc, Brighton, Prahran Crime Cars, Mooroolbark CIB, Dandenong CIB, various task forces and the Homicide Squad. Being a police officer was a terrific job, he thought. Max changed into his uniform and began to plough through the 'mini Kosciusko' on his desk.

THE KILLING ZONE

5

Sunday – 9.30 p.m.

Sarah Knight, 15, went upstairs to her bedroom at 6 Ramsden Street, Clifton Hill. Her mother, Pamela, a book keeper, was downstairs watching the film, *Rebels*. Sarah's brother, Matthew, 16, was staying overnight at their grandparents' in Hawthorn, while Julian, 19, was in his bedroom. He had been to the Royal Hotel in nearby Spensley Street and she had seen him return at about 9.00 p.m. He had slammed the front door as he had entered the house and gone towards his bedroom at the end of the hallway. Sarah could hear him going through the boxes where he stored photos, personal papers and military clothing on top of the wardrobe next to his bedroom. He then went upstairs where Sarah and her mother had their bedrooms. At the top of the stairs on the landing, Julian kept more of his army equipment. Sarah approached him, telling him about a phone call from a woman who was interested in buying his Holden Torana, but he was uncommunicative and seemed unhappy. There was nothing about his speech or manner that suggested to Sarah that he was affected by alcohol. He had been drinking coke earlier in the day and Sarah had been told that he had had one beer at their grandparents' house. She had seen Julian drunk and she felt that this was not one of those occasions. She left him and went upstairs to her bedroom. Soon after, Pamela heard the front door shut.

Sang Wang drove his Holden Commodore stationwagon off the Heidelberg Road exit ramp and into Hoddle Street. As he travelled down the ramp he accelerated towards the Clifton Hill Railway Station. He heard a loud bang on his left and, almost instantaneously, the passenger-side window of his car shattered. His right, ring finger and his left side were cut by flying glass. He realised he was being shot at and did the only thing possible. He lowered himself across the seat and accelerated harder as more shots were fired into his vehicle. Two bullets penetrated the front windscreen and a third, the passenger-side, rear door. As he drove further south along Hoddle Street he heard what sounded like fire crackers. He knew differently.

On the first floor of the Russell Street police building, in the duty officer's room, Adrian Fyfe and Pat Murtagh drank tea and talked about the previous week. Adrian was as interested in what had happened during daylight hours as Pat was in what had occurred during the night shift, as they were overlapping each other's worlds. When working night shift there is a tendency to feel isolated from everyone not working the same hours. One misses out on the day-to-day gossip and police politics.

Adrian advised that the afternoon shift had been quiet for him. There had been no problems with the prisoners and he had not had any supervision problems. Pat was pleased to hear this as it often followed that the next shift experienced similar problems. In the background they could hear the police radio. It was just loud enough to hear, like muzak. Between them they had fifty years police experience and they knew that if they missed anything important then someone from D24 would contact them. Pat lit another cigarette and said that he hoped his night shift was going to be quiet.

Alan Jury drove his mother's 1986 Toyota Crown sedan west along Heidelberg Road then left down the Hoddle Street entrance ramp. Alan and Monica Vitelli, his girlfriend of four years, were arguing about Alan's sister who was to have come with them to the nightclub. Danielle Kissas was in high spirits and sat in her usual place, the middle of the back seat. In the three years they had known each other Danielle had always sat in the middle of the back seat, so she could look at her two friends while they all chatted. While the song *Shattered Dreams* played softly on the radio Danielle shifted from her usual position and sat directly behind Monica. Usually the three friends chatted and laughed the whole time they were in each other's company but tonight was different. There was tension between Alan and Monica.

Alan turned his head to check for cars on his right travelling past the entrance ramp along Hoddle Street. There were no cars in front of him or to the side as he drove off the ramp and south into Hoddle Street.

As they approached the Clifton Hill Railway Station Danielle was looking at the billboards on the left and then into the park on the right. Monica was moody and thinking about where her relationship with Alan was going. She stared blankly out of her side window. As they passed the railway station and approached Ramsden Street their car was hit by what they thought was a stone.

Alan momentarily closed his eyes and braked, waiting for the windscreen to shatter. When he opened his eyes a fraction of a second later he realised it was no stone that had struck the window. Almost dead centre in the windscreen was a small hole which he recognised from television as a bullet hole. If Danielle had not earlier shifted her seating position the bullet's trajectory would have passed through her. Having shot rabbits Alan knew it was a .22 rifle that was being fired at them. He yelled to the others. "Duck! We're being shot at!"

For the first time that evening Monica did not question Alan's judgement. She slid down in her seat and leaned over to the centre console as more shots could be heard. Danielle blamed Alan, believing a passing motorist had shot at them.

"Who's after you?" she screamed.

The volley of shots continued into the passenger side of the Toyota sedan as it passed the bushes opposite the rail lines, showering the women with glass as the passenger windows shattered. Alan felt a burning sensation on the side of his neck about two centimetres below his left ear. He accelerated hard towards the Mobil Service Station asking himself who might want to kill him. Who were his enemies? He braked to go into the first driveway of the service station but overshot it, turning quickly into the second.

Dianne Fitzpatrick noticed that she was the only car on the road in Hoddle Street as she approached the Ramsden Street intersection. She travelled down the outside lane and thought it unusual that there were no pedestrians on the footpaths, not even a dog in the parklands. The overhead street lights produced a yellow haze and reflected off the car bonnet.

As Dianne crossed over Ramsden Street with the railway crossing on her right she heard what seemed to be an explosion directly behind her. It was so loud she thought a house had fallen onto the car roof but realised that that was ridiculous. Then the side passenger window behind her shattered, followed by something punching her – it was a .22 bullet – in the back of her right shoulder. The bullet had slowed on impact with the passenger window and had penetrated the backrest of the drivers seat stopping short of actually entering Dianne's body. The bullet was held fast, caught in the woollen fibres of the feather and fan stitch of her jumper. The jumper an eighty-year-old woman had knitted for twenty dollars.

"Don't stop! Don't drive fast! Get to safety!"

Dianne felt her insides were exploding. There was a terrible pain, as bad as childbirth, throughout her torso area. Then she felt a burning sensation which overrode that initial pain. She felt blood trickle down her back and felt that she was going to die.

"Don't stop! Don't drive fast! Get to safety!"

It was the voice again, a presence she felt, which led her to believe that she was going to survive. She continued past the Collingwood Leisure Centre and the Clifton Hill Railway Station, turning left up the exit ramp onto Heidelberg Road and crossing over Hoddle Street. The voice kept repeating, "Don't stop! Don't drive fast! Get to safety!"

As she entered Heidelberg Road a white Holden stationwagon drew up alongside, the occupants looking in at her. She stared straight ahead, fearing that they would shoot her. Then the stationwagon accelerated away. Dianne felt relief and continued to drive slowly along Heidelberg Road. Four hundred metres further east she approached a red traffic light at Fenwick Street. The voice told her to stop and she waited for the light to change.

As the white Volkswagen stationwagon travelled north in Hoddle Street the three friends talked about their work and the film they had just seen together. Raewyn Crighton, a nurse, checked the rear-vision mirror then diverged to the far, left lane as they approached the Mobil Service Station on their right. Bernd Micheel, a sewing machine mechanic, who was sitting next to Raewyn, heard three loud bangs. He was not sure where the noise was coming from and made no mention of it to Raewyn or to Dianne Arnold who sat directly behind him.

As they crossed over Ramsden Street the banging sound was more audible. Bernd looked about trying to see what was making the noises but saw nothing other than a small number of other cars in Hoddle Street. He was sure the sound was coming from near the railway station. He mentioned it to the others but as they could see nothing unusual Raewyn kept driving. She thought it may have been fire crackers and estimated that about ten had gone off.

As they approached the swimming centre on their left, they felt something hit the car twice from the rear. All three ducked. Raewyn said, "I think we're being shot at."

Bernd did not want to believe that this was happening. There was no reason for anyone to shoot at them. Dianne looked behind them and saw sparks flying off the road. In the next lane was another car which appeared to be travelling normally, as was the car in front.

"Pull over and we'll see what's happened," Dianne suggested.

Raewyn briefly took her foot off the accelerator but continued driving. They were scared. They turned left onto the Heidelberg Road exit ramp. As they drove along Heidelberg Road heading for their homes in Northcote, Bernd and Dianne looked down over Hoddle Street and the railway station. The 'bangs' were still happening with such frequency that they believed they had been mistaken about the cause. It had to be fire crackers.

No one was aware of the .22-bullet damage to the air-cooled, inlet vents to the motor, or the ricochet damage to the panel behind the driver's door. The bullet that had struck the inlet vents had travelled through the back seat and into the driver's seat. Under Raewyn's seat lay the .22 bullet.

An excited Alan Jury rushed into the Mobil Service Station shop. The afternoon-shift operator, Keith Halge, 19, looked up as Alan approached saying he had been shot and asking him to call the police. As Alan spoke, Keith could hear the sound of shots being fired outside. He picked up the phone and rang D24, then turned off the petrol pumps and switched off the lights.

It sounded like youths again, letting off fire crackers in the pedestrian subway, thought Station Master, Giovanni Di Vincenzo. He went to the windows but was unable to see the subway. Fernando Myra thought the noise was a car backfiring and went outside, closing the door, and ran across the tracks to the Hoddle-Street side of the station.

Giovanni walked out onto the platform and looked around, waiting for the youths to appear. Then he looked behind him towards Ramsden Street, where he heard what sounded like shots from a .22 rifle. A Chinese man waiting for the next Melbourne-bound train said it was the sound of fire crackers.

Giovanni heard screaming coming from Hoddle Street but was unable to see anything because of the billboards and the bushes on the west-side of the station. He looked back towards the Heidelberg Road overpass and saw two cars coming down the exit ramp for Hoddle Street, then, simultaneously, heard rifle cracks and saw two sets of headlights swerve left as they passed the station. He saw the partial outline of cars stopping near Ramsden Street. Giovanni rushed back inside the office and rang Control which had a direct line to D24.

"Someone is firing a gun, get the police!"

As he spoke he heard the shots again. He looked about the office and noticed that Fernando was missing. The person from Control suggested that they get down on the floor, but Giovanni felt that that was useless as aluminium walls were no barrier to a shotgun.

Michael Anthony, 19, and his friend, Colin Smeelie, 16, were in Plenty Road, Reservoir, when Michael decided it would be good, for a change, to drive into the city by a different route.

"We'll go down Hoddle Street," he said.

Michael turned left into Albert Street and adjusted the volume control on his cassette player. The two friends were in good spirits and sang along to the rap music. Colin talked of seeing his new girlfriend again. The three were going to meet at the Billboard disco. At the Heidelberg Road intersection the red Holden Camira sedan turned right and continued west for the next two kilometres, past the shops, petrol stations and parks, across the bluestone bridge under which the Merri Creek flows north-west towards North Fitzroy and Rushall, past the flats and houses, and across the overpass. Michael turned left onto the Hoddle Street exit, giving way to a white, Mazda sedan coming from the High Street end of the carriageway. He followed it into Hoddle Street.

Con Vitkos and his wife followed the bend along the nearside lane into the straight, then past the Clifton Hill Railway Station in their white, Mazda sedan. They had been to visit friends in Lalor and were on their way home where they had left their two daughters.

As they passed the railway station there was a loud boom, then Rita's side window shattered. At first Rita thought someone had thrown a stone at them but the left side of her head and face were bleeding and her left eye was cut. She covered her face and bent down, frightened to remove her hands for fear the insides of her head would gush out.

Con considered that maybe a stone had been thrown up from the road. Rita said that they were being shot at and indicated the rear passenger seat, behind Con, where their daughter would have sat. There was a hole the size of a fist through the side window.

Glass shattered all over the back seat of Michael Anthony's Camira sedan. Pieces of glass showered his head and he looked behind to see the damage to the rear, passenger window, behind Colin.

"They wrecked my window!" he shouted believing the Mazda in front of them was responsible.

He asked Colin if he saw what it was that had been thrown from the Mazda. Was it a bottle? He accelerated to catch up with the car, flashing his headlights at it. He was angry; pumped up and was not going to let them get away with it.

Gregory Elliott was on his way home to East St Kilda driving a white, Datsun 200B sedan. In front of him, in the same nearside lane, were the Camira and the Mazda as they passed the railway station. His passenger-side window suddenly showered the inside of his car. He noticed the cars that he was following stop near the Mobil Service Station.

Isaac Lohman, 31, had been out of work since April that year and was bored. He left his flat in Thornbury in his 1969 Ford sedan for a drive around Melbourne. He turned left into Hoddle Street from High Street and cruised past the railway station. He noticed cars moving from the centre lane and stopping beside the kerb. As he approached Ramsden Street, he heard a cracking noise and felt something whizzing past his head. He looked to his left and saw a small hole through the middle of the rear passenger window. Someone was throwing rocks. Isaac checked his rear-vision mirror, indicated and moved from the centre to the nearside lane. He pulled over ahead of a Mazda and a Camira and other cars which were behind them.

The Mazda stopped just past the service station. Michael Anthony and Colin Smeelie quickly jumped out of the Camira. Michael Anthony went for the driver's door of Con Vitkos saying, "Smart arse! What do you think you're doing?" Gregory Elliott got out of his car and checked the damage to his car asking, "What's happening?"

Psychiatric nurse, Reginald Dutton, turned his HR Holden stationwagon into Hoddle Street from Queens Parade. He and Dana Sabolcki, a hospital domestic worker, had been visiting friends in Sunshine and were driving to Dana's home in Abbotsford. As they passed the railway station there was a loud bang, then something hit the car, followed by a second loud bang. Reg thought the car had been hit by a stone or, perhaps, they had suffered a tyre blow-out. Whatever it was he was not confident that either answer was correct. Dana was scared.

"Stop, stop!"

Reg continued on, south along Hoddle Street, and pulled onto the apron of the Mobil Service Station on his left. It was well lit and he could check the car, even change the tyre if necessary.

Rita Vitkos thought she was about to be attacked as Colin Smeelie came to her door. Colin noticed the windscreen glass on Rita and stopped. Michael Anthony let go of the driver's door when he, too, noticed the damage to the Mazda and the pale, open-mouthed expression on the driver.

As Reg Dutton and Dana Zabolcki pulled over, a group ran up to them.

"You've been shot!" they screamed, pointing to the passenger side of the stationwagon.

Reg and Dana got out and examined the car. There was a .22 bullet hole in the roof above the front, passenger-side door, and another below the door handle. Dana started to cry with the realisation that she could have been killed. Isaac Lohman looked along the line of cars outside the service station and saw that each of them was damaged on the passenger side.

Council worker, Michael Pearce, 25, had just picked up his fiancée Jacqueline Langosch, 24, a nurse, from the Eye and Ear Hospital in East Melbourne. She had finished working afternoon shift and they were returning home to Thomastown in Michael's blue-striped, white Datsun 1600 sedan. They noticed cars stopped on the east side of the road as they approached Ramsden Street and then again as they got closer to Clifton Hill Railway Station. As their sedan went past the station they heard two loud bangs, like an explosion. Jacqueline thought a tyre had blown or something mechanical had gone wrong with the car. She became scared when she felt a current of air around her legs.

"I'd better stop and have a look," said Michael.

He slowed the car but Jacqueline urged him to go further.

"Don't stop here, wait till we get a bit further up."

Michael accelerated under the Heidelberg Road overpass and followed the left-hand curve in the road. He mounted the curb and stopped on the nature strip about one hundred metres east of Queens Parade. He got out to check the car and, as Jacqueline opened her door to do the same, they heard a volley of about ten shots.

"Someone's shooting at us! Get back in the car!" Jacqueline yelled.

At the Mobil Service Station someone said, "Some bastard's shooting at us; we're being shot at."

Reg Dutton and Dana Sabolcki ran into the service station toilets with some of the others.

Still in their car, Con Vitkos looked across at Rita.

"Get to a hospital!" she screamed.

Con accelerated down Hoddle Street heading for Prince Henry's Hospital where they would be safe and his wife could have her injuries treated.

Colin Smeelie and Michael Anthony ran back to their car, some fifty metres north of the Mobil Service Station driveway. As they approached the car more shots were fired. Colin stopped, turned and sprinted towards the shop in the Mobil Service Station while Michael got into the driver's seat. He started his car and drove quickly into the service station, stopping near a factory wall, which offered some protection. Gregory Elliott, in his Datsun 200B, was close behind. Isaac Lohman ran to the service station and yelled for the police to be called. The attendant, Keith Halge, nodded that he had already done so. Isaac saw the injured Monica Vitelli and Danielle Kissas outside the service station and ran towards the centre of Hoddle Street.

Trevor Robinson was on his way to the Jolimont railway yards to start the night shift as a shunter for MetRail. He passed the railway station on his left and heard cracking sounds. Someone must have thrown stones at his car, but he had not felt any impact. Further south, just before the pedestrian crossing near Ramsden Street, he saw a man kneeling down beside the door of a light-coloured sedan talking to the driver. He then looked over his left shoulder and saw that there were holes in the windows of the front and rear passenger doors. For a moment he was unsure what to do next and considered stopping, then from behind he heard another volley of shots. Trevor accelerated. One-hundred metres further, he drove to the Mobil Service Station and ran inside.

Eddy McShortall had spent the day in Ivanhoe with an actor friend, rehearsing his lines for the part of a burnt-out prison officer. On Monday he was to audition for the role, in an old, Port Melbourne factory. At 28, Eddy had been a stunt actor for eleven years with more than thirty film and television credits in Ireland and Australia.

At 9.15 p.m. he started home still not satisfied but feeling better prepared than before. As he travelled along Heidelberg Road in his white, Datsun Sunny stationwagon he went over his lines "I'm sick; I'm leaving; I'm gone." He tried varied facial expressions and experimented with the tone and inflection in his voice. His mind focused fully on the part he desperately wanted to win as he turned into the exit ramp for Hoddle Street.

"I'm sick; I'm leaving; I'm gone," he repeated to himself.

Eddy passed the railway station and heard a bang. A hole suddenly appeared in the windscreen, sending pieces of glass flying through the cabin. He thought stones were being thrown. His face felt warm and his nose started to bleed. He wanted to touch his face and check that it was still there, but was frightened of what he might find. Maybe his nose had been sheared off or his mouth torn. Almost immediately, there was another bang and six holes simultaneously appeared in his windscreen. He realised then what was happening but he had no idea from where the shots were coming or why anyone would want to shoot him.

Eddy glanced in the rear-vision mirror at his face. He touched his nose and mouth, relieved that everything was where it should be. Then he touched his jugular vein, the right one in his neck. He felt blood, but knew it was not serious – just a nick where a bullet had grazed him. He looked for his attacker but could see no one. He accelerated over the Ramsden Street intersection and pulled over to the kerb before the Mobil Service Station.

"Keep driving, someone is shooting!"

Eddy caught a glimpse of a man who ran from the footpath onto the road towards his car, yelling, "Get off the road, there's a guy with a rifle!"

It was Isaac Lohman who then sprinted across Hoddle Street towards the parklands as shots could be heard behind them. Eddy accelerated and drove onto the apron of the service station. He saw people inside the service station behind the counter area; many were crying and one man's face was covered in blood. People seemed to be bumping into one another. There was confusion. When the police arrived everything would be all right, he reasoned. More shots were being fired behind him and he felt his life was in danger.

Eddy put the car into gear and drove out of the service station and into Hoddle Street towards South Terrace. Then he decided to go back to see if he could help. He drove up on to the footpath and got out of his car. As he did so six lead pellets fell from his lap on to the floor of the car. Eddy walked quickly up to the service station. A girl gave him a tissue which he pressed against his wounds. Outside there was the constant repetition of shots being fired. He had to get to hospital and went back to his car, wondering whether he was doing the right thing leaving the others. His heart was thumping.

Steve Wight looked up at the metal roof of the swimming pool. He thought someone was throwing gravel. Then he heard the sound of detonators outside, near the railway station. He looked through the window and saw the silhouette of a male with a rifle hiding among the bushes between the footpath and the railway fence. He saw the gunman look around as if he were a hunter stalking prey.

Matthew Morrow was on his way home from the Loaded Dog Hotel in St George's Road, North Fitzroy, where he worked part time. A technical-school teacher during the week, he drove his white, Holden Commodore stationwagon south along the outside lane of Hoddle Street. He felt a dull thud and thought that a stone had hit the car. He looked to his left at the car that was beside him and noticed nothing unusual. He reduced speed then felt the impact of a shotgun blast as his windscreen exploded leaving three holes in the glass. Matthew pulled over to the kerb and stopped. He ran his hands over his body to check if he had been shot, then he got out of the car. Isaac Lohman was standing in the middle of the road near the Ramsden Street intersection yelling at him, "Run! Get out of here!"

"Where? Where?" Matthew yelled back, confused.

"Down that way!" Isaac continued, waving his hands and pointing south down Hoddle Street.

Shots from two different weapons discharged from the railway-station side of the street. Matthew bolted in the direction suggested, running crouched for the fifteen metres to Ramsden Street. Isaac was gone. Matthew ran the further eighty-five metres to the Mobil handy-mart where he saw damaged cars and broken windows. People were in a panic, asking each other, "What's happening?"

Matthew stopped and tried to gather his thoughts.

Jayne Morris was having trouble with her Toyota Celica sedan so as she turned from Queens Parade into Hoddle Street, she attributed the banging noises to the backfiring of her car. Kay Edwards was seated in the front with Jayne, and a friend's eleven-year-old daughter, Cecily Caulis, was in the back. As the

Celica followed the bend in Hoddle Street, Jayne listened to the engine. As they came into the straight of Hoddle Street, she saw ahead, a red, Toyota Corolla sedan followed closely by a Holden Gemini sedan. They were only three of the approximately 1,300 vehicles that travelled along that section of Hoddle Street every Sunday between 9.30 p.m. and 10.30 p.m.

Vesna Markovska was a broadcaster, on community radio and an active member of the Australia Macedonia Theatre Group, where she performed in a variety of roles ranging from stagehand to actor. Vesna met her boyfriend, Zoran Trajceski, 24, during rehearsals in January and they had been going out together ever since.

That weekend, Vesna had been to three parties beginning with one for her beloved father who had turned 54 on Friday. Then there was another birthday party for a friend on Saturday. On Sunday she spent hours on the telephone counselling migrant women who had problems coping with domestic violence, separation or divorce. She worked as a social worker and carried a pager all the time. As an accredited English-Macedonian interpreter she was always in demand in one way or another. She liked to be busy and to be helpful to others less fortunate than herself.

After lunch with her parents, Vesna had attended another party with Zoran. They had left the party early to pick up her father's Toyota Corolla sedan following repairs. From the garage in Preston, Zoran followed in Vesna's Holden Gemini to Clifton Hill and into Hoddle Street.

It was an orange and white flash that Steve Wight saw. It came from the barrel end of the gunman's rifle. The flash was about a metre wide as the windscreen of the red Corolla shattered. Vesna Markovska stopped against the kerb and got out to check the damage.

Steve Wight heard some more shots then saw Vesna fall across the footpath, her feet in the gutter. She had been shot in the forehead, the right shoulder, the right upper arm, the right elbow, and there was a 6cm x 4cm wound to the right side of her trunk.

Zoran saw her windscreen shatter and pulled in behind, as a burst of thirteen shots pierced his windscreen causing pellet wounds to the left side of his head. His hand was lacerated. The Gemini he had been driving touched the back of the Corolla as he almost fell out of the car and ran to Vesna.

Jayne Morris's Celica was about sixty metres behind when she saw the spray of windscreen glass. At first Jayne thought the Corolla was about to blow up; that it had serious engine trouble. She did not recognise the noises she heard and suggested to Kay Edwards that they should stop and help.

"Put your foot down! Duck!" screamed Kay.

Kay had turned in her seat pushing Cecily down to the floor. To her, it looked as if the drivers of the Toyota Corolla and the Holden Gemini were shooting at each other. As Jayne accelerated towards the Ramsden Street intersection Kay noticed a man standing on the side of the road, holding a rifle, facing the two cars.

"He's got a gun!"

In 1985, Englishman, Robert Mitchell visited Australia for a short holiday. He enjoyed the weather, the space and the fact that everyone seemed to be equal, unlike in his country. He hated the English class system; in Australia you could make it if you worked hard. When he was back home in Essex, he made up his mind to return. He said goodbye to his family in 1986 and migrated to Australia.

No sooner had he found a place to live than Robert was working as a sales representative for an envelope-making company. He was 27, loved sports and began playing soccer for Mitcham. Then there was golf, cricket and snow skiing. Such was his enthusiasm for his new job that he was soon promoted to marketing, and then asked to set up the Melbourne branch of a West Australia based stationery company. Robert became the State Manager, driving a company car and earning a good wage. Very soon the only thing he missed about his former life were the Tottenham Hotspurs. He could no longer see them play live and had to settle for the occasional match on television during which he would wear the team's scarf and shirt, and wave their colours.

For three months he had lived in a red brick house in New Street, Brighton with Sue Rodaughan, an intensive care nurse, who was three years his senior. They had met at a party and were inseparable within weeks. Sue was attracted to his outgoing nature, his cheerful and positive attitude. They were always going away with friends for trips along the Great Ocean Road, to the snow and to Indian restaurants. It was a close relationship. Sue was his family, and he was accepted by her family as one of their own. That Sunday some friends, who were also from England, dropped over. They went, as a group, to The Victoria Hotel in Albert Park for lunch. Robert's cheerful cockney accent could be heard by anyone who entered the dining area. It was uplifting and people felt glad to be around him. Then at 4.30 p.m. the group went their separate ways. Robert and Sue went home.

Robert debated whether to go to Reservoir and visit some friends who had just returned from England. Sue said she would stay home and get herself ready for work the next day. It was her first day at a new job and she wanted to create the right impression by being punctual and looking her best. Robert decided to go.

Errol and Angie dined with Robert at an Indian restaurant in Coburg then, just after 9.00 p.m., returned to their unit in Sturdee Street, Reservoir. Conscious of the time, Robert declined an offer of coffee.

"I better get back to Sue," he said cheerfully, and he drove towards High Street in his bronze-coloured company car. The most direct way home to Brighton was down Hoddle Street.

School teacher, John Holland, turned his Holden Commodore stationwagon left into Hoddle Street from Queens Parade and travelled in the outside lane. As he approached the overpass, he was alarmed at two sets of headlights coming towards him at great speed. John pulled over to the kerb as the two cars continued on their way towards Queens Parade. With the danger gone he continued along Hoddle Street under the overpass and beside the railway station.

There was a loud noise and his car shuddered as it was hit five times by gunfire. John braked then reversed and crossed over on to the north-bound side of Hoddle Street as the drivers side window shattered causing cuts to his right shoulder. He turned quickly left into the exit ramp for Heidelberg Road and accelerated.

Keith Wing Shing, 24, turned his Datsun 180B sedan right into Hoddle Street from the Eastern Freeway. He had been in North Balwyn having dinner with people he considered his family. When he was ten years old, his parents were killed in a car accident. As an intern at St Vincent's Hospital in Fitzroy he would usually have worked at the hospital and would not have travelled along the freeway and Hoddle Street to go home. He would have driven from the hospital along Nicholson Street, right into Alexander Parade, and then left into Queens Parade, to his home in Northcote. He would pass Hoddle Street as he approached the railway bridge and cross over the Merri Creek.

Keith drove north along Hoddle Street passing the Mobil Service Station which was on his right. As he approached the intersection with Ramsden Street, he saw the bloodied body of Vesna Markovska lying on the footpath on the south-bound side of Hoddle Street. Zoran Trajceski was standing helplessly beside her. Keith pulled over to the left side of the road slightly north but opposite them to offer help. He assumed that Vesna had been hit by the car that was stopped further south of her. Perhaps Zoran had been the driver of that vehicle. Keith turned off the motor and reached for the door handle. There was a loud bang. He thought he had blown a rear tyre.

As he opened his door there was another loud bang and the left-hand side windows sprayed him with broken glass. The rear-vision mirror and the dashboard were damaged. A shotgun pellet would later be located on the driver's seat amidst the glass and his blood.

Keith felt immense pain in the right side of his face and he felt his jaw hang loose. The bullet had passed through his bottom lip over his back teeth and had then shattered the jawbone.

Keith looked around to see who had done this but he could see no one. He had no idea where the shots had come from. He pulled his door shut and restarted the engine. He applied pressure to the arteries of his neck believing this would best reduce blood loss, only removing his left hand to change gears. He kept his head low, spitting blood onto the passenger seat, his mind totally focused on St Vincent's casualty department. He had to get to cubicle seven as quickly as possible. He knew that he would survive no matter how much blood he had lost, once there, in the resuscitation cubicle.

Keith flattened the accelerator and raced along Hoddle Street towards Queens Parade. He worried about passing out on the way; losing control of the car; maybe killing someone. At the same time, speed limits and red lights were not going to deter him.

Zoran Trajceski bent over Vesna Markovska's body, unsure of what to do. He looked north towards the railway station as Fernando Myra, the station assistant, appeared from inside the main entrance. Two Japanese boys had told him that something was on the road because every time a car went past there were bangs. Zoran was yelling something but Fernando could not hear and he stepped onto the footpath and began walking towards Zoran, his eyes centred on Vesna Markovska.

Shots rang out again. They were close by. Fernando froze, then ran back towards the station entrance. On the platform, he saw people waiting for the next north-bound train. Fernando called them together and hurried them across the tracks and into the station-master's office where he told them to lay low.

Zoran Trajceski tried to lift Vesna Markovska in his arms, as twenty-one-year old student, Georgina Papaioannou, stopped opposite them in her blue Datsun 200B sedan. The cassette playing Bruce Springsteen stopped mid-song. He was her favourite singer and she often identified with his lyrics as he sang about relationships, struggle and hard times. Springsteen was almost an obsession. Even her boyfriend, Con, bore a striking resemblance to the singer.

Gina, as she was better known, knew what it was like to go through hard times. Her mother had died when she was twelve and for the past nine years she had helped run the house with her sisters, Vicki and Rikki, while their father, Christos, 55, worked twelve-hour days in a plastics factory. They matured quickly having to combine school with home duties, then university with work. Earlier in the year, Vicki had married and moved out of home, so it was left to Gina to cook and clean. When she was not at university she worked at the Oakleigh Market selling chickens.

Gina was in her final year as an arts student at Monash University, having transferred from La Trobe University. During the week, because of the distance, she lived with Rikki, the eldest of the three girls, in Northcote, and went home on the weekends. Gina was the youngest and was close to both her sisters. Rikki was feeling the pressure of being separated from her husband and the first woman in the family to file for divorce. Sometimes Gina would find Rikki looking glum and offer encouragement. With the slight lisp Gina carried she would say, "Wash a matter? Give ush a hug," and Rikki's troubles seemed to wash away.

She was relieved to transfer her studies over to Monash University for the 1987 year as it was much closer to home and she could help Vicki run the house. She was excited to be studying Law the next year. Gina wanted to be a lawyer and help the underdog in society.

Clutching her car keys, Gina rushed across the road to offer some help. As she reached the centre of the road, Robert Mitchell's bronze Mitsubishi Magna pulled into the kerb in front of Zoran and Vesna. Robert and Gina reached the pair together. Robert told Zoran not to lift his girlfriend, but to wait for an ambulance.

Jacqueline Turner, 22, was on her way home from nursing duties at the South Caulfield Hospital when she saw Gina leave her car and rush over to help Vesna. It looked to her as if Vesna had been struck by the Toyota Corolla with the shattered windscreen. Jacqueline pulled in behind Gina's car and made to get out to offer help, but just then she saw, behind a billboard advertising the new Honda Accord sedan, the silhouette of a man, his arm outstretched as if he were holding a rifle. Jacqueline was frightened. She threw herself towards the passenger side as shots were fired again.

Robert Mitchell had his back to the bushes and the railway line when the shooting resumed, and he dropped with a .308 bullet wound to the right side of his head. The bullet produced a 1cm diameter entry wound and a 2cm diameter exit wound. Then Gina was felled by the same weapon, leaving a thirty-eight-by-twelve centimetre hole in her left side. Zoran lay low on the footpath hugging Vesna, and trying to give her comfort, when he felt her body jolt as two more bullets penetrated her body. He could hear a man crying.

Steve Wight could not believe what he had witnessed. This was Australia – not Ireland, the USA or the Middle East. As he went to the telephone and dialled 000, he could still see the flash from the rifle every time a shot was discharged. He had done first-aid training and knew that it was imperative to remain calm and help those who had been shot.

Andrew Hack was on his way home when he decided to buy Chinese food from a city take-away. A friend had recommended the shop to him. He was singing along to AC/DC's *Back in Black* which was playing loudly in his car when he turned off Heidelberg Road and left into Hoddle Street. It was a spur-of-the-moment decision; he usually went to the city via Queens Parade. He just felt like a change. He travelled down the exit ramp, enjoying the music, when he saw sparks fly on the road, between the wheels of a car ahead. Then he saw the bodies of Vesna Markovska and Robert Mitchell just past the railway station. As Andrew slowed to stop and lend assistance, an explosion entered the car and the sound system cut out.

Andrew felt himself lift off his seat and slam against the driver's door. He felt the left side of his body spew out, like red-hot lava. He felt numb and then a burning sensation. He couldn't move, and then found that he couldn't feel anything. He flexed his hands and feet, trying to regain some feeling.

Andrew stopped outside the entrance to the railway station and held on to the roof, lifting himself out of the cabin. He managed to walk towards the bodies. When he got to the front of his car there was a loud bang. He recognised it as coming from a rifle, the target this time the car behind him. It was then he noticed that his T-shirt was soaked in blood, and his shoulder hurt. He got back into his car and did a U-turn, thumping over the concrete median strip to get back into Heidelberg Road. He put two fingers deep into the gaping wound on his left side and almost fainted.

Dusan Flajnik, 53, worked as a fork-lift driver at the Carlton and United Brewery in Abbotsford. He had worked there for twenty-five years and had accumulated almost six months of sick leave. When he migrated to Australia from Yugoslavia in 1960, he had no money but he was a hard worker and it had paid off. He had come from having nothing to living in a comfortable red-brick house with his wife, Elefteria, and their sons, Steve and Tony, in a street of otherwise weatherboard houses in Preston.

During the day, Dusan took it easy and tried to rest. He did some gardening and checked on the lemon trees he had recently planted. He was looking forward to retirement and was making plans for an easier life. But tonight he had to work; he was taking someone else's place – it meant overtime.

When his older brother, Jimmy, came over at about 5.30 p.m., they played billiards in the garage. Then when Jimmy left at about 7.00 p.m. he had some pita that Elefteria had made. They watched television together, relaxing on the couch, while Tony was in his bedroom and Steve was in the garage playing billiards.

Just before 9.30 p.m. Dusan drove his brown Sigma sedan to work. It was a ten-minute drive to Hoddle Street and another ten to the Brewery. He would have time to park the car and have a coffee with his workmates. In the morning, he was to take Steve to his new job as an apprentice cabinet maker.

As he travelled south along Hoddle Street, in the outside lane, he passed Andrew Hack's car and the railway station. There was a loud noise.

The front passenger-side door was struck by a .308 bullet fired from approximately forty-five degrees from the front of the Sigma. The bullet passed through the lower end of the door and the front passenger seat before lodging in the door behind Dusan's seat. A portion of the bullet was lodged in the back seat. A second .308 bullet left a hole in the front, passenger-side window that fractured into a star pattern just above the door knob. The bullet struck Dusan's left shoulder, leaving a 2.5 cm v-shaped tear. It continued on, severing the carotid artery and, finally, lodging in his chest. Dusan slumped against the driver's door, held upright by the seat belt. Later, his family would learn of his death from television footage during a news flash, and from photographs in the newspapers.

In the bathroom of the Mobil Service Station, Michael Anthony was beside himself. His car was damaged, there were two windows shattered and he had found a bullet hole in the front, passenger-side door. There were people crying and shaking, injured and bleeding, or covered in blood and windscreen glass. Michael wanted to get up to the railway station and stop the shooting. He made a start to go outside. Reg Dutton held him by the shirt and told him to settle, that there was nothing he could do. Besides, shots were still being heard and he could be killed.

John Delahunty drove the police car quickly along Miller Street, North Fitzroy. He had been doing the files in his area for several hours and was thinking of returning to the station when the watchhouse keeper, Margaret Kidd, gave him a job. A woman was concerned about her elderly mother, who was not answering the telephone. In half-an-hour he was due to go home to Flemington. While it had been an uneventful day, he had accomplished all that he had set out to do.

He had slept in until 9.30 a.m. before driving to Russell Street Police Station where he left his car and ran through the city streets and then along the Tan Track which bounded the Botanical Gardens. Once back at Russell Street, he worked out using the weights in the gymnasium for an hour. He then headed to his mother's house, stopping on the way, at a heated pool where he swam twenty 50-metre laps. His mother gave him lunch and, as usual, she spoiled him. She wanted to pack a meal for him to have at work but he told her not to worry, he could look after himself.

John scribbled down the details of the job on his running sheet. He reasoned that it would take only a few minutes and, as he was close to his own mother – she had raised him and his two sisters on her own – he could understand the concern. As he approached the elderly woman's house, he heard the Fitzroy van accept a job – an "offenders on" call in May Street, North Fitzroy.

At Collingwood Police Station, Detective Tony Doherty picked up the radio transmitter in the watchhouse and advised D24 that the call should be treated with some urgency. The D24 operator asked if Tony was attending. His private car was parked outside the station and he put the keys back in his pocket. Tony had been on duty for thirteen hours and intended to go home. Jenenne Stiles came running down the stairs and checked Byron Sedgewick who wanted to go with the detective.

"You look after the watchhouse," she said to the trainee, and she and Tony Doherty left in a marked police car for May Street.

When John Delahunty pulled up outside the block of flats in May Street, Constables Bill Taylor, 23, and Jenny Leuther, 26, had the offender in custody. For several months, the offender had been breaking into the victim's flat and masturbating over her bed. John recognised the offender as the boyfriend of the victim. He had been caught looking through her window from a trellis fence against the outside wall. When Tony Doherty and Jenenne Stiles arrived seconds later, the boyfriend denied that he was the offender and that he had been hiding in the bushes waiting to catch the real offender.

John Delahunty turned his head in the direction of Clifton Hill, some four kilometres away. He heard what he thought were fireworks.

Kenneth Stanton was named after his mother's younger brother, but he was his own person and everyone knew him by his middle-name, Shane. He was never called Kenneth.

Shane, 21, loved playing the organ and the guitar but could not be persuaded to sing even if his life depended on it. He took the music no further than his bedroom yet he had talent. Occasionally, he would jam with some friends but he desired nothing more than that.

There were three things that mattered to him: his wife Debra, 20, who he married in 1986; his family; and his friends. Everything else was secondary. A quiet person who enjoyed ten-pin bowling, Shane kept his friends and stuck by them. Even when he moved to Melbourne in 1986, he stayed in touch with his Shepparton friends.

Shane's first big break came when he started work as a postal officer with

Australia Post. The job offered security and an opportunity for him and his wife to eventually leave their rented Fairfield house for one of their own in Wantirna South. While the overtime he worked on day shift was handy, the penalty rates for working night shift were greater. He and Debra were hopeful that the extra income from night shift would be worth its intrusion into their time together. They reasoned that together with the money she earned working at a local cake shop, it would get them into their house sooner.

During the day they watched the Brisbane-Collingwood football match on television and discussed whether Shane should take their new car, a Holden Camira, to work and risk it being stolen.

Shane kissed Debra goodbye saying he would be home at 6.00 a.m. He zipped his leather jacket, secured the two-tone helmet on his head, and rode off on his green, Kawasaki 250cc motor cycle. The short, red beard that he grew during the winter months would keep the cold air off his face as he travelled along Heidelberg Road. Because it was his first ever night shift, he wanted to get to work early, find a secure place to park the motor cycle, and settle in.

Shane was unaware that he was actually on a rostered day off. He was not expected at work until the following night.

"Collingwood 311 with one reply," Belinda Bourchier said.

"Collingwood 311," Mick Hogan replied.

"Collingwood 311, er 303. Your last in Mayfield Street was an enquiry in relation to a theft that had happened there previously. All apparently correct."

Mick Hogan grinned. Everyone who had been on night shift and was working the "quick change-over" seemed to be using his or her night shift call sign.

"Roger. We've got you saying it now," Hogan said.

A policewoman cut across the transmission.

"'On you', Frenchie, (sic)" she said to Belinda, using her Academy nickname.

Glen Sheluchin turned left from Johnston Street into Hoddle Street. He decided to drive up to Hoddle Street and onto the Eastern Freeway, where there were no traffic lights or stop signs.

Salvation Army worker, Sharyn Maunder, 19, drove her Honda Civic sedan north along Hoddle Street. She had just left church in Camberwell and was on her way to visit a friend in Northcote. As she was passing the railway station, she jumped in fright at what sounded like a car backfiring three times. She thought that it might even be her own car but kept driving. She noticed, in passing, an orange car and, close by, a man standing next to a taxi. She continued along Hoddle Street unaware of shotgun damage to her driver's-side front mudguard and door.

Steve Wight locked the door to the swimming pool and put the keys in his shorts pocket. He left his sport bag inside the building then went into the park, immediately regretting not having worn something warmer. A singlet and thongs were no insulation against the cold, night air. He reached a tree and stood behind it.

Peter Gauci, 22, and John Muscat, 26, came out of 23 Turnbull Street which was opposite the railway station. They had been there for several hours with their friends. Peter, who lived in a boarding house at 5 Ramsden Street, was unemployed and broke, and had been invited over for dinner, but he had arrived too late. The friends watched television for a while in the lounge room then began to discuss near-death experiences.

John, who organised city newspaper deliveries for Mitty's Newsagency in Bourke Street, Melbourne, told of getting stabbed when he went to help someone in a fight. He was not a good fighter but it was not unusual for him to step in to help someone being bullied. He recalled an incident when he went with his sister, Mary, to Fitzroy Street, St Kilda. Mary received some unwanted attention and John stepped in to protect her but it was Mary who had to rescue him from a beating; but he didn't care – no one was going to hurt his sister.

John grew up in Yambla Street, Clifton Hill, in a single-fronted, two-bedroom, weatherboard house and went to St Thomas Catholic School until Year 10. Each school day he would walk to school, crossing the train tracks at the Hoddle Street intersection on his way.

When his parents had saved enough to buy a bigger house in Montmorency, John continued to see his friends in Clifton Hill, catching the train or getting a lift to visit them on weekends. As he had to be at work early in the mornings and went to bed late, he was often seen asleep in a train carriage as it passed through Clifton Hill. Once he slept through to the end of the line and had to get a taxi home, as it was the last train. At the Bourke Street newsagency, where he had worked from the age of fifteen, he was popular with customers who knew him as fun loving, good natured and reliable. In all his years with the newsagency he had never taken a sick day.

Peter Gauci related how he had received an electric shock connecting 240-volt motors into 1.5-volt racing-car motors. Another friend talked of being hit by a car. Peter told of going to the Thomastown cemetery, near where he lived as a boy, and looking down the cracks of graves. He said it made him feel that the dead were nothing to be afraid of.

Sarah was in bed when she heard what seemed like four gunshots. She got out of her bed and looked through the window and saw the silhouette of a man, who appeared to be Julian, with a rifle slung over one shoulder and another in his hands. He was running towards the Clifton Hill Railway Station. She lost sight of him through the trees and bushes. She heard rapid gunfire and then nothing. Then further rapid gunfire. The gunfire seemed to be from different calibres. She ran downstairs to Julian's bedroom. He was not there. She then ran to her mother who was still watching television and had not heard any gunfire. They went upstairs and looked out of Sarah's bedroom windows. They could not see Julian or anyone else in either Ramsden or Hoddle Street.

Pamela Knight then checked her wardrobe in her bedroom. A box of ammunition was missing. Julian had stored the rifles and ammunition in his mother's room while he had not been living at home. His bedroom had been converted into a lounge. Since his return, he had been sleeping in a makeshift bedroom. She ran down the stairs to Julian's room. She now heard gunfire. Behind a couch, she saw an empty gun box and a rifle carry-bag. She went to the telephone and dialled 11444 – the direct emergency line to police at D24. The operator took down the details of Julian Knight.

9.37 p.m.

The Collingwood divisional van had entered the nearside lane to exit Hoddle Street for the Eastern Freeway, to travel east. Belinda Bourchier saw the headlights of a car flash repeatedly on the south side of Hoddle Street. It was travelling quickly, its horn blasting. It then weaved across the four lanes to the centre median strip. Jayne Morris leaned her head out of the car window as Belinda Bourchier leaned over to the dashboard and switched on the flashing blue lights. Glen Sheluchin proceeded across the four north-bound lanes and stopped beside the Celica. Jayne Morris was frantic.

"Get up there! Get up there!" she screamed, indicating further north in Hoddle Street.

Steven Mihailidis was driving his 1979 Ford Cortina stationwagon south along Hoddle Street to start night shift at the Carlton and United Brewery in Richmond. As he passed the railway station he watched the green, Kawasaki 250cc motor cycle, ahead and to his right, suddenly drop to the road and roll over. Before he had a chance to go to Shane Stanton's aid he heard two loud bangs. Instinctively, he leaned towards the driver's door. His left ear suddenly blocked and the steering wheel went loose in his hands. A bullet had struck the steering column and shattered the steering wheel.

Steven looked over his left shoulder and saw that his back passenger window was shattered. In the front, he saw .308 calibre bullet holes in the bottom, right-hand corner of his windscreen. Inside the dash and door was a .308 calibre jacket. Steven continued at slow speed along Hoddle Street, towards Ramsden Street, one hundred and eighty metres away. Isaac Lohman waved him on.

"Don't stop! Keep on going! There's a man with a shotgun!"

Steven Mihailidis accelerated and was not going to stop his car until he got to work.

Peter Harvey sat in the A signal box, a weatherboard structure, at the Ramsden Street and Hoddle Street intersection. He switched on the light and started to shave when, outside, he heard the sound of glass breaking. Peter opened a window and tried to see who was causing the problem. Youths were always throwing stones or bottles at the signal box.

Peter looked north along Hoddle Street when he heard rifle shots, but was uncertain where they were coming from. Having served in the Army Reserve he recognised that the shots came from a shotgun and a high-powered, military rifle. He saw cars swerve across the road, some trying to U-turn, and he saw shattered glass spread about the lanes. Some cars had stopped by the side of the south-bound lane. A driver, with wounds to his chest area, stood at the front of a car looking dazed. Peter saw his legs buckle as he fell to the ground. He leaned out of the window to improve his view but jumped back inside when two more shots whizzed past the signal box. Peter kept close to the floor, went for the telephone, and dialled 000.

Belinda and Glen remained calm. "What's the problem?" they asked. Traffic which had been stopped at the Johnston-Street traffic lights began to surge forward. Belinda looked at her watch. It was 9.37 p.m.

"Cars are being shot at!"

"What sort of cars were shot at?" Glen asked.

He believed, as did Belinda, that it was nothing more than the nuisances with their sling shots and ball bearings. During the last night shift they had attended several such calls. Belinda reached for the radio transmitter. It was just another routine call. Like a theft report or a cyclist without lights on his bicycle. She spoke calmly and without fear in her voice.

"Collingwood 303. We've just received a call from a passerby, there are two cars being shot at in Hoddle Street just after Roseneath Street."

D24, the police communications section, was housed on the mezzanine floor of the Russell Street police building. Sergeant Mick Hogan pressed the foot pedal that enabled him to reply. To his left sat Sergeant Gary Ricardo, who took phone calls and passed 'yellow job' cards to Hogan as the jobs occurred.

The Killing Zone | 55

"What did she say?" Mick Hogan asked.

They had been leaning back in their chairs and looking up at the clock, looking forward to having a couple of drinks and then going home.

"Hoddle Street near where?" Hogan asked.

Glen Sheluchin accelerated.

Belinda opened the Melway street directory and ran her finger over Map 44, along Hoddle Street, stopping at the grid reference, E1. She was more specific.

"Collingwood 303. Corner of Ramsden Street."

Mick Hogan asked for back up assistance and called Collingwood 250. While he felt it was probably the youths with their sling shots again, there was no room for chance. D24 was the lifeline for the police cars on patrol. He pushed aside his newspapers and magazines and made space.

Paul McNicol, the Collingwood Sergeant, and his driver, Shane Keogh, were in a street off Johnston Street. Shane was in a milk bar buying milk for the station, while Paul was in the police car listening to the radio. He heard the call and sounded the horn then ran from the car to the milk bar window and rapped on the glass.

In Carlton, Phil Bradley mentioned to Gary Maddern that the call was probably nothing. While Phil casually turned the police car into Lygon Street towards Victoria Street, Gary increased the volume on the radio.

Inspector Pat Murtagh was in mid-sentence when he heard Belinda Bourchier report shots being fired. Neither he nor Inspector Adrian Fyfe was concerned about the call. Police were always receiving reports of shots being fired and most were found to be hoaxes. They put it down to youths firing sling shots again.

A blood-stained Zoran Trajceski ran into the middle of the road and flagged down David Clement, 24, a semi-professional basketballer with the Sunbury Jets. David pulled in against the kerb in front of Robert Mitchell's car. Zoran led David by the arm to the motionless bodies of Vesna Markovska, Robert Mitchell and Gina Papaioannou. Gina blinked her eyes. It was the only movement.

"You must get these people to a hospital," Zoran said.

"Don't touch them," David replied.

In the distance they saw the fast-approaching Collingwood divisional van. It was making a silent approach, in order to catch the supposed offenders with the ball bearings. Zoran was frantic and ran towards it. Shots rang out again. David Clement ran into Ramsden Street and took cover behind a parked car.

The patrol car from Russell Street Community Policing Squad was in Rathdowne Street, Carlton as part of its general patrol for the evening. Andrew Hiam, 26, was the driver and had earlier remarked to his partner, Michelle Young, 21, that the evening was dead boring.

Andrew revealed that he had attended behavioural science lectures at La Trobe University during the week. He found it difficult to combine study with police work and he had spent an hour at the books before coming to work. Michelle said that she had slept for three hours between the time that she got home at 8.00 a.m. and when she started again at 3.00 that afternoon.

"I slept all right. I didn't get up 'til about eleven," Andrew said.

They listened to the radio and thought that the call from Collingwood 303 was most likely a hoax – nothing more than vehicles backfiring.

It took only a matter of seconds for the Collingwood van to travel the six hundred metres to Ramsden Street. Belinda Bourchier remarked to Glen Sheluchin on how dark it had become all of a sudden. As they approached the Mobil Service Station, it seemed as if they were going into a darkened tunnel.

6

With the sound of wailing police sirens, everyone who was jammed into the small toilet in the service station burst out and into the shop area looking for their saviours. Someone lit a cigarette, others cried in relief, while others hugged. Some stayed close to the floor just in case.

The Collingwood divisional van passed over Ramsden Street approaching the pedestrian crossing which extended across the width of Hoddle Street. Stopped, one behind the other, in the inside lane, were two cars facing south. Set back between the footpath and the railway line was a V-shaped billboard which extended from the railway signal box up to the Clifton Hill Railway Station.

This billboard advertised, "Tastes so good, it's uncanny. The Stubby," while the billboard facing south-bound traffic promoted *Dear Children*, the latest album by the Australian band, Joe Camilleri and The Black Sorrows. Seventeen metres north of the *Dear Children* billboard and the Gemini and the Corolla, were the bloodied bodies of Vesna Markovska, Robert Mitchell and Gina Papaioannou. Belinda and Glen could only clearly see Gina and note that she was alive. The glass all over the road confirmed in their minds that youths had again been firing ball bearings from sling shots.

As Glen brought the divisional van to a stop almost five metres past the pedestrian crossing, Belinda saw the silhouette of a tall, thin man under the *Dear Children* billboard. He looked in their direction from among the bushes. Belinda made to get out of the van while Glen took the transmitter from the dashboard clip.

"Collingwood 303. Can you get a unit down here? There's (sic) been three or four cars shot," Glen said.

Mick Hogan called for the Collingwood 250 car. Paul McNicol advised that it was "on the way."

"303. Could we get an ambulance here too, thanks!"

"Roger. What's the situation there, 303? Who's injured?" Hogan asked.

"One female has been shot, I believe, or glass wounds."

Suddenly, there was a rapid burst of gunfire from a high-powered rifle. Belinda counted five shots. Almost simultaneously, Glen reversed the van, tangling the transmitter cord around his left hand in his hurry to get going. Belinda stretched over trying to free his wrist from the cord.

Donna Randall and Tim Edgeworth were in the office of the District Support Group preparing to go home. It had been a quiet night and it seemed as if the drug dealers were home before a warm fire rather than on the cold streets of St Kilda. It had been the first shift for nine months where they had not made an arrest. They listened to the monitor in their office about shots being fired in Hoddle Street and felt that the report was nothing out of the ordinary. There was always someone somewhere reporting gunfire in Melbourne, and more often than not, they were hoaxes.

Michael Baretti rushed back inside the house and dialled for the police. He told John Muscat and Peter Gauci that someone was shooting outside. It was all they needed to hear. The two men raced out the back door to the front of Turnbull Street, crossing the road and heading through the park before pausing next to the blue Datsun sedan that Gina Papaioannou had been driving. They were unsure of what to do next. They could see the bodies on the eastern side of the road and the Collingwood divisional van approaching from the south. Steve Wight ran towards them, yelling to them to be careful, that they would get shot.

"Is an ambulance coming?" Peter Gauci asked.

Shots rang out as John Muscat stepped onto the road. He yelled and fell to the ground. He had been shot twice in the left shoulder, in the left side of the chest and in his right ear, his head and his neck. There were more shots and Peter Gauci's right shoulder jerked forward and he felt an intense burning sensation throughout his whole body. He stepped back behind a light pole, initially unaware that he had also been shot in the right arm, chest and thigh. When the shooting stopped he called out to John but there was no answer.

Steve Wight heard Peter Gauci cry out for help; that his mate John had been shot. Steve waited behind a tree for a moment hoping the gunman had left or run out of rounds. When it seemed there were no more shots he walked quickly over to the men. He was about five metres from them when another series of shots rang out. He saw the muzzle flash from two rifles being discharged at the same time by one person. The windscreen of Gina's car was peppered with shotgun pellets.

His head felt as if it had been struck with a baseball bat. He saw stars, blinding stars, and fell backwards towards the ground. He maintained his balance and sat without falling. Steve wiped the left side of his forehead and saw blood on his hand from the shotgun blast to his head. He got on his hands and knees and began to cough up froth and blood. As he struggled for breath, he noticed a small hole in his chest, and realised he had also been shot with a .22 rifle. He rolled over and lay on his back thinking that he would never again see his wife, Lucy, and Jesse. He couldn't see properly; it was as if he was looking through a plastic bag; the back of his eyes felt sticky. He sat upright and, slowly, his eyesight returned to normal. Steve told Peter to relax and not to panic. Everything would be all right.

Paul McNicol and Shane Keogh, in Collingwood 250, drove quickly down Johnston Street and then left into Hoddle Street overtaking other cars as they proceeded north. Their flashing blue lights bounced off the walls and windows of the buildings as they passed.

"Rifle's being shot now; we're reversing ... " Glen Sheluchin said, aware that north-bound traffic was approaching.

At D24, Mick Hogan counted the seconds as he waited for more information from the Collingwood van. When there was none he thought that its occupants may have been killed.

"Roger. VKC to Collingwood 250. VKC to another unit in the Collingwood area," Mick Hogan said.

Michelle Young picked up the radio transmitter.

"Russell Street 603. We'll head that way," she said.

Andrew Hiam accelerated towards Pigdon Street while Michelle activated the flashing blue lights and the siren. She opened her folder and wrote the details down on the running sheet.

9.38 p.m.

"Roger, 603," Mick Hogan said, "Collingwood 250, you take charge of the scene. Russell Street 603, we've got a fellow going through the Clifton Hill Railway Station at the moment in relation to this one, if you can head that way."

Michelle opened the Melway. Neither she nor Andrew were familiar with the Clifton Hill area. Apart from Hoddle Street, the street names meant nothing to them.

Constable Shane Cross, 23, waited in his police car outside Russell Street Police Station while his partner went inside. The passenger door opened and Inspector Pat Murtagh got in.

"Quick! Down to Hoddle Street!" the Inspector ordered.

"We're Russell Street 203 Sir. I'm not your driver," Shane said, while putting the car into gear.

Inspector Murtagh stretched across to the dashboard and activated the flashing lights and the siren.

"You are now, mate," he said.

Glen Sheluchin reversed the van so that it blocked both north-bound lanes, the sweep of the headlights tearing into the bushes and across the billboard where they had seen the thin man, and then across and into Mayors Park. A taxi driver, seeing its north-bound passage blocked by the police van, mounted the western nature strip and began to manoeuvre its way around the van. Belinda Bourchier yelled at the driver to stop. At first he ignored her and concentrated on his manoeuvreing. Frustrated, she could see other motorists wanting to follow the taxi, she pulled the switch for the flashing blue lights on the roof.

Belinda got out of the van, taking the portable radio from the briefcase, and ran, crouched, over to the taxi. At last the driver stopped. As Glen got out of the van, two men came running towards him from the middle of the road. One of them, Zoran Trajceski, had been shot on the left side of his face and shoulder. Blood was running down his neck and back. Belinda signalled to them to come behind the van. Glen was leaning inside trying to get through to D24 on the radio.

Peter Harvey hurried down the steps of the signal box and onto the trainline towards the next station which was a kilometre further south. There was a train due to arrive at Clifton Hill shortly and he had to stop it. He heard another shot and sprinted.

At Russell Street Police Station, Ralph Lockman was already in his uniform when he realised the urgency of what he was hearing on the police radio in the room opposite. He heard someone increase the volume of the wall monitor. When Belinda Bourchier came back on the air a second time, Ralph knew that something was terribly wrong. She had originally spoken in a calm, routine-like manner. The second time there was tension and fear in her voice as she spoke of being unable to get near the other cars and of reversing the van.

Ralph went into the room with the monitor and listened with the other police. He then grabbed his cap and ran down the stairs to the reception desk. He took out a .38 Smith and Wesson revolver and hurried to a police car. He roared down Victoria Street, north into Nicholson Street and east along Alexandra Parade, stopping outside the United Kingdom Hotel in Queens Parade. They got out and stopped all traffic coming into Queens Parade.

Mick Hogan directed the Carlton 310 van, to check the Clifton Hill Railway Station. Russell Street 302 and 303 advised that they would back up the Carlton van. Belinda Bourchier, her voice wavering, suggested that they come in through the other end, the east side, of Ramsden Street as shots were still being fired. They seemed close – too close for comfort.

Glen Sheluchin took the radio transmitter from her and said, "It sounds like a shotgun. He's moving further north."

9.39 p.m.

Hogan, whose concentration was being tested by interruptions from other police, was given a note from another operator. Hogan broadcast that the offender was "heading north in Ramsden Street."

It was the start of the general misinformation that would confuse and hinder everybody but the offender.

"About two hundred yards north of Ramsden," Glen Sheluchin corrected. "Two hundred yards north of Ramsden and extreme caution should be exercised. He's in possession of a shotgun, apparently ... "

Police in cars from Russell Street and Royal Park also volunteered their services and Hogan directed them to the area of the railway station.

"St Kilda 500 to VKC," Syd Hadley said.

"St Kilda 500."

"St Kilda 500. We're in the city. Do you want us to head that way?"

Glen Sheluchin and Belinda Bourchier saw north-bound Hoddle Street traffic, and vehicles from the side streets, approach them. Further south, Isaac Lohman tried to get traffic travelling towards Ramsden Street to turn back. While many motorists took notice of his hand signals, many ignored him. Glen Sheluchin leaned into the cabin of the van.

9.40 p.m.

"303. Could we have a unit block off Alexandra Parade, there's (sic) units coming down past the area."

Royal Park volunteered and Hogan directed them to block traffic at the intersection of Wellington Street and Alexandra Parade, where traffic splintered into the side streets. Glen Sheluchin had meant to ask that Heidelberg Road be cut off. He could see vehicles travelling along Heidelberg Road and westbound traffic coming down the overpass and into Hoddle Street. When he tried to correct his mistake he could not penetrate the airwaves because of the intense activity.

"Royal Park 203. What's the vehicle's description?"

"We've a fellow on foot at this stage," Mick Hogan replied.

Driving a marked police car but calling themselves Fitzroy 500, the CIB call sign, Tony Doherty and Jenenne Stiles approached the Heidelberg Road overpass from Queens Parade. It was a challenge for Doherty as he cut through the one-way streets and bounced over the speed humps from North Fitzroy to Clifton Hill. Even though the siren and flashing blue lights were activated, he was concerned to make sure that he avoided a collision and thereby not get to the scene at all. Mick Hogan directed them to go to the railway station and take charge of the scene.

"Roger," Jenenne Stiles said, "We're a couple of minutes off."

Peter Gauci lay over his friend John Muscat and tried to stop the bleeding from his neck. The blood ran down the gutter, thick like paint. He could feel John breathing and he talked to him, constantly trying to reassure him, but he felt helpless. Peter felt that, at any time, the gunman would come out of the darkness and kill him. He understood how a rabbit must feel about the hunter waiting for its head to appear above the grass. Peter wished he had his own rifle. He felt so defenceless.

The 1978 Holden Gemini panelvan turned left from Heidelberg Road and then down the exit ramp to Hoddle Street. Nurses, Michael Smith, 27, and Jacqueline Megens, 19, had, five minutes earlier, left Fairfield Hospital for Windsor where they lived. As they came down the ramp approaching the railway station, Jacqueline saw the flashing blue lights of the Collingwood van as it straddled the north-bound lanes of Hoddle Street.

"Coppers up ahead, there must be an accident," Jacqueline warned her boyfriend.

There was a loud noise, then the windscreen shattered over them. Michael thought a passing car had thrown up a stone until they heard it a second time.

"Stop the car! We're being shot at!" Jacqueline said.

Michael pulled over to the kerb and started to get out of the van. He was stopped by Jacqueline who told him to stay and lock the door. They lowered themselves in their seats, and as far under the dashboard as possible. Street lighting illuminated the interior and it was then that Michael saw that he was hurt. His right thumb had been split open like a block of wood and the left side of his face and neck, and his left shoulder were peppered with shotgun pellets. Blood from his face trickled down his neck.

Jacqueline felt pain in her right shoulder. There was a hole in her jumper and she could feel blood on her back. Behind them, close by, they heard five or six blasts from a shotgun. Jacqueline looked up and saw other vehicles passing, with their windscreens shattered. Michael looked out and saw a car with four passengers move slowly past. The woman in the front passenger seat was staring at him. He watched it continue down the road and then he heard a single shot. This was followed, a short time later, by another shot, that sounded the same, but further away.

Some seven kilometres further east along Heidelberg Road police cars, with their blue lights flashing and sirens screaming, raced past Dianne Fitzpatrick. She considered trying to get their attention but decided against it. She didn't know if she could last much longer. She wanted to get to the nurses home, where she had lived most of the time, since her second husband had died several years before. She wanted to be with people she knew and where she could feel safe. She pulled up outside the main doors of the hospital and pushed open the car door. She walked towards the supervisor's office and was met by a nurse who greeted her.

"Come in Dianne, come in," he said opening his arms to her.

"I've been shot!" she said. She turned her back to the nurse and collapsed.

Dr Keith Wing Shing stopped in the ambulance bay of St Vincent's Hospital and staggered into the casualty area. His injuries initially made him unrecognisable to those he frequently worked with. They thought his injuries were from a serious assault. They did not believe him when he said that he had been shot. An ambulance officer came into casualty and told of five people having been shot in Clifton Hill. There was no doubting Keith now, as he asked for an intravenous line, morphine and a drug to prevent nausea, before being taken to X-ray. Specialists, including a plastic surgeon, were contacted.

The train was pulling out from the Victoria Park Railway Station when Peter Harvey ran into its headlights. He waved his arms frantically, hoping to catch the driver's attention as it moved away from the platform. It slowly stopped. Peter tried to get in to the driver's cabin but the driver would not let him. Of all the nights that Peter Harvey had wished that he was wearing his railway uniform, this was the one.

Senior Constable Stephen Aylward stood outside the Richmond factory with his partner, Constable Simon Black, and took down the details of the burglary. He was asking the proprietor questions when they heard something about a hold-up on the police radio. Stephen stopped writing in his folder and listened as Simon adjusted the volume of the portable radio. There was something about someone being shot in Hoddle Street. They apologised to the proprietor saying they would come back to him, then ran for the divisional van parked on the street.

Simon started the motor while Stephen flicked the switch on the instrument panel for the blue lights and pulled out the siren button.

Sang Wang went to the Prahran Police Station, checking his car before going inside to report what had happened. He noted the damage to the windscreen and the passenger-side window and door, then he stopped at his driver's seat. There was a bullet hole through the head-rest. He had been luckier than he had at first realised.

John Holland caught up with a police car in Heidelberg Road and followed it through the back streets of Clifton Hill. It turned into Hoddle Street and pulled into the Mobil Service Station with John close behind.

At the Fitzroy Police Station, Acting Sergeant Charlie Machen, 31, and Constable Margaret Kidd, were locking up the prisoners for the night. The counter area in the watchhouse and the telephones were unattended. Charlie had turned up the volume control of the police radio before they entered the cell block. As they stopped at the door of one cell the excitement from the radio monitor in the watchhouse caught their attention. They locked the last prisoner in his cell and Charlie ran to the exercise-yard door with Margaret behind him. He ran into the watchhouse looking for a torch, then to the Sergeant's office pulling open drawers and searching through briefcases. He burst out through the front door telling Margaret he could not find a torch and that he was going to put in a report about there being too few on issue at the station.

As he got into the Sergeant's car, Margaret answered the phone. She had just put the phone to her ear when the other telephones in the station rang. All lines on the switchboard were full.

Paul McNichol and Shane Keogh in Collingwood 250 advised Mick Hogan that they had arrived at the scene as they pulled up behind the Collingwood 303 van. The Collingwood van was stationary across Hoddle Street facing north-east towards the billboards. Glen Sheluchin was at the rear of the van and Belinda Bourchier at the front with the radio.

"Complete sit rep ASAP." Mick Hogan said.

"Roger that. (sic)" Shane said and placed the transmitter back on the dashboard clip.

Other police tried to get through to Mick Hogan at D24 to advise where they were and to be given direction as to where they could best be utilised. Mick asked for the Collingwood van again.

9.41 p.m.

"Collingwood 303," answered Belinda Bourchier with the portable radio. Mick Hogan asked if there was only one minor injury caused by broken glass.

"Collingwood 303. Unable to get through to the cars that have been shot and see (sic)," Belinda added.

"Roger. What is the exact location of the person? Do you have him in sight?"

"Collingwood 303. Negative. We reversed the van when we heard the shots."

Glen Sheluchin, who was leaning into the van, took over.

"Collingwood 303. He could possibly be; it sounds like it is east of Ramsden now."

Hogan checked his Melway.

"East of Ramsden. Roger, 303. Presumably still on foot, is he?"

"He's still firing!" shouted Glen as he ducked below the dashboard.

It sounded, to him, like a shotgun but he was unsure of where the shots were coming from other than in a north-east direction. Belinda tried to get through to Hogan.

"Collingwood 303!" she screamed.

When nothing else was said Mick Hogan thought that she had been killed. Glen tried to tell Hogan that rapid gunfire was taking place but he could not get through. City West 203 advised Hogan that they were travelling towards Hoddle Street. They were in Carlton, in Cemetery Road. Hogan instructed the police to "back off to a safe position."

Constable Phil Bradley braked heavily as he was about to turn left and enter Hoddle Street from Victoria Parade. On his right, in Hoddle Street, tearing through the intersection, against the red light, was the Richmond divisional van with its lights and siren operating. Phil looked across at his partner who had the Melways open on his lap. Gary was looking straight ahead, his finger firmly on the grid reference they were heading for. Since taking the call they had not spoken to each other, despite the many risks involved in weaving in and out of the traffic travelling east along Victoria Street. Phil turned left into Hoddle Street and accelerated hard, overtaking the divisional van that they had almost collided with seconds earlier, and making it look sluggish.

Glen Sheluchin and Belinda Bourchier were crouched behind the divisional van, guns drawn, as shots bellowed throughout the night air. Behind them, in their car, Paul McNicol and Shane Keogh slumped as low as possible in their seats. Shane heard two, deafening shots. A sedan travelling west along Ramsden Street powered over Hoddle Street and into North Terrace, the continuation of Ramsden Street. It flashed past the Collingwood vehicles. As it passed them, Shane Keogh was momentarily dazzled by what he thought was muzzle flash from the passenger-side windows.

"He's got a gun!" Shane shouted.

Paul McNicol put the car into gear and accelerated left into North Terrace.

"Collingwood 250." Shane said," We're in pursuit of this vehicle."

"Right. Go ahead 250. The description." Mick Hogan was leaning over his desk and trying to remain calm. If the D24 operator spoke with panic in his voice then it filtered through to the police on the streets in the danger zone. He wrote down the time on a scrap of paper and waited.

9.42 p.m.

"Collingwood 250. It's a Ford sedan, looks like about a 1975 model. They're firing from the vehicle; they're now heading down in Hodgkinson Street. They have turned left into Hodgkinson Street. The registration is India Quebec Echo 3-6-3. They're pulling up in Hodgkinson Street - can we have assistance at this scene here?" Shane gasped for air with almost every word he spoke.

Mick Hogan checked the Melway. He reasoned that Fitzroy 500, with Tony Doherty and Jenenne Stiles, would, by now, be in the vicinity. He called them and Jenenne advised that they were turning into Hodgkinson Street. Hogan's assistant, Gary Ricardo, typed into the computer the registration details of the vehicle being pursued by Collingwood 250. Hogan called Collingwood 250. There was no response and Hogan dropped his head. The seven seconds of silence seemed like an hour. He was sure they had been killed.

Paul McNicol and Shane Keogh pulled up behind the Ford sedan a hundred metres into Gold Street. The policecar's headlights were on high beam, the blue lights flashing. Travelling towards them from the opposite direction were Phil Bradley and Gary Maddern in Russell Street 213. Shane Keogh, crouched down using his passenger door as a shield, and trained his revolver on the driver of the Ford who came running up to them. He was waving something in his hand, shouting that he was "in the job."

Paul McNicol relaxed when he recognised a 'freddy', police slang for the identification badge, in the driver's hand. The driver shouted that he had his wife and child in the car. He had seen what was happening and wanted to get them to safety. Paul wrote down the registration number on the running sheet. Instinct and ten years as a policeman told him that there was no need to take any further particulars.

"All right mate," Shane said.

Phil Bradley and Gary Maddern holstered their firearms and started to walk back to their car. Suddenly there was a burst of gunfire coming from the direction of the Clifton Hill Railway Station. The walk became a run.

7

"Give me your gun! Give me your gun! I'll get him!" Zoran Trajceski demanded, seemingly unaware of the blood and glass over his face and clothes. Belinda Bourchier tried to settle him, but Zoran was persistent. He lunged at her revolver, still holstered on her right hip.

Kevin Farmer drove slowly along Hoddle Street while Tracey bottle fed Adrian in the seat beside him. Adrian was ready for bed, dressed in his pyjamas and dressing gown. As they approached the railway station Kevin noticed a brown Sigma sedan stopped in the centre lane. He thought the car had broken down and continued on, slowing almost to a crawl, as he approached what he assumed was an accident. He could see cars and bodies on the left side of the road. Suddenly the front, passenger-side window seemed to explode as a .308 bullet made impact.

"Get down Tracey!" he yelled.

Kevin felt her head touch his knee and was relieved that she had done as he had said. The first shot was followed by another five. Kevin saw, to the right, the bodies of Steve Wight, John Muscat and Peter Gauci. Kevin pushed his foot down hard on the accelerator but the car struggled. He willed it not to stall. It coughed and barely moved but he kept the motor running, until it quickly surged forward. He kept his head up as he accelerated towards the Collingwood divisional van, where they would be safe. He wanted to stay as low in the seat as possible but was frightened of running over anyone who may be in his path.

Belinda Bourchier wrestled with Zoran Trajceski behind the divisional van. He was like a madman, screaming for her gun. Belinda held the gun firmly in its holster. It was a difficult task for her as, at 175 cm and slim, she was not physically strong. Where she found the strength to ward off Zoran she did not know, but she managed to.

Zoran ran over to Glen Sheluchin who had his back to him, still trying to get through on the radio. Zoran reached for his revolver. Belinda pulled him away and was struggling with him as shots were fired from the billboard area. Belinda wondered which shot was going to strike her down like the others. Zoran continued to yell that he wanted to get the gunman; that he wanted to kill him, "the weak bastard". Shots could be heard ricocheting off the road and the kerbs. Eventually, Belinda and Glen gained control of Zoran and convinced him to stay behind the van. They told him to sit on the road, to take cover. They tried to calm him and they told him that they understood his frustration. Belinda went out from behind the van and directed traffic away.

Kevin Farmer looked down at his lap. Tracey was dead. "He's killed my wife! My wife is dead! Give me a gun, I'll kill him!" he screamed as he brought the Datsun to a stop. Adrian stood facing his mother with his arms outstretched crying out, "Mummy! Mummy!" and opening and closing his fingers. It was a shock. Kevin had thought that they had all survived.

"How do you know? She might be all right." Belinda tried to comfort him. The left-side of his face and neck was stained with blood and tissue.

Then she looked across at Adrian and his mother. She saw the severe head injury to Tracey. Wedged between her and the back support of her seat was Adrian's plastic milk bottle. Belinda urged Kevin to drive to the Mobil Service Station where he would get help. Tracey Farmer had been shot in the face, leaving a 15 cm x 10 cm wound.

Matthew Morrow and Zoran Trajceski ran behind the trees on the west side of Hoddle Street.

"I've got to get my girlfriend; my girlfriend's up there," Zoran said.

"No, you can't," said Matthew.

"You can't, now get out of here!" Belinda Bourchier said.

Matthew Morrow grabbed Zoran by the jacket and ran him to the Mobil Service

Station. Zoran made to run back but Matthew and another man held him.

"We've got to go back," Zoran said.

Russell Street 603 pulled in against the kerb in North Terrace facing Hoddle Street. Michelle Young and Andrew Hiam surveyed the scene about them and could not believe what they were seeing. There were bodies and damaged cars on both sides of Hoddle Street. They felt powerless watching the arm of Gina Papaioannou rise and then slowly fall. In the intersection before them was the Collingwood divisional van. Michelle stood beside the police car until she was stung into action by another police officer in Mayors Park.

"For Christ's sake! Get behind a tree, he's still firing!" yelled Paul Storey, 21, a constable from City West.

Paul was lying prone below the bluestone kerb in Turnbull Street. It was the third major incident he had experienced in less than two years service. The first was a search for Pavel Vasilof Marinoff, who had shot and wounded police during burglary investigations. In four separate incidents, between 1982 and 1986, Marinoff or Max Clarke (or 'Mad Max' as he was called in the media) shot and wounded seven police officers.

Paul's second major incident took place when he was working day shift at D24, and Russell Street Police Headquarters was bombed.

Paul felt safe lying on the road against the bluestone blocks. He was reed thin, and because of this, was known as Rex (from anorexia) more widely than by his proper name. His partner, John Anderson, 21, took cover behind a tree. John had been two blocks away from Russell Street when the bombs went off in 1986. He wondered if his luck was going to hold out again.

Michelle drew her revolver and ran for cover behind a tree. She did not know what to do next and felt helpless. There had not been any training at the police academy for this type of situation. She saw people coming out of their houses in North Terrace.

"Get back inside! Go on, get back into your houses!" Michelle yelled.

Andrew Hiam ran from the police car into the park and took cover behind the largest tree he could find. He could hear shots but couldn't make out from which direction they were coming. Andrew knew that the weapon being fired was not a .22 rifle or a .38 revolver; the noise was too loud. He suspected it was a shotgun.

"VKC, Collingwood 303."

Mick Hogan was relieved to hear Belinda Bourchier's voice, relieved to know that she was alive. He continued to speak matter-of-factly and acknowledged her call sign.

"Collingwood 303. Can we have an ambulance at the Mobile (sic) Service Station. It's probably the safest place for them to go," Belinda said, her voice quivering.

The word mobile spilled involuntarily from her mouth. Mobile was what she said when she was a little girl, and she was asked by her parents to name the various landmarks she saw when they were driving in the family car. She felt foolish and hoped no one would pick up on it.

"Mobil Service Station location again 303?" asked Hogan.

"It's in Hoddle Street, we have one person's (sic) been shot in the neck. It's not very serious."

"Stabbed in the neck is it (sic)?" asked Hogan. Belinda had been cut across by other police trying to speak to him.

"303. Shot."

"On the way 303," said Hogan, while Gary Ricardo made contact with the Ambulance Service.

Sergeant Terry Howard had been to a hotel brawl in Swan Street, Richmond and was travelling to the Collingwood Police Station as part of his divisional supervision duties when he heard the call to Hoddle Street. A no-nonsense person, who had experienced personal tragedy several times, he drove quickly through the back streets of Richmond and into Hoddle Street. As he approached Ramsden Street he saw the Collingwood van blocking the northbound lanes from Ramsden Street. Hearing gunshots, Terry turned into Turnbull Street and made a U-turn to provide cover for an ambulance that was turning into the street from the west end. Terry could see Steve Wight lying in Mayors Park. He tried to get through to D24 but the airway was jammed.

"There's something going on in Collingwood," said Constable Jenny Leuther. She and her partner were still in May Street with 'the boyfriend' suspect when she heard Belinda Bourchier's distressed call. John Delahunty went over to his police car and turned up the radio. He listened to what seemed like a vehicle pursuit. The Collingwood sergeant's car was chasing someone. There were car chases nearly every shift and he began to walk back to Jenny Leuther and Bill Taylor.

" ... one person's been shot in the neck," he heard Belinda Bourchier say.

He could tell it was serious by the tremor in her voice. While Jenny Leuther and Bill Taylor continued to take personal details from the suspect, John

Delahunty was already heading east along Miller Street. He increased the volume of the radio, the adrenalin already pumping through his body. Whatever was happening in Hoddle Street was more than a car chase, more than someone being shot in the neck. In the five years he had been a police officer John had not heard such confusion and terror over the airwaves. He flicked the switch on the dashboard to flash the blue lights as he approached a major T-intersection. It was clear on both sides as he turned right and accelerated into St Georges Road. He drove over the tram lines passing several cars, including another police car which was cruising. He looked at the speedometer. He was travelling at 80 kilometres an hour and decided not to go any faster in case he passed the offender travelling in the opposite direction. That is, if the offender was heading his way. He didn't know. No one did.

8

Acting District Officer Darrell Rintoule had been in the radio room of the communications department, when the first call was received. It had been a quiet shift with few serious calls since he had started work at 1.00 p.m. The radio operator took the call and gave the job to City 15, staffed by ambulance officers Shane Gleeson and Campbell Trewin. It was despatched and taken by City 15 as nothing more than a routine call. Then there was a second call during which the radio operator advised that several people had been shot.

"Probably an armed robbery in the service station and someone's been shot," Darrell said to the radio operator.

Noel Shiels put down the telephone and told Peter Collins about the call – something about a man going crazy with a gun. Peter laughed and they remarked together that it was probably a hoax. As their MICA ambulance travelled quickly down Victoria Parade, Fitzroy they were told not to approach via Hoddle Street, but to go through Princes Street and stop at Turnbull Street. The radio controller advised that it was an "ongoing shooting incident".

At D24, Constable Greg Splatt took the call. The woman, from John Street, Clifton Hill, was reporting that she had seen two men, both over two metres in height, wearing army clothes and firing rifles near the railway station.

Wayne Monohan was waiting for his evening meal of Kentucky Fried Chicken to warm in the oven. He watched *Risky Business* on his portable television and considered the irony. It was against the rules to watch TV. Still, it was quiet and it did not distract him from his duties as a railway signalman at the B signal box. He checked his take-away food and it was still cold. A truck in Hoddle Street backfired, doing so again and again. He opened the door to the signal-box office and walked over to Hoddle Street and onto the east-side footpath beneath the overpass. Unable to see anything out of the ordinary he returned to the signal box. He looked along the train lines coming from Clifton Hill and then dividing. One line went north-west towards Rushall and Epping, the other north-east towards Westgarth and Hurstbridge. He returned to the signal box and rang the A signal box where Peter Harvey worked. There was no answer. Wayne sat down and resumed watching the film.

Darrell Rintoule got into the Ford stationwagon which carried the word AMBULANCE on its bonnet and sides. He followed the MICA ambulance into La Trobe Street, activating the flashing red lights and siren.

Shane Gleeson was stopped by police from going any further. At Ramsden Street, he could see that the intersection was blocked by a police vehicle, and cars were being made to U-turn. Shane, who had been an ambulance officer for eighteen months, and his partner, Campbell Trewin, went in to the Mobil Service Station, where they were quickly acquainted with the situation.

"We've got eight patients," Campbell advised the communications department.

The MICA ambulance was doing 90 kilometres per hour when its occupants heard that City 15 had eight patients. It was just a routine job, nothing out of the ordinary, Peter Collins still thought. The radio controller called them and Noel Shiels answered, expecting to be told to cancel – that it was not a job for the MICA ambulance crew. The radio controller again directed them not to go into Hoddle Street, but to go to Turnbull Street. They were to go 'code nine' – without the red flashing lights and siren. It was "an unsafe situation."

Darrell Rintoule was puzzled. Turnbull Street was some distance from the Mobil Service Station where the injured were waiting. He followed the MICA ambulance into Turnbull Street where he saw many uniformed and plain-clothes police taking cover behind the trees in Mayors Park. Other police were taking refuge behind their cars. They all had their revolvers drawn.

A police officer ran to the two ambulances and told them to turn off their headlights. He directed them to park at the end of Turnbull Street. Darrell Rintoule suggested that the two vehicles park so as to form a V shape. It offered greater protection and allowed them to work within the V relatively safe from bullets. The police officer guided them into position.

"Get behind your car," the police officer said, as shots could be heard from the eastern side of Hoddle Street, near the railway station. Everyone spoke in whispers. It was very dark apart from the yellow glow of the light over Hoddle Street.

As they took cover, one of the police officers told Noel Shiels that they were in the 'killing zone'. That was what they called a situation like this when he was in the Vietnam War. He told Noel that the injured were in the park. Noel grabbed his kit, trying to see where they were in the darkness. As he walked towards Steve Wight and Peter Gauci, a policeman behind a tree yelled "Get down!"

Glen Sheluchin hit the passenger-side window of Gina Papaioannou's blue Datsun with the butt of his revolver. He was unable to open the doors on that side as they were locked and it was too great a risk for him to move out into the open to try the driver's door. He wanted to pull John Muscat into the Datsun and reverse it to the ambulance in Turnbull Street. The window wouldn't break. A policeman from within the park yelled at him and he moved away from the car. One hundred metres south from where Glen was, other police began to edge their way towards the blue Datsun.

Constables Phil Bradley, Gary Maddern and Andrew Hiam crawled through the park and used trees as cover to reach the car. Glen Sheluchin was white, as if he had been dipped in flour, and his eyes were wide. He held his revolver in both hands and asked the others what he should do. He was not sure whether he should fire some shots across Hoddle Street and he didn't know then where the gunmen were anyway.

Phil Bradley did not answer him as he had no answers himself. Instinct told him that the gunmen were on the opposite side of Hoddle Street but, like Glen, he was unsure. All he knew for certain was that there were seven people lying dead or dying on both sides of the roadway. Phil felt distress at seeing Gina Papaioannou's arm rise, her hand wave, then her arm drop and rise again. Glen had applied his handkerchief to John Muscat's neck wound and Gary Maddern covered him with Peter Gauci's jacket. The four then dragged the heavy Muscat across the park grounds and into Turnbull Street where Peter Collins waited with a stretcher.

On the railway side of the street a strong smell of gun powder drifted through the night air into the houses of residents who had opened their windows.

Steve Wight's breathing sounded like the noise a whale makes from its blow hole when surfacing. Steve was telling Peter Gauci to relax and that everything would be all right. At the same time Steve worried that his talking would be heard by the gunman, who would stalk and shoot him. Noel Shiels crawled on his stomach towards them.

9

Noel Shiels lay on the grass and checked the injuries to Steve Wight and Peter Gauci. There was little he could do away from the ambulance. He considered trying to drag or lift them one at a time but it seemed physically impossible and anyway, to attempt it would place them all in greater danger. The risk of being shot was too great and their wounds were not life threatening. Gunfire started again and Noel ran to a tree for cover. He yelled out to a police officer near him.

"How am I going to get to the ambulance?"

"Very quickly!" came the reply.

Noel managed a grin as he raced to the MICA ambulance. At the sound of more shots, he threw himself onto the roadway tearing his trousers and bumping into Peter Collins who was struggling to maintain John Muscat.

"What are you doing?" Peter asked.

Noel didn't answer as the policeman who spoke to him at the tree threw his kitbag as arranged.

Noel held a pen torch in his mouth and tried, for what seemed like hours, to find a vein in John Muscat's arms in order to insert an intravenous needle. It was frustrating to use the pen torch, he could barely see what he was doing. It was too dangerous to put John in the back of the ambulance as the interior lighting would make everyone a target, so he and Peter continued working in the night air. Peter passed an endotracheal tube down John's windpipe to get oxygen into his lungs using an oxy-resuscitator.

Noel went into the back of the MICA ambulance and searched for extra IV catheters, conscious that he was visible from the outside. He considered turning the interior light off but still felt that he would be a target and it would take him much longer. He'd just returned to his partner and John Muscat, when the area around them suddenly became as bright as day as the police helicopter flew over them. With what seemed like his last IV needle, Noel found a vein in the sudden burst of light, inserted the IV and got the drip going. Then he joined those around him shouting, "Get the fuckin' thing away!"

Moments later, Air 495 shifted the *NiteSun* away.

Broadmeadows ambulance officers Barry Sidebottom and Kevin Carter wheeled a stretcher over and pushed John Muscat the 200 metres to their ambulance in Hodgkinson Street, where they no longer had to keep their heads down.

9.43 p.m.

"Collingwood 250. The vehicle we've had – it seemed as if shots came from him (sic) but this guy's in the job, he's a member. It's not him at all; you can clear him from any enquiries," said Shane Keogh.

Shane got back into the front passenger seat. Paul McNicol pulled away from the kerb and turned left into South Terrace and left again into Hoddle Street. He pulled up close behind the Collingwood van.

"Roger. So we're back to where we started then, are we? North of Ramsden Street in Hoddle?" asked Hogan.

"Affirmative to that," Shane said.

"VKC to all units, we're back to square one." Mick Hogan said.

Mick Hogan advised Fitzroy 500 to take charge at the Mobil Service Station. Jenenne Stiles and Tony Doherty did not know why they were being sent there. Hogan told them that someone there had been shot.

"Roger. We're on the way," Jenenne Stiles said as they travelled along North Terrace.

9.44 p.m.

At Hoddle Street they turned left and pulled up behind Kevin Farmer's car which was hard up against the kerb. Hogan directed St Kilda 500 to attend where the Collingwood van was and to take charge of the original crime scene.

"We're on the way now," Constable Syd Hadley responded, calm and unaffected.

Syd had volunteered to partner Rick McIntosh, a St Kilda detective, rostered to work on his own that Sunday, rather than complete his correspondence at the police station. Working with a detective was better experience and a chance to get out of the office. Together they had arrested a youth for criminal damage, and obtained a statement from an armed-robbery victim. They were beside the CIB car checking two youths in Fitzroy Street, St Kilda when they heard the radio come to life. Rick accelerated rapidly through the streets and into Hoddle Street. He stopped outside the Mobil Service Station where there were people and cars everywhere and he could hear shots being discharged. He ran up to Ramsden Street and saw bodies on the road, the footpath and in cars. Behind him, near the service station, two police cars collided, one, a marked police car, and the other, a CIB car.

Steve Wight tried to crawl over to where it was safer, in Turnbull Street, but he had no energy despite being fit and strong from years of playing A-grade water polo. Phil Bradley, Gary Maddern and Andrew Hiam moved quickly across to the solidly built Wight. They grabbed an arm or leg and carried him to where Noel Shiels and Peter Collins were still working on John Muscat. Exhausted, they put Steve on the nature strip by the road, lifting him again as another ambulance arrived. They carried him towards the second ambulance as more shots pierced the air. The sudden gunfire and the weight proved too much for the police officers and Wight was dropped, his head hitting the road like a coconut falling from a tree.

"Sorry, mate."

They lifted him again and, with aid from Nunawading ambulance officers John Newnham and David Hadj, Steve was placed into the back of their ambulance. Dressings were applied and he was placed on a drip.

"I hope they shoot the bastard," Steve said.

Glen Sheluchin urged Peter Gauci towards him during a lull in the gunfire. It was not safe for Glen to go to him. Peter staggered a few steps before Glen and Darrell Rintoule reached for him. Darrell lifted him under the arm while Glen held him from the other side. Shots rang out as they hurried him over behind the ambulance and made him lie on the road. Peter kept wanting to sit up and stand.

"He's hit me in the leg," he said.

Darrell led Peter to his ambulance where Steve Wight was being treated. The interior light was bright and Peter was worried about being seen by the gunman and being shot again. When the ambulance left for St Vincent's Hospital, he felt an overwhelming sense of relief.

Jacqueline Megens counted six police vehicles and an ambulance further south from where she and Michael Smith were stopped. She looked at Michael's injuries and held a cardigan in her hand intending to push the windscreen out to make it easier to see.

"You need help, there's an ambulance up ahead," she said.

Michael stopped her from pushing out the windscreen and started the engine. They drove forward staying as low in their seats as possible, shots continuing behind them. They passed the brown Sigma where Dusan Flajnik had been killed, still held upright by his seat belt. On the footpath and in the gutter were the bodies of Robert Mitchell, Vesna Markovska and Gina Papaioannou. They passed the flashing lights of the Collingwood van and stopped before the first driveway of the Mobil Service Station. Jacqueline got out and some police rushed to her aid. Ambulance officers were brought over to the panel van from which they took Michael and Jacqueline to the back of an ambulance where they waited. Alan Jury, then Kevin and Adrian Farmer got in the ambulance with them. Everyone was covered in blood.

Ambulance officer Campbell Trewin carefully examined Kevin Farmer looking for injury to account for the blood and matter on his head and clothing. "That's my wife; she's dead."

10

At Northcote Police Station, Sergeant Graham 'Yabby' Larchin had hoped for a quiet afternoon shift. He was due to take 28 days leave, which included the rest days he was owed, so he wanted to complete any outstanding paperwork. He had a large crew to supervise and at the start of the shift organised for Constables Anita Adair and David Depyle to work the van. He hurried them out of the station so that by 3.15 p.m. the divisional van – the work horse of the police force – was on patrol. The car crew and the spare member remained in the station to complete their paperwork. His driver, newly promoted Senior Constable Betty Roberts, typed a statement in the muster room. Domenic Cannizzaro, the watchhouse keeper, could cope on his own with telephone and counter enquiries.

Graham Larchin was about to sit down at his desk when Domenic Cannizzaro gave him details of a man threatening to kill his de facto wife. He had tried to force his way into their house with a large knife. Graham yelled out to Betty Roberts and together they raced down the steps to the parked police car. Betty went to the passenger side as Graham liked to take the wheel. They drove a few hundred metres from the police station to the Helen Street address, but the offender had already left. His wife was hysterical. He was coming back, she said, with a gun.

Graham Larchin and Betty Roberts shifted the police car to a position where it couldn't be seen and waited for the offender to return. When there was no sign of him, after several hours, Graham decided to return to the house and reassure the wife. They would then check the locks and the backyard, and leave.

They were about to do this when they received a call to assist other police in searching for an offender armed with a firearm. He had wrecked one house in West Heidelberg using a firearm, then another one in Preston. No one was really sure why this had happened but the two police officers assumed that it involved drugs or a domestic dispute. They commenced the drive north to Preston but were redirected back to Northcote.

Graham Larchin reversed the police car into a lane behind the Northcote Fire Station and from there they watched a flat in Frederick Street. They were tired and hungry and lack of sleep was beginning to tell.

Betty looked at the new stripes on her jacket and marvelled at the difference they had made, apart from the small increase in salary. Even though she had been promoted for only a few days she had noticed that the public gave her more respect. Even her workmates at Northcote were more respectful, despite their jokes. They remarked that the shine from the stripes hurt their eyes and some wore sunglasses when around her.

Graham Larchin said that he could eat a horse. He wanted the offender to arrive soon so that they could hand him over to detectives and return to Northcote. They were discussing what they were going to eat when they heard shots. Graham thought it was a car backfiring, or fire crackers. Whatever the source of the noise, it was probably not serious. It was coming from the bottom of Ruckers Hill, down near Westgarth Street.

Darren Anderson replaced Domenic Cannizzaro as the watchhouse keeper. The Northcote van had been waiting in Separation Street for a window-shutter service to arrive at a shoe-shop but it was taking longer than expected. Darren was in the kitchen washing the evening-meal dishes while watching *Risky Business* when the front-door buzzer sounded.

Michael Pearce, 25, was waiting at the inquiry counter. He told Darren that he had heard, what sounded like, eight explosions as he had driven past the Clifton Hill Railway Station.

"Explosions?"

"Like incandescent light bulbs being thrown onto the ground," Michael explained.

Darren was not sure what to do. It seemed to him, a minor thing – perhaps detonators left on the train line. He took some details and promised to ring it through to D24 for Collingwood police to investigate. Michael opened the door to leave. A short man came through waving his hands and speaking quickly.

"I wanna charge him with murder! I wanna charge him with murder!"

The man thumped his fist on the counter as two other men came in to report a theft and, what was more appealing to Darren Anderson, that they knew who was responsible.

"Someone shot my car! Someone shot my car!" the man said.

He said someone had tried to shoot his mother. Darren asked the men reporting the theft to wait, then went outside the station to inspect the man's Commodore sedan. The quarter-vent window behind the driver's seat, where his mother sat, was shattered.

North-bound traffic was becoming congested. Simon Black braked hard to avoid hitting the rear of the utility whose driver seemed oblivious to the screaming siren and the blue flashing lights coming up from behind. There was a break in the median strip. Simon indicated and cut across and into the south-bound lanes. Cars were still coming towards him but this was an emergency and they moved out of his way.

Senior Constable Dennis Harnetty, 27, came into the Richmond Police Station about an hour before his rostered starting time. He had the sergeants on his back about a file that he had to complete. He stopped at the Sergeant's office where Max Drake was putting on his jacket and listening intently to the police radio.

"Coming for a drive?" Max asked.

Dennis rushed to the watchhouse, took out a revolver and hurried out of the station to the police car parked in Bridge Road. Max put the car into gear and tore into Church Street towards Clifton Hill. Dennis adjusted the volume of the police radio so that they could hear it clearly over the siren.

As Darren went back up the steps into the police station, Michael Pearce walked quickly over to him. Together they examined the Datsun sedan where Jacqueline Langosch was waiting. Michael showed him a bullet hole through the driver's door, just above thigh level. Then lower again another bullet hole. Darren opened the door and scratched his head. There appeared to be no exit point for either of the two bullets. Michael showed him the bullet hole in the boot. They were all the size of a ten-cent piece. Darren ran up to the steps of the police station and grabbed the radio transmitter.

Messages from a police station to D24 had to be given by telephone and not by the transmitter in the watchhouse. The stations were not licensed by Telecom to transmit messages, even though most police stations had a hand-held transmitter. Darren felt that there were times when rules were made to be broken. He told the men reporting the theft to wait.

"Northcote 900. Urgent!"

Darren told the channel 67 operator what he had seen. In a calm, almost detached manner, the operator told him to change over to channel 36 and repeat the message. Channel 67 covered B district which included the Northcote area, while channel 36 included Clifton Hill. Police on one side of the Merri Creek would not know what was happening on the other side of the creek due to the different channels.

Terry Howard stepped out in front of the police car and waved it down. Max Drake had already seen him squatting behind a parked car and turned the wheel to park alongside a police car. He and Dennis Harnetty got out as Terry explained what had been happening. Max walked over to two constables, a male and a female, taking cover beside their car at the Hoddle and Ramsden Street intersection. Each was wearing a white peaked cap and holding their revolvers pointed towards the railway station.

"Take them off and get behind the engine or something," Max said. "I don't want to do your eighty-threes."

Max paused for a moment and caught his breath. He tried to relax but it was impossible. Tension always affected his breathing.

Graham Larchin and Betty Roberts heard Darren Anderson's call and told the channel 67 operator that they would respond to the call. Both assumed the problem concerned new migrants shooting rabbits along the Merri Creek. It was a regular problem for the Northcote police. Betty suggested that the Collingwood van meet them and, together, they would search for the wayward hunters. They would probably charge them with shooting in a populous place, and, more than likely, they wouldn't be licensed.

They drove out from the lane, down Frederick Street, along Mitchell Street and south along High Street going down Ruckers Hill where, earlier, they had thought a car had backfired. Graham stopped the car at Westgarth Street and waited for the red light to change. The D24 operator asked them to change channels, to go to channel 36. It made sense as they were entering the A district area. There was no alarm in the voice of the operator.

Terry Howard walked over to the barricade of police cars at the Ramsden Street intersection. Police officers were crouched behind the cars, revolvers drawn and pointed north along Hoddle Street. A policewoman started to shake and cry, and Terry Howard worried that it would have a domino effect on the other officers. Almost everyone who was there was in his or her twenties, and had not been involved in such a life-threatening situation before. It was important that they remained cool. He tried to reassure the policewoman but she began to develop signs of hysteria. Terry slapped her face, telling her to relax and not panic; it would soon be over and she was safe if she remained calm. But the policewoman's condition became worse and she started screaming. Terry went to the front of a police car and removed the keys from the ignition. He took the policewoman by the arm, opened the boot door and pushed her inside, slamming it shut.

Darren Anderson walked out of the Northcote Police Station and stood on the steps looking south-east towards Clifton Hill. The others followed and stood by him and listened to the 'ka-boom, ka-boom, ka-boom' in the distance. Even though it was happening several kilometres away he felt vulnerable and unsure of what to do. He went back inside and took down the details from the motorists on a crime report pad.

Betty Roberts turned the channel selector to 36 and heard Mick Hogan checking Collingwood 303's update.

"Stabbed in the neck is it (sic)?" Mick Hogan had said.

Betty pressed the transmit button cutting out any dialogue between D24 and other police, being heard in the car. Betty checked the Melway and continued trying to get through.

"Northcote 253. We're coming down High into Hoddle. Where do you want us?"

Mick Hogan directed that they take the signal box at the Clifton Hill Railway Station and confirm if there was anyone injured. Before Betty could reply, Collingwood van 303 interrupted. There was a distinct tremor in the voice of Belinda Bourchier.

"We have a really badly injured lady, she's been shot bad (sic)."

"Collingwood 303, what's the location?"

"Collingwood 303. We're still at the Mobile (sic) Service Station."

Hogan reassured Belinda. The ambulance was on its way and the Fitzroy CIB were also coming.

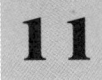

9.45 p.m.

When John Delahunty reached the Eastern Freeway he turned left and then left again into Queens Parade, overtaking cars as he went. He scanned both sides of Queens Parade, looking for any sign of the offender – there may be two, he had heard on the radio. As he drove up Heidelberg Road approaching the Hoddle Street overpass, he switched off the blue lights, then the headlights and pulled over to the side of the road. Further east along Heidelberg Road he saw another police car blocking traffic travelling west towards Clifton Hill. Cars were made to U turn or turn into a side street. Shots continued. John had never been interested in firearms and listened carefully to try and determine what type of rifle was being used and where the shots were coming from.

He looked behind to see someone running towards him. John braced himself but, as the jogger came closer, he relaxed. It was a teenager and instinct told him that this was not the offender. Further shots were heard and John motioned for the jogger to crouch down. John ran his hands quickly over the teenager, just to be sure, and together they remained beside the police car taking shelter. When there was a lull in the shooting, John told the jogger to run down to the other police car and to keep his head down.

Kevin Farmer had driven his car past the Collingwood van. He had been travelling slowly, weaving between the two, south-bound lanes concerned that he might hit someone with his car. As the Datsun coupe approached the Mobil Service Station, Isaac Lohman, who was still directing north-bound traffic away from the Ramsden Street intersection, yelled to Farmer, "Come on, don't stop. Move, move, move!"

The Datsun coupe pulled in outside the service station behind a white Holden stationwagon. In the CIB car, Rick McIntosh and Sid Hadley pulled up on the opposite side of the road.

"I'll kill the bastard! I'll kill the bastard!" cried Kevin Farmer as he struggled to get out of his car. Matthew Morrow helped him stay on his feet.

"My baby! My baby!"

He was screaming; crying out.

"He's killed my wife! My wife is dead!"

His cries alerted Michael Anthony about what to expect inside the car. Adrian's arms were still outstretched towards his mother. The left side of her face was blown away. He wanted her to cuddle him just as she always did when he was upset. It was a sight that everyone who was present would never forget. Like everyone else, Michael Anthony was more confused and scared than ever. Jenenne Stiles went over to Kevin Farmer. He was shaking his head, yelling and swearing.

"I'm going to kill him! My wife! My baby!" he cried beside his wife's open door. Adrian remained standing between her legs. Tracey had pushed him onto the floor only a moment before she was murdered.

Max Drake opened the boot of the police car and helped the policewoman climb out. She was composed and he gave her hand a squeeze.

"You'll be fine," he said.

Tony Doherty asked those still outside the petrol station to go inside where it was safe. With the help of other police, he persuaded them it was the safest place. The gunfire resumed. Many of them thought it seemed closer and they panicked, rushing the door of the shop as if at a huge sale. Many rushed for the toilet, and even those who had no intention of heading that way were pushed along in the rush.

Detective Tony Doherty entered the service station shop and told the twelve or so people to lay low on the floor. He explained that he did not know what was happening, but would keep them informed. Everyone did as the detective suggested. Some started to read the magazines from the rack, while others ate food bars and chips. There was a general fear that the gunman would enter the shop and start shooting. Michael Anthony checked the walls. He commented to Colin Smeelie that they were paper thin – they had no hope.

"If you want to help your wife, calm down," Jenenne said to Kevin Farmer. Then, "I'll have a look at her and see if I can get some medical help, but you must calm down."

"What the fuck are you talking about? She's dead!" Kevin Farmer replied.

Jenenne Stiles looked into the car and immediately felt foolish. She reached in and grabbed Adrian. She handed him to his father who wrapped his arms around the boy and held him tightly. "Look after your child," she said. Tony Doherty waited with Kevin and Adrian. Two ambulances drove up to the service station and Tony directed them to the Datsun coupe. Ambulance officer Campbell Trewin examined Tracey's body from inside the car, then walked away to check another patient. He said just one word.

"No."

Rick McIntosh drove his CIB car into Ramsden Street and surveyed the scene in front of him. It was chaos and no one could do anything.

Robert Boscia was watching the film *Atlantic City*, with Leanne, his wife, in the loungeroom of their two storey house in John Street. They had heard noises outside but put them down to work being done at the railway station. Then they heard a noise that changed their minds. It sounded like gunfire. Robert and Leanne went outside. He stood in the doorway while she spoke to Urania Michaelides, their next-door neighbour. There was a burst of about thirty shots; it was hard to tell from where. Robert yelled to Leanne and they went back inside, and up the stairs to the glass balcony doors. There they saw a thin man running from the southern end to the northern end of the station platform, then dropping out of sight. He was carrying a rifle.

Rick McIntosh edged his way slowly north along the footpath and gutter on the eastern side of Hoddle Street in his newly-purchased grey suit. Seeing the rise and fall of Gina Papaioannou's arm was too much; he had to do something. He crawled towards her slowly, on his hands and knees. At any second he expected his head to splatter, but there was Gina and her waving hand. Phil Bradley watched Rick pause briefly. Phil rushed to the side of a car and edged along the footpath behind Rick.

Wayne Timms, 27, and his pillion passenger, Jayne Timbury, 19, travelled south along High Street then under the railway bridge and into Queens Parade. Wayne indicated to turn left into Hoddle Street but slowed when he saw an east-bound car stopped at the entrance. In front of this car was another which was reversing towards Queens Parade. Wayne looked over his shoulder and moved his Norton 850 Commando motorcycle to the right side of the cars and passed them. He and Jayne were on their way home to Carlton after having had dinner in a Chinese restaurant at South Morang. Earlier they had visited Wayne's parents in Doreen. Wayne changed gears and accelerated to go under the Heidelberg Road overpass.

With north-bound traffic stopped in most lanes, Simon Black drove the Richmond divisional van over the centre dividing plantation and continued north along the south-bound lanes approaching the Mobil Service Station. The lights inside the shop area of the service station had been turned off but they suddenly flickered back on. Some felt safer with the lights on.

Domenic Cannizzaro had predicted to his wife of six months that there would, one day, be a mass murder in Australia. He reasoned that it had to happen as Australia seemed to follow American trends, even if years later. Even when he was working in non-operational areas, Domenic carried a revolver. He wanted to be prepared. The window-shutter service had relieved him at the shop window in Separation Street, Northcote. Domenic heard talk on the radio of shots fired in Hoddle Street and he assumed that there was an armed robbery in progress. He crossed over to channel 36 and travelled quickly through side streets and west along Heidelberg Road. As he approached the exit ramp for Hoddle Street he saw police cars near the Clifton Hill Railway Station, and, near Ramsden Street, he saw police redirecting traffic.

As Wayne Timms and Jayne Timbury rounded the bend under the Heidelberg Road overpass they heard muffled noises. The balaclavas and helmets they wore made it difficult to identify the sound; they assumed it was a car backfiring and continued south along Hoddle Street. A panel van was in front of them and Wayne was anxious to overtake but the opportunity didn't present itself. Twenty metres ahead, as they came out from under the overpass, they saw twenty-two-year-old postal worker, Shane Stanton, fall and slide under his Kawasaki motorcycle.

The burst from the .308 M14 military rifle was like that of a machine gun. The stream of bullets struck the bitumen and the centre-dividing strip, and ricocheted from south to north in a straight line up and into the rider. Shane Stanton's body jolted from the impact. He sustained multiple gunshot wounds to his chest, arms and legs.

Domenic Cannizzaro heard the gunfire as it echoed around the concrete ramp. He looked down to Hoddle Street and saw, in the centre of the road near the railway station, the body of Shane Stanton under his motorcycle. Shane had been shot in the left thigh, the bullet leaving a 19 cm x 8 cm exit wound, the groin, the left arm, twice in the right side of the chest, the right shoulder, the right thigh, and four times in the left shoulder leaving a 4 cm x 2 cm wound and 5 cm x 3 cm wound. Domenic reduced his speed to 40 kilometres per hour and travelled down the exit ramp towards the Clifton Hill Railway Station, not knowing where the shots were coming from. In front of him was a red Ford Falcon XD sedan which had stopped.

Dimitrios Collyvas, 21, was driving his Ford Falcon XD sedan down High Street from Reservoir. Sitting next to Dimitrios, in the front passenger seat, was his seventeen-year-old girlfriend, Renata Coldebella. Behind them sat her brother, Daniel, and his friend, Danny De-Luca, who were both sixteen years old. They were looking forward to spending a few hours at the Chevron Hotel Night Club in Prahran but first they had to go to Glen Iris where Dimitrios lived. He wanted to change his clothing before they went out.

They turned left into Hoddle Street and followed the bend in the road as they travelled under the Heidelberg Road overpass. On the west side of the road, Dimitrios saw the flashing blue lights of police cars opposite the railway station, and other cars spread about in different positions on both sides of the road. They all thought that they had come across an accident as there was the motor cyclist on the road and he appeared to be dead. Dimitrios reduced speed and was almost stationary when he heard two loud bangs.

Domenic Cannizzaro, who was following them in the police car from the exit ramp, saw their back window shatter. At first he thought he was being shot but then realised the shots were hitting the red Falcon. Renata Coldebella felt a heavy blow to her head as her side window shattered. She felt that there was something strange about her left hand and looked down. It was bleeding and she started to scream. Her brother Daniel shouted that he had been shot in the back.

"Get down! Get down!" Dimitrios shouted.

Danny and Daniel lowered themselves down in their seats as another volley of about ten shots was fired, several hitting their car while the other rounds could be heard whizzing past them. Dimitrios had no idea where the shots were coming from but knew that they were not safe remaining where they were. He reversed quickly.

Domenic reversed about twenty metres towards the ramp as other motorists proceeded down the exit ramp towards him. He stopped the police car. He could go no further because of the cars banking up behind him. He turned around in his seat to watch the red Ford reverse quickly at an angle towards him. The driver's-side rear of the Ford struck the driver's-side front of the police car damaging the bumper, headlight and bonnet.

Carlton North 150 travelled quickly north towards the Mobil Service Station. Inspector Pat Murtagh urged his new-found driver, Shane Cross, to continue past the service station. As they crossed over Ramsden Street at high speed, they noticed the bodies on the east-side of Hoddle Street – it was obvious that more than ball bearings were being fired. They saw the flashes from the northern end of the railway station. Shane braked hard and steered the police car towards the kerb, its tyres scraping against the gutter and stopping near a light pole opposite the railway station. Opposite them was Dusan Flajnik held upright in his Sigma sedan. As the gunshots continued Inspector Murtagh pushed his door open and scrambled out of the car with Shane close behind. A police officer fired a shot towards the gunman; a single shot that sounded pathetic compared with the canon-like sound they had heard while driving into Hoddle Street.

Wayne Timms told Jayne Timbury to lie on the ground while he held up the Norton motorbike with the foot peg resting against the concrete kerb. It was the only cover the Norton offered.

Alexandra Stamatopoulos, her brother, Steven, and their friends, Pana, Vicki and Irene Fountis, were returning home from a family party in St Albans. It had been a good party, with much singing and dancing. In Alexandra's car, a Ford Telstar sedan, they continued with the party mood by playing cassettes loudly. Pana liked the George Michael song "I Want Your Sex" so Alexandra increased the volume. The car vibrated with the sound as she steered it around the bend under the Heidelberg Road overpass and south along Hoddle Street.

As they approached the railway station Alexandra pointed at the red Ford as it reversed into Domenic's police car.

"Have a look at the cop car!" She laughed.

The others joined in the mocking and laughed at what they had seen. Alexandra slowed down.

The Richmond divisional van approached the Ramsden Street intersection against the trickle of south-bound traffic. Until they got closer, it looked to Simon Black and Stephen Aylward like a major car-accident scene. There were bodies and cars scattered across both sides of the road.

"We're supposed to be having a quiet shift," Simon said.

It was pointless stopping at the Mobil Service Station as other police were already there. As they travelled towards the railway station Stephen Aylward saw Shane Stanton's motorcycle directly in front of them.

"Stop! Don't go any further!" Stephen said.

He leaned across and disengaged the siren and blue lights, while Simon turned off the headlights.

Simon swung the van to the right and parallel to Shane Stanton, and stopped across the south-bound lanes. Stephen felt his life was about to end and bailed out of the divisional van screaming out to the Ford Telstar, "Reverse! Reverse!"

Alexandra Stamatopoulos wondered what she had done wrong, as she saw Stephen Aylward run around to the front of the van. She looked to her left, something compelling her to do so. There was a tall, thin man on the northern edge of the railway station, behind the fence. He was looking in the direction of the divisional van and had a rifle aimed in its direction. Frightened, Alexandra quickly reversed her car towards the centre reservation as Stephen Aylward dropped down beside his driver's-side wheel. Alexandra couldn't hear any shots for the music of George Michael was still playing in her car. The thin man lowered the rifle as Stephen dropped out of sight. Alexandra reached for the radio control and turned off the cassette.

Rick McIntosh was about five metres from Gina Papaioannou when there was a volley of shots. He could not determine where the shots came from or if they were aimed at him but he decided to go back. There was nothing he could really do to help Gina, her injuries were too serious, but he could report back to D24 that she needed urgent help. The other two were definitely dead. He crawled backwards over the same area feeling the blood and glass against his hands and legs, waiting to hear the shot that would paralyse or end his and Phil Bradley's lives. Phil Bradley paused and checked behind himself then crawled towards Ramsden Street.

A cameraman walked onto Hoddle Street from Ramsden Street. He was carrying his equipment and the area was suddenly lit up by his floodlights as he took footage of the area. Shots rang out in the distance. Rick McIntosh ran at the cameraman yelling, "Turn it off! Turn it off!"

Rick knocked him to the ground, then dragged him and his camera equipment back behind the police cars.

"That's 50,000 dollars worth of camera equipment you've just damaged," the cameraman complained.

"You put our lives at risk again and I'll shoot you," said McIntosh.

He grabbed at his back and limped away from the cameraman, stooped over like an old man. He leaned against the side of a police car and looked at his suit, at the blood and the tears in the trousers. Now his back was strained as well.

Wayne Monohan had seen the cars banked up on the Hoddle Street entrance ramp when he went out again to investigate the backfiring noise. Looking south down the tracks towards the Clifton Hill Railway Station he saw Fernando Myra herding people over the pit, from the north-bound to the south-bound platform. He heard the backfiring noise again, this time clearly, and knew he had been mistaken. Wayne ran back to his signal box and rang the MetRail train controller.

"Someone's shooting the shit out of everything," he said. "I'm going to stop the trains; there's one coming from Eltham any minute."

Wayne pressed a button on the control panel in the signal box and pulled a lever. The south-bound train stopped over the Urquhart Street bridge.

The wheels hit the edge but would not go over. In her sights Alexandra Stamatopoulos saw the exit ramp for Heidelberg Road on the north-bound side of Hoddle Street. She had to get over the reservation and then to the safety of Heidelberg Road. Pana and Steven tried to calm Irene and Vicki who were screaming that they were going to be killed. Unable to get over the concrete strip Alexandra turned the steering wheel and reversed her car towards Domenic Cannizzaro's police car then under the overpass where she stopped, feeling that the concrete walls offered some protection. The five friends sat upright in the car until a policeman told them to get down.

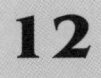

12

Graham Larchin and Betty Roberts made their way down High Street over the Merri Creek and into Queens Parade. In front of them a tramway bus carrying several passengers was turning left to go into Hoddle Street. Graham accelerated and cut in front of the bus forcing the driver to reverse and take another route. Graham waved another car away from Hoddle Street and when he saw that there was no traffic along Queens Parade and High Street he returned to the car. There was the injured man at the signal box to see . . .

Wayne Monohan stood by the bus lane in Hoddle Street and saw two cars reverse quickly away from the Clifton Hill Railway Station. Gunfire was loud and rapid and he felt it was coming from the south. He hurried towards the stationary train, its headlight drawing him like a magnet and distorting his vision. When he was about 100 metres from the train, Tom Harris the driver, put his head out of the side window and yelled, "Look out! Behind you!"

100, maybe 200 metres away, it was difficult to tell in the light, Wayne saw the figure of the gunman, holding his rifle waist-high, approaching the train. The gunman fired randomly into the air and towards the ground.

Graham Larchin drove the police car about twenty metres into Hoddle Street when Betty looked up from the Melway. She saw someone carrying what appeared to be a shotgun across his chest. As a country girl she had used a shotgun once while shooting rabbits with her brother. Being petite, she had fallen over from the kick in the discharge.

At first she thought it was a detective or a member of the Special Operations Group who was running along the railway line. Graham had seen the gunman jump over the fence erected along Hoddle Street, north of the Clifton Hill Railway Station. He saw the gunman walk towards and then run along the railway line and, like his partner, believed he was a police officer – probably a detective.

Graham Larchin unbuckled his seat belt. He told Betty to check with D24 if there were other police searching along the railway line. He left the engine running and the headlights on high beam. They picked up the gunman and the rifle. Graham got out, leaving the door open wide and walked towards the "detective". Then he saw the man run towards him, stop and crouch, and bring the rifle up. Graham turned and ran back towards the police car. He screamed at Betty to get out of the car – to get behind it – as he zig-zagged across the road, running hard, just as he had been taught in the Army Reserve.

Graham had spent five years in an infantry battalion to improve his firearm skills and to increase his skills of self-preservation. Pistol practice in the police force then was irregular, and limited, due to expense, to thirty rounds a year. The army reserve taught you how to react if you were under fire and what cover to take. He was taught survival drills which became instinctive, and the cost of ammunition was not such a problem.

Betty reached for the transmitter, "Northcote 253. Urgent. Man coming towards us with a gun. We're in High Street. Urgent."

Mick Hogan asked for a repeat. He wanted to get the street name. He heard Betty say High, but he wanted to be sure. More importantly, he wanted her to be sure, as he felt that maybe she meant Hoddle Street. Detective Rick McIntosh, who had been stationed at Fitzroy for several years and knew the area well, cut in and suggested cordoning off various streets.

Mick Hogan asked Rick and other police to stand by while he tried to get help to Graham Larchin and Betty Roberts. He asked for any unit to come down High Street and assist Northcote 253.

Betty had already dropped the transmitter when Mick Hogan had asked for a repeat of her message. The gunman fired five times at Graham and Betty, striking neither them nor the police car. It was something they could not understand for they were under bright street-lighting, their headlights were on high beam and the interior light was on. They hid behind the car, almost merging into one another. There was silence after the five rounds were discharged, and Graham reasoned that the gunman was reloading.

As Wayne ran up to the driver's cabin, he could hear the shells being ejected onto the stones after each discharge, and he wondered if he would be killed. Tom Harris reversed the train a short distance as the gunman disappeared from view. The two men determined that if the gunman came back into view again and approached the train, there was nothing else to do but go forward and, hopefully, run him over. Tom stopped the train over the Urquhart Street bridge with the rear half straddling the Merri Creek, and switched off all the carriage and train lights.

Domenic Cannizzaro hurried out and went behind his police car. Carrying the revolver in his right hand he waved traffic down and stopped any more cars from proceeding further down the exit ramp. He told the driver of the first car to keep his head down, then ran to the red Ford. He checked Daniel Coldebella and reassured him that he was all right. There was a 4.5 cm x 8 cm laceration to his back, where a piece of metal had become embedded. Below the laceration were three puncture wounds which had made superficial entry into his chest cavity.

At Domenic's urging, Dimitrios Collyvas tried to start the Ford but the engine would not turn. Renata was hysterical then suddenly silent. Domenic went to her side and slapped her face gently to bring her around. He told everyone to keep down, that there were gunmen nearby. He had no idea where, although the damage indicated that the shots had come from the front and the railway-side of the car.

Domenic went back to his police car to contact D24 for an ambulance. Those in the Ford cried out, "Don't go away!"

As he reached the door to the police car he looked up at the full moon.

"It figures," he said.

9.46 p.m.

Like many of the police officers at Hoddle Street, Dennis Harnety was not familiar with the area. Not knowing the street names and their locations made him feel extremely vulnerable. He opened a Melway and ran his finger over the page trying to understand where he was and where the gunmen might be. If he were in Richmond, the area he knew, he would have felt more confident. He dropped the Melway through the car window and made his way to the back of the car where Max Drake and Terry Howard, with their revolvers drawn, had taken cover.

Standing outside the Northcote Police Station looking south-east towards Clifton Hill and the Merri Creek, Darren Anderson heard the shots. Everyone who had come to the station was there with him and they were all silent. The phones began to ring again and he rushed inside.

In the five years that Betty Roberts had been in the police force, no one had tried to take her life. Behind the police car in Hoddle Street, where she faced the prospect of losing her life, she became angry and upset that she had yet to achieve her goals. She wanted to have children; wanted them badly, and now she was aware it might not happen. Someone she did not know was trying to murder her and end her five-month marriage to a Brunswick detective. She wanted to know why this person wanted to kill her. She had done nothing to deserve it.

Graham Larchin told Betty to stop traffic coming into Queens Parade from Alexandra Parade. He told her he believed the gunman was reloading and if she was quick she could escape to Queens Parade unharmed. He would cover her with his revolver.

Betty ran from behind the police car. Her legs were like jelly, as if she had just finished a marathon. She had done a lot of running in her youth and had belonged to an athletics club yet her legs seemed to be bogged in quicksand. While she ran south along Queens Parade towards Alexandra Parade, a couple in a sedan pulled up behind Graham Larchin. Graham ran towards the sedan yelling at the driver to go back and waved them away with his revolver. The sedan quickly reversed, back into Queens Parade and under the railway bridge.

Graham ran towards Queens Parade. He continued to zig-zag along the road wondering where the gunman was and if he had reloaded. When he ran into Queens Parade, he saw a man waiting at the tram shelter, oblivious to the danger. Graham yelled at him to leave, to get out if he valued his life for he was about to be shot at. The man ran south towards Alexandra Parade without a word. Graham's shirt was saturated with sweat and his heart thumped. He was aware that the gunman had the advantage of being hidden among the bushes in the dark, while everyone else was in the open and exposed by street lighting. Graham had to ensure that no one else entered the killing zone.

He stepped onto the road aware that at any second the gunman could shoot him. He made the north-bound vehicles along Queens Parade turn. The vehicles that were travelling south along High Street towards the bridge, with their indicators flashing left for Hoddle Street, he directed back again. He waved his revolver frantically and kept moving, again, just as he had been trained in the army reserve. He went from one side of the street to the other.

Mick Hogan called for other police cars to back up Northcote 253. He called for Graham Larchin and Betty Roberts but there was no response. For some seconds the air was quiet then a Dog Squad unit, Canine 267, coming from another area and a different radio channel, volunteered to assist. Hogan directed the unit into the area, warning that people had been shot.

Again, Mick Hogan called for Northcote 253 but suspected that the worst had happened. Domenic Cannizzaro called him giving his call sign clearly, enunciating the 2-1-3 so no mistake could be made.

"Northcote 213," Hogan responded.

"Northcote 213. I'm just off the ramp at Hoddle Street just reaching the railway station. I've got some people injured (sic) in the car here who've been shot, one in the shoulder."

"Stay with them," said Hogan. "You're on top of the ramp, are you?"

"Underneath the ramp," corrected Domenic who added that traffic down the ramp was banked up and that he had stopped the traffic going into Hoddle Street.

9.47 p.m.

"Roger. How serious are the injuries there?"

"He seems to be moving, I've just kept him still. He's hit in the shoulder, he tells me."

"Roger. If you stay with him," Mick Hogan said.

Mick Hogan believed Northcote 253 had been killed. He called for them again. When there was no answer he called for a unit in the High Street area.

"Fitzroy 303," said Bill Taylor who, with Jenny Leuther, had cleared the North Fitzroy inquiry.

Bill Taylor told Mick Hogan that they were travelling south along High Street towards Clifton Hill and had not sighted Northcote 253. Could they get their exact location? Mick Hogan called Northcote 253 again, hoping that his gut instinct was wrong.

Stephen Aylward and Simon Black heard the shots but could not tell where they were coming from. They had tried to get under the police vehicle but they were keen body builders and were too big. They leaned against the side of the divisional van and took in the scene, each holding a revolver in the ready position.

"Require an ambulance here, thanks. We've got about five or six people who're shot, at this stage," Stephen Aylward said into the portable radio.

Everywhere Stephen looked there were bodies, broken glass and blood oozing its way along the gutter towards Ramsden Street. His eyes fixed on the centre plantation that separated north and south-bound traffic, and the missing chunks of concrete that were now spread around Shane Stanton.

"Yeah, we've got them all over the place. What's your location, Richmond?" Mick Hogan asked.

"Beside the Clifton Hill Station."

"In the station itself, is it (sic)?"

"Beside the station in Hoddle Street," Stephen said.

9.48 p.m.

Mick Hogan ran his hands through his hair, and pawed at his face. He wanted to get the ambulance officers safely into the scene. If they were shot there was no one else to take their place. He pressed the foot pedal and called Collingwood 250 and Collingwood 303. There was no immediate answer from Paul McNichol who was at the Mobil Service Station or from Belinda Bourchier and Glen Sheluchin. Paul McNichol was unsure what route the police, let alone ambulance officers, could safely take.

Stephen Aylward thought it ironic that at the start of the shift everyone at Richmond agreed to take a low profile so that they could celebrate the end of night shift and the birthdays of Belinda Bourchier, and Leigh Wisbey, who was stationed at Richmond. He had a quiet chuckle to himself as he looked at what was around him. His hands were cold like ice and he wished his overcoat was in the van and not in his locker at the station. His whole body felt cold.

He and Simon Black crawled over to Shane Stanton. The hole in his Kawasaki's petrol tank was huge. Neither had experience with rifles but they knew that whatever caused the damage was more powerful than a .22 rifle. What was it they were up against? As they reached him Shane let out a deep sigh.

"Hang in there, you'll be okay," Stephen said.

Simon checked Shane's pulse and found no movement. Although his eyes were open and his body warm, he was dead. Stephen crawled back along the road to the divisional van.

John Delahunty got back into the police car. He could tell the shots were nearby – somewhere in Hoddle Street – and he wasn't able to help from where he was. Quickly he drove across the concrete strip dividing Heidelberg Road, and down the entry ramp towards the Clifton Hill Railway Station. He had travelled only a short distance along the entry ramp when he stopped, unable to pass several stationary cars in front of him. He saw the red Ford with the shattered back windscreen and noticed that it had collided with the Northcote police car. John drew his revolver and ran down towards the end of the ramp. He stopped at each car and checked the occupants, telling them to remain calm and to stay in their cars. Everyone he saw was frozen in their seats, too terrified to move.

The old man touched Shane Keogh's arm to get his attention. He pointed to the Datsun Coupe parked outside the Mobil Service Station.

"There's someone injured in there," he said.

Shane told the man he would check and walked over to the Datsun and opened the passenger-side door. He put his hand against Tracey Farmer's jugular vein, felt nothing, then leaned further into the cabin. He recoiled, stumbling over to the old man. "She's dead! She's dead!"

Stationmaster Giovanni Di Vincenzo put the phone down and raced across the train tracks, up onto the other platform and out to Hoddle Street. He saw Domenic Cannizzaro beside his police car and walked quickly to him.

"Get down!" Domenic yelled.

Giovanni crouched down and continued towards Domenic. He told him that the gunman had been sighted by Wayne Monohan near the sub-station, a locked concrete building which was at the point where the Epping and Eltham lines divided.

"Stay here, there's more than one," Domenic said.

Giovanni got inside the back seat of the police car and listened to the police radio.

Clint Morrison stood on the footpath in Hodgkinson Street. He lived nearby in a terrace house. He looked through the Darling Gardens towards where the shots had come from. A criminal-law barrister and solicitor, he had for years taken a stand against what he perceived to be injustice and police brutality. He shook his head in disgust. Hoddle Street was a mass of police and ambulance vehicles, and police wielding revolvers. Clint was joined by several other residents to watch the drama as it unfolded.

"It's the fuckin' police again!" Clint shouted, waving his hands about.

The veins in his neck bulged like a Carlton football coach's during a tight game. Clint stamped his feet and shook his head.

"Typical. Fuckin' typical of the bastards. They shoot first and ask questions later. They're as bad as the fuckin' yanks. What sort of a country have we got? A fuckin' police state!"

Everyone kept their attention fixed on Hoddle Street. There were people looking out of partially opened front doors and through cracks in blinds. Some men cradled babies in their arms. One walked out into the middle of the road in North Terrace to get a better view. His wife called him back, to give her the baby. If he wanted to get killed that was fine, she screamed, but not the baby.

"Pack of gun-happy bastards," Clint Morrison cursed.

Constable Anita Adair lit up another cigarette and wound the window down another centimetre. Her partner, David Depyle, was a non-smoker and was the junior partner and observer for the Northcote afternoon shift divisional van. They were returning from West Heidelberg as a back up to a reported attempted murder when they heard Darren Anderson tell of the shooting down by the Merri Creek. Then they changed from channel 60 to 67 to listen to the progress of their sergeant's inquiries.

They were in Merri Parade, Northcote, near the railway bridge. The two thought it best to prevent any trucks going under the bridge as, in the past, there had been several that had got stuck. They waited for ten minutes and no trucks passed by. Anita removed the spotlight from the side pocket and shone it over the banks of the Merri Creek and up towards the Rushall Railway Station on the Fitzroy side of the creek. She reasoned that if the gunmen were following the railway line, then there were plenty of places to hide in trees, bushes and long grass. She wished she knew the best place to be to cut the offenders off but there were a hundred other places for the gunmen to go. Anita tried D24 again but the air was congested. She switched back to channel 60 and advised the B district operator that they were moving to the Rushall Railway Station.

Inspector Adrian Fyfe told his driver, Robert Kovacs, to turn left into Queens Parade. Robert was happy to oblige as he was concerned for Belinda Bourchier and had wanted to attend earlier. Inspector Fyfe had decided to help rather than continue on home. What was happening was much more than "shots being fired".

Graham Larchin was taking refuge behind a tree on the footpath near Brennand Street, a short distance from the railway bridge. Graham and Betty Roberts could hear the engine of their police car idling in Hoddle Street more than 100 metres away. In their haste to escape they had left the portable radio in the car. They felt vulnerable not knowing what was happening, even though they could hear some of what was being said on the car radio.

When motorists by-passed the roadblock near Michael Street, Graham waved them down, revolver in hand, making them turn back, while Betty covered him. Graham flagged down the approaching police car and told Inspector Fyfe what had happened. Betty and Robert Kovacs laid five flares across the road further south, near Michael Street. Betty, who was directing traffic away from Hoddle Street, was given a white reflector vest by a detective.

"You'll get run over," he said.

Graham Larchin yelled at Robert Kovacs to shelter behind a brick wall while the Inspector took out a white, reflector coat from the boot and put it on. On the other side of the Merri Creek they could see the flashing blue lights of a police car.

Colin Chambers directed traffic into Urquhart Street, away from Hoddle, while his partner, Michael McCormick, was further north at the Westgarth Street intersection. Traffic was still getting through from Westgarth Street so Colin returned to Michael, who had only a torch to direct traffic. It was obvious that some motorists were having difficulty seeing Michael. So Colin, thinking that Michael was in a more dangerous position than he himself was, gave him his cap with its bright, white-and-navy chequered band.

Colin felt that they were balancing on the edge of a razor blade. Was it better to be killed or injured by a non-observant motorist or by the gunman? Was it more important to divert traffic to safety and risk your own life, or to abandon the traffic duty in order to preserve your own life? They both secretly considered whether what they were doing was worthwhile. Several motorists argued or questioned them, while residents from the flats and houses nearby gathered behind a cyclone-wire fence on the west side of High Street not far from where shots had been heard.

Colin Chambers drove back to the south-side of the Urquhart Street intersection and parked the police car, blue lights flashing, across the path of south-bound traffic. No one should be able to get past Urquhart Street, he reasoned, unless they drove around the police car. He ran to two police officers who walked about with their hands in their pockets, smoking cigarettes, 100 metres further east in Urquhart Street. They had been sent from the Preston area, unaware of what had been happening in Hoddle Street, and with no portable radio.

Simon Black and Steve Aylward ran crouched towards the Heidelberg Road overpass reaching Wayne Timms and Jayne Timbury who were taking refuge behind Wayne's motorcycle. They were pale-faced, asking, "What's going on?"

Simon and Steve led Wayne and Jayne back to the divisional van. They half-crawled, half-carried them to the side of the van, not sure that they had taken them to a safer position.

Inspector Adrian Fyfe tried in vain to get through to D24. The airwaves were jammed. He tried again.

"150. Afternoon urgent," Mick Hogan responded.

"I've just spoken to the crew from the Northcote van. We believe that that man is on the railway-cutting on top. He may be shooting at police vehicles so try and keep the police cars away – with their blue lights off, please – before someone gets hurt."

Asked for further details, the Inspector explained that Graham Larchin and Betty Roberts had been shot at, and that they had last seen the gunman on top of the railway bridge where it crossed over High Street, south of Urquhart Street.

Inspector Pat Murtagh trained the revolver north of where he and Shane Cross were pinned behind the police car.

"I've got you covered," the Inspector said.

He searched for any sign of movement among the bushes as Shane dashed across the north-bound lanes of Hoddle Street and over to the Sigma sedan. Shane opened the driver's door and while at first Dusan looked to be sleeping, beside him his lunch in a brown paper bag, there was no mistaking the fact that he was dead. Shane rushed back to the police car feeling particularly vulnerable without his revolver. The Inspector had taken it. At any moment he expected to hear rifle shots and he hoped that the Inspector was a better shot than the gunman, as he had nothing to defend himself. He felt naked without his revolver. It was a feeling he was going to have for the rest of the night.

Jacqueline Turner slowly looked up over the dashboard of her Toyota Corona and decided now was the time to get to safety. She started the engine, worried that, at any moment, one of the gunmen would see her and cut her down like the others. She looked over her shoulder, fighting back the tears, and quickly reversed towards Ramsden Street. A police car pulled up alongside, a policewoman in the front-passenger seat yelling, "Get out of here!"

Jacqueline pressed the accelerator a little harder and, when she saw that she was opposite the signal box, changed gears, turning left into North Terrace, then right into Turnbull Street. She was not familiar with the side streets of Clifton Hill and one-way and dead-end streets only added to her confusion and distress.

9.49 p.m.

Bill Taylor from Fitzroy 303 told D24 that he and his partner were travelling south along High Street with the blue lights off. Jenny Leuther pulled into the service lane and stopped the divisional van opposite a church. Having heard Inspector Fyfe's transmission they decided to abandon the police car in High Street and approach the scene on foot.

They were in a quandary as to how to leave the divisional van. Locked or unlocked? If they left it unlocked there was the chance that equipment could be stolen and damage done. Yet if they left the van locked it might mean the difference between living and dying. Keys in or out of the ignition? Leaving the keys in the ignition meant that they could get away quickly. At the same time it allowed someone, maybe a gunman, an opportunity to steal the van.

They decided to lock the van and not to wear their chequer-band caps. Bill Taylor reasoned that the caps would make them more visible to the gunmen. The two police officers moved quickly, although crouched along the footpath to the Urquhart Street corner. Bill motioned to Jenny to remain there while he checked deeper into Urquhart Street. Jenny spoke to residents who had come out of their houses and told them quietly but forcefully to go back inside. She felt the cold and wished she had worn a jumper under her overcoat. It seemed much colder in Clifton Hill. Shots could be heard in the near vicinity. Bill returned and told her that the gunmen were close by. She followed him into Urquhart Street towards the overhead bridge that carried trains to and from Clifton Hill along the Hurstbridge railway line.

"Carlton North 150. Urgent. This is obviously a job for the SOG. Call them out. We've got about six people shot," Inspector Pat Murtagh said.

"Will do," said Hogan, unaware that the Special Operations Group had already been despatched by another D24 operator.

Glen Sheluchin from Collingwood 303 advised that ambulance vehicles could enter the scene from the west in Turnbull Street.

A policewoman from Royal Park 203 volunteered to go to the Rushall Railway Station, the direction in which the gunman was thought to be heading.

"Keep west of the situation," Hogan directed.

Glen Sheluchin advised that it was safe in Turnbull Street and he reported that four or five people had been shot. Other police advised of people in need of medical attention and the need for extra ambulances.

"We're trying to get more there at the moment," Mick Hogan said.

For every voice he heard there were several others that withered and disappeared in the background. He had to go with the strongest signal, which might not have been the most important transmission. Sometimes he had two strong signals cut across one another and he could not understand either of them.

Mick was conscious of the need to remain calm despite the enormous pressure; the responsibility. While he leaned over his desk and wrote brief notes on scraps of paper and on the job cards, he was being bombarded with notes from more senior police wanting updates. How many were injured? How many were dead? What was happening? The telephones were ringing constantly with calls from members of the public and from police at various suburban police stations. Everyone wanted to talk to Mick Hogan. An inspector reached over to take a job card.

"Fuck off!" he was told by Mick, and the job card remained where it was. Mick did not want his focus to be compromised for one second. In times of urgency, rank meant nothing to him. Deputy Police Commissioner Kel Glare entered the control room.

"The braid's coming," Greg Splatt said.

"What do they want me to do? Put me (sic) cap on?" Mick said.

The Deputy Commissioner remained in the background and observed his troops in action. Mick glanced across to his right and saw Dianne Smith, another member of his Crew Five team, writing on the white board. Dianne filled in the positions of where police were and the sightings of the gunman. Dianne was very conscious of the fact that her husband, Colin Chambers, was at Hoddle Street.

Colin Chambers ran to the silver train which had stopped over the Urquhart Street bridge. Some passengers were hanging out of an open door. He yelled at them to move back inside, then ran, crouched, back to his police car in High Street with the revolver in his right hand.

9.50 p.m.

"VKC to Russell Street, correction, St Kilda 150 Afternoon," Mick Hogan said.

Inspector Adrian Fyfe recognised that the incorrect call sign was meant for him.

"Russell Street 150 Afternoon," Inspector Fyfe said.

"Which direction of travel was he last seen heading?"

Inspector Fyfe crouched beside the front, passenger door of his police car and pressed the transmitter button, the cord stretching from the dashboard and out of the window.

"Heading along the railway line towards the Rushall Railway Station."

"Roger. How long ago was it now, 150?"

"A matter of two minutes."

Royal Park 203 advised that they had heard the transmission. They were caught up in traffic which had been diverted from Hoddle Street, but would get to the Rushall Railway Station as soon as possible.

Inspector Pat Murtagh was becoming increasingly frustrated. He could not move from the side of the police car for fear of being shot, and whenever he tried to transmit to Mick Hogan at D24 there were other police attempting to do the same thing. Around him were dead and injured people, and ambulance crews who were unable to do their job. At Ramsden Street he saw a police officer herd spectators and media away. It was like a war zone.

Mick Hogan wanted a police car to get to Rushall Railway Station as soon as possible. With Royal Park 203 delayed, he asked for Carlton 302. They responded by calling themselves Carlton 310 – the night shift call sign. Mick continued to call them Carlton 302 but was unable to shift their location. They were in Heidelberg Road, on the overpass, blocking traffic entering Hoddle Street. Mick asked for a police car to come down St George's Road. City West 303 volunteered; they were close by. Mick's instructions were not received as other police cut in.

9.51 p.m.

Stephen Aylward reached inside the cabin of the divisional van for the radio transmitter.

"Richmond 310. Urgent," he said.

Mick Hogan at D24 pressed the foot pedal.

"Richmond 310. We've a solo down, we believe he's thirty-three. It looks like he might have a gunshot wound; between South Terrace and the Heidelberg Road overpass."

He was trying to control his breathing. He tried to speak normally but the adrenalin rush was overpowering.

"Roger, if you remain and preserve the scene," Hogan instructed.

Frustrated, Stephen cut in.

"We're doing that. Can we have an ambulance just to confirm that please?"

"Roger and which way is it safest for the ambulance to get through?" Mick Hogan asked, ready to write down the direction.

"If it comes north in Hoddle Street, it would be the best bet. There's cars (sic) banked up both ways."

Inspector Pat Murtagh called for VKC several times without any response or sign of recognition from Mick Hogan. To send the police or ambulance crews in would be asking them to commit suicide. He pressed the transmit button again.

9.52 p.m.

"I've got the station master and he's got some information on where this person could be," Domenic Cannizzaro said from the front seat of his police car.

"Go ahead," Mick Hogan replied.

"Air 495," the police helicopter, interrupted, but was told to stand by, then Mick Hogan suggested that they cover the Clifton Hill Railway Station area, "at this stage."

"Northcote 213 go ahead," Mick Hogan said, pressing the foot pedal.

"From what I can gather he is behind the ... sub-station ... between ... the Eastern Freeway ... and we're not sure of the street ... but the street where the station is, that runs across Hoddle Street," Domenic Cannizzaro said, pausing as he repeated, almost verbatim, what Giovanni Di Vincenzo was telling him from the back seat of the police car.

Before Mick Hogan could reply other police tried to engage his attention. The strongest signal was from Carlton North 150.

"Carlton North 150," Inspector Murtagh yelled into the microphone, "It's a containment situation. I don't want people rushing in."

In his hurry to get to the scene he had not taken out a firearm. It was a bad mistake on his part, one that he would never allow himself to repeat. He blamed himself for thinking that it would all be over by the time he reached the scene and that it would be nothing serious anyway. Never again would he treat any calls lightly.

It was a hard lesson to learn, particularly as in the past he had been to several firearm incidents. At Fawkner an offender fired a shotgun at him while trying to avoid a vehicle intercept. Then at Broadmeadows, children held as hostage were released by an offender after Pat, who was then a sergeant, had negotiated with him. When negotiations broke down, the offender attempted to shoot him, but Pat knocked him out with a single punch to the face.

Inspector Murtagh paused, holding the transmitter to his mouth, and listened to more shots being discharged in the near vicinity.

"It sounds like we've got gunshots going now," he advised D24.

9.53 p.m.

Giovanni Di Vincenzo made to leave the police car but stayed put when he saw a man carrying a revolver run down the exit ramp. It was not a police officer as he was not wearing a uniform and Giovanni could not see a badge anywhere. He felt his heart beat hard and fast and his breathing quicken as the man came closer. As the man came down the ramp, he turned his whole body from one side to the other. This reminded Giovanni of what he'd seen police do on television and in the movies and he assumed that maybe the man was, after all, a police officer or a detective. Believing that the man posed no threat to him he made to run over to the railway station.

The blue Toyota stationwagon, a DSG vehicle, was travelling along Canterbury Road, South Melbourne when Peter Butts took the transmitter from inside the glove box.

"Prahran 452. We're available," he said.

"452, if you could come down to the vicinity. We're looking at a general direction. If you could take charge. We'll have to block off traffic from, say, Johnston Street and Hoddle. A unit for Johnston and Hoddle?" said Hogan.

"Take charge!" Peter said looking across to Bruce Lowe, "Get fucked! What about the other sergeants already there?"

Peter put the magnetic blue light on the roof and plugged the lead into the connection for the cigarette lighter. Bruce accelerated quickly through the streets of South Melbourne, proceeding against red lights and one-way signs till they got closer to Hoddle Street.

The Northcote divisional van pulled up outside the Rushall Railway Station with another police car pulling in behind. Anita Adair steered the van onto the footpath outside the station as a Clifton Hill-bound train pulled onto the platform. As she and David Depyle left their vehicle, Glen Sheluchin, who was still in Hoddle Street, contacted D24 expressing concern about the next train due to arrive at Clifton Hill from Rushall Railway Station. Anita returned to the cabin of the divisional van and told Hogan that they were "right beside the train".

With the other police they hurried to the train to speak to the driver. None of the four had been issued with a portable radio so that they could be aware of any developments.

Domenic Cannizzaro repeated what Giovanni Di Vincenzo was telling him. He told Mick Hogan that the trains had been stopped.

9.54 p.m.

Mick Hogan directed Carlton 310 to the intersection of Johnston and Hoddle Streets where they were to prevent north-bound traffic approaching the scene. Pat Murtagh advised that there were about twenty police cars on the west side of Hoddle Street. He wanted to know how many were on the eastern side of the railway station, on the side of John Street. Victoria Dock 210 and another police car responded.

Murtagh advised that there were at least "six or seven people down" and that ten ambulance vehicles were required. They could come in under escort as it appeared to be safe on the western side of Hoddle Street. They were not under gunfire.

Gary Ricardo pressed the foot pedal while Mick Hogan checked the Melway. Gary told Pat Murtagh that two MICA's and five ambulances were on route and that they were to approach from Turnbull Street. Was that the route to take?

Murtagh paused before answering as he listened to the gunshots again. He tried to get a fix on them. They seemed further north, towards the railway bridge at High Street.

9.55 p.m.

Jenny Leuther was sick of carrying the revolver, it seemed to get heavier every minute she held it in her hand. Her hands were freezing and she felt terrible because of a cold which she had picked up from the night shift sergeant. She really wanted to be home in bed. Jenny wanted to put her revolver back in the holster but was too scared to; that couple of seconds delay in retrieving it could mean the difference between living and dying.

She was standing under the Urquhart Street railway bridge with her partner Bill Taylor when they saw the lights on the train above them go out. Immediately they trained their weapons on the train. A carriage door opened and they could see the silhouette of two men in the doorway. The two constables held their guns tightly, a micro-second away from pulling the trigger, when Bill lowered his arms.

"Step back Jenny," he said as the two men urinated on to the road below them.

"Not only are we getting shot at, but we're getting pissed on as well!" Bill said.

As the carriage doors closed, further east, in Urquhart Street, a car door slammed and an engine revved loudly. Then the car accelerated rapidly. Bill ran after the car trying to get the registration details but lost it as it turned left to travel north in Ross Street. He stopped a car coming from High Street and got in, directing the driver to pursue the fleeing car hoping to get close enough to see the registration plate. He lost sight of the car and felt frustrated at not having a portable radio. The motorist drove him back to High Street, where the Fitzroy divisional van had been left. Bill thanked the motorist and told him to go, then he ran back towards the bridge where he had left his partner. When Bill arrived, she had disappeared and, again, he felt frustrated at the lack of portable radios. He did not know where Jenny was and she did not know where he was. He looked back towards High Street and saw the open driver's door of Colin Chamber's police car.

The middle-aged woman with the handbag came out from the pedestrian underpass and up the footpath towards the Clifton Hill Railway Station.

"Get back! Get back!" Domenic Cannizzaro yelled, waving his hand at her.

The woman continued walking towards the railway station.

"Get back!" Domenic yelled again.

She continued approaching the station then suddenly stopped as she surveyed the scene in front of her. She put a hand to her mouth, quickly turned around and went back, disappearing into the underpass.

The four police went through each carriage advising the wide-eyed passengers of what was happening and suggesting that they keep their heads below the window line. Before the police had returned to their vehicles beside the Rushall Railway Station the train driver had already extinguished the lights in the carriages and the train. Anita Adair reached in to the divisional van for the transmitter.

"Northcote 303. Myself (sic) and another unit are at the station with the train and it will not be going."

As John Delahunty reached the police car, he saw Domenic Cannizzaro crouched by the driver's side and he ran to him.

"I'm from Northcote," Domenic said.

"Fitzroy," John replied, scouring the landscape south along Hoddle Street.

He saw the motorcycle on its side and, until that point, had thought that the "solo down" had been a police officer. Further south he saw various stationary cars and windscreen glass across the road. It all looked surreal.

"It could be another Mad Max," Donna Randall said, as she and Tim Edgeworth gathered their equipment and ran from the DSG office to their Ford XC sedan parked outside.

Traffic was light as Tim Edgeworth accelerated hard towards Hoddle Street. They had no blue light or siren and Donna asked him to slow down believing they should arrive at the scene as carefully as possible. As they approached intersections where police were directing traffic Donna pressed her police badge, the 'freddy', against the windscreen and they were given access. They propped momentarily at red-light intersections and when clear, charged through. North along Hoddle Street the traffic slowed to a bottleneck. Tim turned back, and east into Roseneath Street then north into Gordon Street. As Tim turned the car left into Ramsden Street he and Donna saw several police taking cover behind cars parked along both sides of the street. Residents in their dressing gowns and slippers stood on the footpath or hid behind their knee-high front fences. Tim parked the car opposite house number six.

Domenic Cannizzaro and John Delahunty ran to the Clifton Hill Railway Station covering one another as they ran through the main entrance. As John came onto the platform he saw Fernando Myra and about a dozen people standing on the Melbourne-bound platform.

"Get the people inside! Lock the doors and stay down on the ground!" John yelled.

Fernando Myra quickly moved the others into the portable ticket office.

Another police officer entered the shop area of the Mobil Service Station. He told those gathered there that it was believed two men wearing army gear were responsible and that they were heading away from the Clifton Hill area, towards North Fitzroy. The sense of relief was almost palpable.

Colin Chambers heard a shot. At almost the same time he felt an impact on his right side, then a burning sensation just above his hip. The impact pushed him forward; he almost fell onto the road; but he maintained his balance and kept running towards his police car. Everything seemed to be happening in slow motion, like in the movies, but he was running faster and harder than at any time in his life.

He dived under the police car, his handcuffs digging into his left side. He could feel blood from where the handcuffs had cut into him. Colin tried to see where the gunman was. He fingered his tunic in the region where he had felt the impact. He felt a horizontal tear in his jacket, as if it had been slashed with a sharp knife. His finger explored inside the tunic and found that his police shirt and singlet had also been slashed. His skin was sensitive to touch and blistered. It was pitch black and he could see no sign of the gunman, who was already running down to the Merri Creek from the west side of the High Street bridge, near the footpath, where he had taken aim.

Fiona Weightman, 23, was watching television in her third-floor flat in Hales Court, Northcote when she heard, what she thought, were railway detonators. As the Epping line and the Rushall Railway Station were a short distance away, over the Merri Creek, it was not an unusual sound. When she continued to hear the bangs she realised that she was wrong. The police helicopter was making a lot of noise as it hovered nearby. She walked onto her balcony and saw police cars in High Street and, further east, the train, stopped on the Urquhart Street bridge. There were cars banked up along Heidelberg Road. She heard a shot; it was very loud and seemed to come from near a pylon supporting the Merri Creek bridge. It was close to her flat. The helicopter went out of view.

13

It was the loudest shot he had ever heard in his life. The sheer loudness of it stunned Bill Taylor for a moment, and he had no idea from where it had come. There was no muzzle flash to be seen and the location made it difficult to pinpoint where the shot discharged. Then he saw Colin Chambers stagger along High Street screaming, "I've been shot," several times before sliding under his car. Bill ran across Urquhart Street and into High Street where a high fence gave some protection. He knocked on the front door of the house behind it.

"Who is it?"

"Police."

The occupants did not believe Bill Taylor and refused to open the door. Bill took out his freddy and pushed it through the mail slot in the centre of the door. The door opened and he rushed inside where he telephoned D24 telling the operator that he had seen Colin Chambers shot, and giving the location. He advised that Colin was alive. Bill was given a large jacket to cover his uniform, by the male occupant in case the gunman was shooting only at police. He then left the couple and their small child and went back outside to be confronted with what appeared to be a ghost town. There were no police or cars to be seen. Not even the spectators by the cyclone fence.

After checking the waiting rooms, the public toilets and both ends of the platform John Delahunty and Domenic Cannizzaro ran back to Domenic's police car. When John had checked along the platform he had seen more dead and wounded people in their cars or on the ground. The people in the red Ford which had reversed into Domenic were covered in blood. Everything seemed unreal. When he heard more shots being discharged, John left Domenic for his own car. He reversed quickly into Heidelberg Road, heading west and trying to keep himself as low as possible in the driver's seat. He heard on the radio that vehicles were still travelling into Queens Parade, in the direction of the area where the gunman was possibly located. At the intersection of Queens Parade and Heidelberg Road he met another police car that had just entered Queens Parade. The officers were not known to him and were unfamiliar with the Clifton Hill–Fitzroy area. John told them to stop traffic coming into Queens Parade and approaching the railway bridge over High Street.

Fiona Weightman could hear something running through the grass on the other side of the fence that separated the block of flats where she lived and the banks of the Merri Creek. She followed the sound with her eyes and saw a male running quickly towards the Rushall Railway Station. She went back inside and closed the balcony doors then rang the Northcote Police Station.

Tim Edgeworth and Donna Randall got back into the police car. Donna reversed east along Ramsden Street into Myrtle, then west into Roseneath Street and then north into Hoddle Street. It would have been easier to have driven across the Ramsden Street railway crossing – they were parked twenty metres east of it – but other police had advised them not to.

Donna turned into the Ramsden Street intersection and stopped the car on an angle across the south-bound lanes of Hoddle Street. In Turnbull Street groups of residents had stepped out of their homes to see what was happening. Donna and Tim Edgeworth took cover behind the driver's side of their car. As Donna got out of the police car she saw Syd Hadley walking carefully towards the billboards on the east-side of Hoddle Street, with both hands clasped around his revolver. A camera crew followed. Syd stopped and waved angrily for the camera crew to retreat. The *NiteSun* from the police helicopter illuminated the street, and three people could clearly be seen lying together. Donna and Tim thought that they were taking cover, until Gina Papaioannou raised then lowered her arm, as if waving for help.

"Air 495. We're over the top. Have we got a better location please?"

Constable Keith Stewart had served in New South Wales and the Australian Capital Territory, in uniformed police, plain clothes and traffic, for sixteen years before obtaining his pilot licence. He then worked in the Northern Territory mustering cattle. In 1986, he joined the Victoria Police as a helicopter pilot. When D24 contacted the Air Wing at its Essendon Airport hangar, with reports of a man with a shotgun in the Clifton Hill area, it seemed a routine call and nothing was said to indicate any extreme urgency or danger. As there was the possibility that people had been injured the ambulance helicopter was taken out of the hangar. On route to Hoddle Street Air 495 contacted the aviation frequency and advised that all aircraft should stay clear of the Clifton Hill area.

Keith Stewart's crew consisted of observer, Senior Constable Trevor Wilson, trainee-observer, Senior Constable Daryl Jones, and ambulance officer, Allan Scott. As the helicopter surveyed the Clifton Hill area Keith decided it was unsafe to hover. Below them were bodies cut down in motor vehicles, on the footpaths and in the gardens. Several police and ambulance officers waved the helicopter away. The *NiteSun* searchlight made everyone instant targets. Several members of the Air Wing had, for some years, asked for infra-red or other night-vision aid instead of the *NiteSun* spotlight, but had been rejected. The *NiteSun* told everyone the helicopter's location and, since its inception in 1979, the police helicopter had been shot at several times.

As Air 495 flew to the Clifton Hill area Keith debated whether to use the *NiteSun*. Would it help or hinder those on the ground? It could help save lives or put lives at risk with a sniper hiding among the bushes. Keith switched off the navigation, interior and rotating-beacon lights to avoid being seen from the ground. He lowered to 1000 feet. Residents complained to D24 and to Fitzroy, Northcote and Collingwood Police Stations about the noise it made, and the interference to television reception. Some people went outside to see what was happening and others complained that it was flying too low. Some said it was flying at 300 feet.

Air 495 made right-hand orbits scouring the backyards, parks, creek, streets and train lines. Daryl Jones operated the *NiteSun* while the others looked for signs of the gunman or gunmen – any movement at all.

"495, the last we saw he was heading towards Rushall Station on top of the tracks. Where the bridge goes over the Merri Creek – heading on foot towards Rushall Railway Station. Melways 30 Echo Eleven (sic)," Mick Hogan advised.

"Air 495. Received. Thank you," Keith replied.

Other police cut across the final transmission.

Donna Randall crept from behind her car and edged towards the railway line. She felt vulnerable without a radio and approached a divisional van to hear what was happening. A grey-haired man told her, "I think I know who it is. His name is Julian Knight and he lives in that house."

The grey-haired man, a friend of Pamela Knight, indicated 6 Ramsden Street. He spoke reluctantly, but felt he had no alternative but to speak the truth.

Glen Sheluchin took the grey-haired man and placed him in the rear of the divisional van, then drove him to the Mobil Service Station.

Jason Rowbottom was watching TV in his upstairs bedroom when the helicopter flew over his house in McKean Street, North Fitzroy. He went outside and stood in the middle of the road watching the helicopter orbit, when a police car approached without its headlights on. The police car stopped and he was told to go back inside, that there was someone outside with a gun.

He went back upstairs.

9.56 p.m.

Detective Senior Constable Rick McIntosh pressed the transmit button on the portable radio.

"St Kilda 500."

McIntosh advised of three people with a dog near a block of flats on the east side of the Clifton Hill Railway Station.

"Can we get the night light on them please."

John Watson had run out of money and could not afford to pay for a bed at the Gill Memorial, a refuge for homeless men. He camped in a hollow under a large tree opposite the Merri Creek near the Rushall Railway Station. He had covered himself with newspapers and a coat, trying to keep warm. He had heard a loud noise which he believed was a car backfiring and he was not concerned. Then there was the helicopter swooping around and someone running towards him along the train tracks. Some two-metres away, he saw a thin male running with, what he thought, was a shotgun across his chest, the barrel pointing to the left in an upwards position. As a former soldier, John Watson knew it as the high part position.

"Air 495. Has he got a shotgun or rifle – for our information please?"

"The initial report was both," Mick Hogan said.

He then asked for any police to advise on a more detailed description of the weapons being used.

Constables Anita Adair and David Depyle directed south-bound traffic away from High Street, Northcote. Two cars approached from Walker Street, on the west side of High Street wanting to turn right, but were waved to turn left towards Westgarth Street. The drivers muttered under their breath then turned as they were directed. Anita watched another car travel west and approach the High Street lights where other police were directing traffic. The car turned left in to the service road which ran parallel to High Street. She heard one of the police officers yell at the driver to stop, but he accelerated. Anita rushed across to the service lane and put her left hand up while holding her revolver in the other hand. The car slowed to a stop and Anita indicated for the driver to turn around but he remained still. She went up to his window and motioned for the driver to wind down the window. She tapped at the window with the barrel of her revolver to get his attention. The driver and his passengers jumped. A second car pulled in behind the first car.

"Do as you're bloody told!" she said.

Inspector Adrian Fyfe advised D24 that the firearms being used were a rifle and, possibly, a pump-action shotgun. He said that the Northcote police had been shot at five times with a shotgun. With this knowledge, Keith Stewart lowered Air 495 to 700 feet believing it was out of range of a shotgun. It was also the lowest the police were permitted to fly helicopters in the metropolitan area.

9.57 p.m.

"St Kilda 500. Urgent."

Rick McIntosh was puffing. He had been told that the offender lived in the extension to North Terrace which was Ramsden Street, and he was concerned that the safety of everyone had been greatly reduced. He wanted traffic travelling from Heidelberg Road down through Fenwick Street to be diverted. He did not want it travelling into Ramsden Street, which he knew then as North Terrace.

"St Kilda 500. We've been given an address here by a complainant stating that he is probably the man. The address we've been given is number 6 Ramsden Street in Clifton Hill. Apparently a gentleman left there earlier in a very distressed state and he's left home (sic) his empty gun case," said Sergeant Gary Ricardo working next to Mick Hogan at D24.

"What's the name you've got?" Rick asked checking his note book.

Gary Ricardo asked Rick to stand by while he checked the cards on the desk before him. He had two names and he gave the first as being Battie. Before Ricardo could continue, another police car chipped in asking for instructions.

"Julian Knight is the name we have," Rick said.

"That's the second one we've got. That's the one we've got from number 6 Ramsden Street, Clifton Hill. It's his home address," Gary Ricardo said.

Preston 303 came up urgent.

Mick Hogan answered but Rick McIntosh cut in saying he was in Ramsden Street and cars were approaching the address. With that information Hogan gave priority to Rick McIntosh over Preston 303 and asked for any available police to stop traffic entering Ramsden Street from the intersection of Heidelberg Road and Fenwick Street.

9.58 p.m.

Prahran 452 – Peter Butts and Bruce Lowe – volunteered and questioned the fate of the solo – the name given to police motorcycle riders – and if it was a police officer. Mick Hogan commented that he was unable to confirm this and would get someone to check the solo as soon as possible.

Domenic Cannizzaro from Northcote 213, still near the Clifton Hill Railway Station, asked for a description of what the gunman was wearing. Mick Hogan began to give him Knight's description when another police officer cut in and advised that someone with a white shirt was moving west along the side of the train tracks. Before Mick Hogan could respond, Pat Murtagh, Carlton 150, directed that Air 495 concentrate on the Ramsden Street area. It was difficult for Mick Hogan to know the correct course of action to take. As Murtagh was at the scene, Mick Hogan took his advice. Air 495 asked for directions.

9.59 p.m.

Colin Chambers crawled out from under the police car and opened the driver's-side door. He punched out the housing of the interior light to make himself less visible in the cabin and grabbed the transmitter from the dashboard. His side hurt from the bullet graze and where the handcuffs had cut into him when he slid under the car.

" ... just been shot at!" was all Mick Hogan could hear.

"Unit urgent?"

"Northern 232!"

"Northern 232, repeat your message," Mick Hogan said calmly. "I'm at High Street and Urquhart Street. I've been shot at from somewhere towards the railway station, I think."

A policewoman cut in and told Colin to switch his lights off. He had been oblivious to the flashing blue and leaned over to the dashboard and depressed the button. Preston 303, which had minutes earlier given the urgent call, chipped in saying that the shot appeared to have come from near where the train had stopped over Urquhart Street. Mick Hogan called for "any unit that was near."

"Clifton Hill 150," said Inspector Fyfe. He advised that he was located near the tram stop in Queens Parade, opposite Hoddle Street, on the other side of

High Street and the bridge.

"The shot was fired from across where the Northern unit is calling from. We could have two men with firearms, not just one."

10.00 p.m.

Mick Hogan was frustrated with all the conflicting information given by police and members of the public.

"VKC to all units. We're looking for at least one fellow with a firearm – a Julian Knight. He lives in Ramsden Street. He's described as wearing blue jeans, a blue denim jacket, he's six foot, approximately, with brown hair."

Canine 267 requested the location of Carlton North 150.

Rick McIntosh pressed the transmit button on the portable radio.

"St Kilda 500. A witness, five minutes ago, saw the offender running along the railway tracks heading north to Northcote."

10.01 p.m.

Looking up from the side of the Urquhart Street bridge, Jenny Leuther saw a figure get into the driver's compartment of the train.

"Fitzroy 303. Urgent," Jenny said.

Tim Edgeworth of Prahran 421 cut over Jenny's transmission also calling "urgent".

Mick Hogan heard both calls, they were strong and he was faced with the dilemma of which call sign to ignore. He decided to go for the call sign which responded first.

"The unit urgent?" Hogan asked.

Jenny Leuther and Tim Edgeworth, who was in Ramsden Street with his partner Donna Randall, responded at the same time cutting over one another.

Tim advised that Knight may be "in the premises where he lives, at the intersection of John Street and Ramsden Street."

Jenny advised that the train had stopped and someone had got into the driver's carriage.

Mick Hogan stayed with Jenny Leuther as he could hear her transmission clearly.

"The location?"

Jenny put the portable radio close to her mouth, as if she did not want the gunman to hear what she was saying.

"Air 490 are pretty close. They're just about here, they're right on us," Jenny said.

Gary Ricardo took over from Mick Hogan.

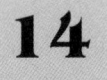

Mick Hogan looked up from his desk and read the whiteboard that Dianne Smith had been updating since the first confirmed reports of the shootings. He noticed that the writing had deteriorated in the last few minutes. It had gone from large print in straight lines to almost microscopic, slanting towards the floor. He watched her write and felt that something was wrong. She was pale and kept wiping her eyes.

Dianne had been on duty at D24 when, on 25 February 1986, Mad Max Clarke was shot and killed during an exchange of gunfire with detectives who were themselves wounded. She had also been on duty on 27 March 1986 when the Russell Street Police Complex was bombed. Now she was on duty when Colin Chambers, her husband, having reported that he had been shot, had not been heard from since.

Mick Hogan rang the telex room.

"Her husband's Northern 232," he said to Caroline Austin who came out of the telex room. Caroline persuaded Dianne to take a break. Dianne wiped her eyes and handed over the marker pen.

Wayne Monohan waved Tom Harris's torch at the police helicopter. He turned the end of the railways torch to produce a red light, thinking it would be more visible from the air than the green or white light. The helicopter's *NiteSun* was focused on Knott Reserve, following the Merri Creek west towards the Eltham train line and then further west to High Street. Wayne yelled directions in the faint hope that if he was not seen he might be heard by the crew of Air 495. At the same time he waved the torch urgently towards the Rushall Railway Station.

"Is that under the Heidelberg Road bridge, is it?" Gary Ricardo asked checking the Melway as he spoke.

"No it's not. It's a bit further east."

Jenny Leuther could give no better detail as she was not familiar with the Northcote area and there were no signs or road markings to be seen.

Keith Stewart of Air 495 advised that they could see the train driver pointing south towards the Heidelberg Road overpass bridge.

"We're over the top now, attempting to locate," Keith said.

10.02 p.m.

Daryl Jones of Air 495 saw Wayne Monohan with other railway staff in front of the train waving the torch towards the creek. As quickly as he illuminated Wayne and the others, he operated the toggle switch to divert the *NiteSun* light. With the gunman so near, the spotlight would give him every opportunity to add to his carnage. The *NiteSun* flashed into the Merri Creek and then travelled west towards Rushall Railway Station.

Pat Murtagh watched the police helicopter follow the Merri Creek towards High Street. He held the transmitter in his hand and gave D24 his location, for the "unit" that had asked earlier, as the eastern side of the Clifton Hill Railway Station. Canine 267 asked if this meant John Street.

Jenny Leuther looked up along the Urquhart Street bridge and heard a carriage door being shut. Then the headlights on the train went out as the police helicopter orbited nearby. She waited a moment then put the portable radio to her mouth.

"Fitzroy 303. The lights have just been turned off on the train. I don't know if that has been organised."

Mick Hogan tried to reach Northcote 213 as he knew Domenic Cannizzaro was with the Clifton Hill stationmaster. He was cut across by another police officer calling, "ETA on the SOG."

There was no response from Domenic Cannizzaro. Mick Hogan tried again.

"Northcote 213."

10.03 p.m.

Pat Murtagh chipped in and asked that ambulances be allowed to progress north, under police escort, along Hoddle Street.

"We've got that (sic) many wounded people we may as well try and move them. Some of them are in a serious condition."

"Just straight north up Hoddle?" asked Mick Hogan.

"They won't be able to go any further, we've got the road blocked up here."

Mick Hogan called again for Northcote 213. He wanted to ask about the lights on the train, but there was no response. Glen Sheluchin from Collingwood

303 advised Hogan that he had a man who could help with enquiries and he wanted the location of Inspector Murtagh, Carlton North 150. Murtagh told Hogan that he was on the west-side of Hoddle Street, almost opposite the Clifton Hill Railway Station. Mick Hogan asked for a repeat of his location.

"Western side," Inspector Murtagh said.

10.04 p.m.

Hogan called Collingwood 303 and heard interference in the return transmission. Glen Sheluchin tried again but nothing he said could be heard. Russell Street 251 advised Hogan that they had left the office with three members. Glen tried again to speak to Hogan, but the static was incomprehensible.

Mick Hogan moved across to Gary Ricardo and asked him to try and get some technical help so that they could hear Collingwood 303.

"VKC to all units – standby."

Mick Hogan hoped that other police would not transmit unless it was urgent, allowing Collingwood 303 a chance to relocate and perhaps be understood.

"Collingwood 303," said Hogan.

Daryl Jones picked up movement in some bushes near the train line. He switched off the *NiteSun* as Keith Stewart orbited clockwise a second time. On the third orbit Alan Scott again saw movement in the bushes. Daryl activated the *NiteSun* and the area below went from night to day.

John Watson was about to call out then stopped himself as the gunman went past his tree, stopped, and took aim at the helicopter. John was not sure what weapon it was but knew it was automatic by the lack of pumping action the gunman used. Watson counted three shots. He remained still.

Fifty metres north of Ramsden Street, in Hoddle Street lay the bodies of Vesna Markovska and Robert Mitchell, and the injured Gina Papaioannou, whose hand continued to wave in the air. Rick McIntosh watched from behind a police car near Ramsden Street. He felt powerless to do anything yet wanted to rescue this woman from further injury and pain. He leaned inside the police car and picked up the radio transmitter lying on the seat. His back continued to trouble him after the altercation with the cameraman.

"St Kilda 500. We've got two on the footpath next to the station. No one has been able to get near them. Can you get the Officer please to do something to get these people into an ambulance."

Mick Hogan was irritated and frustrated. He wanted silence but he got it for only a second. He was concerned about Collingwood 303 who had yet to return readable communication. Then there were the wounded and dying who could not receive the attention they warranted because of the fear of ambulance officers being shot.

John Delahunty parked his police car across the north-bound lanes of Queens Parade with the nose of the car facing into Rushall Crescent. Motorists who had been diverted at the Heidelberg Road intersection had been going through side streets to get back into Queens Parade from Rushall Crescent. With his car there it was one less access available to motorists. John approached a lone police officer standing near the Rushall Crescent intersection. He introduced himself to Ralph Lockman. At the same time, pedestrians were attempting to get past them. A tow-truck driver in a four-wheel drive wandered over and started to ask questions. He was asked to leave but he remained nearby. John told the driver to go back towards the city, that he would only be in the way. The other pedestrians understood but the tow-truck driver remained. John decided to give him one more warning and, if he refused to move, then arrest him.

Some 200 metres further north Air 495 was orbiting around the High Street bridge area. The *NiteSun* was focused on the ground near the bridge and the two men felt confident that the gunman would be located shortly. The *NiteSun* would flush him out.

Darren Anderson picked up the telephone. Another resident was complaining about the helicopter noise. It was impossible to hear the TV or to get to sleep. Others rang wanting to know why it was there.

15

Daryl Jones from Air 495 was looking out of the window at the ground when he saw sparks and felt a dull thud like a sledge hammer under the floor. The impact momentarily hurt the soles of his feet as a bullet hit a wheel strut then ricocheted onto the fuel tank. Keith Stewart turned around in his pilot seat shouting, "What was that?"

Keith checked the instrument panel warning lights and did a function check. The engines, hydraulics, transmission systems and controls were functioning as normal. Thinking that there was still a chance to apprehend the gunman, the helicopter orbited another three times. Although he didn't know, Keith suspected that the helicopter had been shot.

They were about to orbit for a fourth time when they could smell fuel in the cabin of the helicopter. They checked for signs of damage. Keith decided to land when he noticed the fuel gauge for the right engine had dropped.

"There's an oval back there," said Allen Scott who was familiar with the area and had used the bicycle track to ride into the city. Trevor Wilson checked the Melway.

10.05 p.m.

Mick Hogan took down the location details from Rick McIntosh, stamped the job card and passed it on to Gary Ricardo for further attention.

"Air 495 to VKC," said Trevor Wilson calmly.

Mick Hogan felt that they could wait and called for Carlton North 150.

"Air 495 urgent. Air 495 urgent."

Mick Hogan sat upright when he heard the word "urgent" the first time.

"Air 495 go," Mick Hogan said.

"Air 495. We've just been hit underneath the helicopter. At this stage all systems still okay. Roughly where the train is parked on the railway line – we got hit from directly underneath."

"That's the one sitting on High Street is it?"

"That's affirmative."

Mick Hogan needed to know if the lights from the train had been turned off by those inside, or whether the gunman was responsible, perhaps taking refuge there. He called for Northcote 213 again, while Carlton North 150 tried to get through.

"Northcote 213, I presume you've got the station master still with you?" Mick Hogan asked.

"Affirmative," Domenic Cannizzaro said.

"Air 495 the lights on the train were turned off, are they on again?" Mick Hogan asked.

"The lights on the train are off and I'm going to land somewhere," responded Keith Stewart. He moved the joystick in the direction of the Knott Reserve, some 800 metres east of where they had sighted the gunman and the damage had taken place.

10.06 p.m.

Domenic Cannizzaro advised Mick Hogan that the station master would check with the train. Air 495 tried to get through, but Mick Hogan put the call aside while he received a written message from Gary Ricardo.

The Killing Zone | 117

"VKC to all units. We have just received a report that there's a fellow heading down Westgarth Street – can anyone assist further with that?"

"Carlton North 150. Do your best to contain the situation without sending members there. What's the ETA on the SOG?"

"We're trying to ascertain that from the online at the moment," Mick Hogan said.

"Air 495. We've been hit underneath. We have to put down on an oval re check damage."

Mick Hogan asked to be informed of their location on landing.

"Carlton North 150."

"Carlton North 150?"

"Carlton North 150. We've had no luck with the ambulances getting through. Could you check in a southerly direction down Hoddle and see what the delay is?"

10.07 p.m.

Mick Hogan asked for any units to check on the progress of ambulances travelling north along Hoddle Street. South Melbourne 303 and Prahran 303 offered to assist. Carlton 310 advised that two ambulances had just passed the Johnston and Hoddle Streets intersection, approximately 1.2 kilometres south of the Clifton Hill Railway Station.

"If you could make sure there is some sort of access for the ambulances to attend down at the Clifton Hill Railway Station heading north."

Several police cut across one another. Mick Hogan could not decipher any messages.

"Carlton North 150 urgent," Inspector Adrian Fyfe said.

"Carlton North 150."

"The bloke with the shotgun who hit the helicopter is between the railway bridge under High Street and the Rushall Railway Station. He's either side. He could be on the Northcote side of the railway cutting."

10.08 p.m.

"Carlton North 150," said Gary Ricardo. "We've just had a report that he could possibly be in the car park of the Terminus Hotel on the corner of Brennand and Queens Parade."

"Carlton North 150. We're there now," Inspector Fyfe said.

"Roger," Gary Ricardo replied.

Inspector Pat Murtagh tried to get through but his message was damaged in transmission. Mick Hogan could barely understand what was said.

"Unit calling?"

"Carlton North 150."

10.09 p.m.

Mick Hogan recognised the voice of Inspector Murtagh but was confused as to the call sign. Initially Inspector Fyfe was calling himself Clifton Hill 150 and now he was using the call sign of Carlton North 150.

"150 unit?"

"Carlton North 150. You're also going to have to notify the coroner on this, we've got dead ones." Inspector Murtagh said.

"Collingwood 303," Glen Sheluchin said.

"Collingwood 303?"

"Collingwood 303. I'm still trying to find the location of 150 with this gentleman here who knows the person doing the shooting."

"Carlton North 150 is just going down to the Terminus Hotel in Brennand Street and Queens Parade," Mick Hogan said.

10.10 p.m.

"Carlton North 150. I'm still at the scene which is opposite the railway station," Inspector Pat Murtagh corrected.

"Roger," Mick Hogan said.

"Collingwood 303 he's back at, or he's still at the Clifton Hill Railway Station if you'd like to go down there. On the western side," Mick Hogan continued.

Domenic Cannizzaro of Northcote 213 advised that the station master had told him that the lights on the train had been turned out as a safety measure. A police officer called urgent but was cut off by other police trying to get the attention of Mick Hogan.

10.11 p.m.

Brunswick 500, Richmond 250, Flemington 250 and Brunswick 353 offered to assist. Mick Hogan gave them areas to attend. Other units cut across one another wanting such information as the type of firearms being used and the time of arrival of the SOG.

Inspector Adrian Fyfe realised that he had given the wrong call sign when he detected the frustration in Hogan. He corrected this and advised Hogan that his call sign was Russell Street 150 Afternoon and that Inspector Murtagh was Carlton North 150. Inspector Fyfe asked that Brunswick 500, the detective car, meet him at the Terminus Hotel.

CLOSING IN

16

Senior Constable Charlie Machen drove an unmarked police car down Holden Street, past the Loaded Dog Hotel, down towards the reserve which crossed the Merri Creek. The Epping bound train line crossed the creek, and there was a footbridge. A bicycle track followed the path of the creek between Clifton Hill, near where the shots originated, and De Chene Parade, Coburg. With trees and no lighting in the reserve Charlie felt it was an ideal place for the offenders to hide.

He parked the police car as close as he could to the reserve entrance. A barrier had been erected to stop vehicles gaining entry. He reached for the radio and tried to tell D24 his location. He put the transmitter back in the cradle. The air was jammed with urgent voices, some in panic and near hysteria.

Charlie walked over to a garbage skip just in front of the reserve entrance and crouched down behind it. He heard a number of shots in the distance. Minutes later, about 400 metres east of his position, there was another volley of shots. His six years in the army told him that whoever was firing those shots was using a semi-automatic rifle. He touched the .38 Smith and Wesson revolver holstered on his right hip. His heart was pounding as he listened to his portable radio. He heard Air 495 advise D24 that it had been hit and was going to land.

Charlie moved to the side of the skip to get a better view of the reserve. He studied the bushes and the bicycle path. It was hard to see without overhead lighting. He looked back along the railway line and then he saw movement. Coming from under the railway viaduct, where it crossed the Merri Creek, he saw the silhouette of a man carrying what looked like a rifle. The man was running, and keeping pace beside him was a dog. As they approached the skip to go into Holden Street, Charlie felt he was facing certain death again. Two years earlier he had fought cancer and won, and he was determined that a gunman was not going to take him either.

"Police! Don't move!"

Machen jumped up from his crouched position and ran straight at the man when he was less than three metres away. He thrust the muzzle of his revolver into the forehead of the man, his finger squeezing the trigger. He would kill the man if he gave the slightest resistance. The man fell backwards and onto the ground, the piece of wood he carried flying up in the air. The dog sat beside his owner and wagged its tail.

Two uniformed police who had just arrived helped Charlie search the man who explained bitterly that he was a jogger. He had found the wood while on his run and intended to use it as fuel for his barbecue. Charlie let the man up. His forehead carried a red mark. It wasn't safe to go for a jog any more, the man complained. He picked up his wood and continued his run up Holden Street, the dog keeping pace.

They caught a glimpse of movement in the shadows from the west side of High Street. A man came out of nowhere, his hands in his pocket. Anita Adair and David Depyle watched from behind a parked car as he approached them. They felt uncomfortable about his sudden appearance and his pocketed hands.

"Put your hands up!" Anita yelled at him, but the man ignored her.

She stood up straight, revolver in both hands, while David trained his revolver from the front end of the car.

"Put your hands up where we can see them!" she yelled in her Rod Stewart voice, a voice that owed much of its huskiness to cigarette smoking from the age of twelve.

"Do it! Do as you're told!"

The man threw his hands up in the air. David Depyle raced over and searched him. The man was shaking and they could tell he was not one of the men they were looking for.

"Get home," Anita said to him.

Graham Larchin felt his confidence sag when he heard the helicopter had been hit and had left the scene to check for damage. He looked from behind his tree and saw a man running towards them from under the High Street railway bridge. It had to be the gunman. Graham rolled over onto his back believing he was about to face death. He swore and then rolled back onto his stomach and trained his revolver on the man running towards him. In the army reserve he had been taught to let the target come towards you. To keep yourself under cover. Then shoot.

The St Kilda CIB car drove out of Hoddle Street and west along North Terrace, then right into Michael Street. At Heidelberg Road Rick McIntosh directed Syd Hadley to drive towards the Rushall Railway Station, as the shots seemed to be coming from that vicinity. There had been none from the Clifton Hill Railway Station area for quite some time. McIntosh, Hadley, Phil Bradley, Bruce Lowe and another detective, Kim Cox, knew that the train was stopped near Rushall. They believed that there was a chance that the gunman was on the trainline. Syd Hadley stopped the car outside the railway station and the five fanned out.

Rick McIntosh and Kim Cox moved out into the car park area checking behind trees and seeking them for their own personal protection, while Phil Bradley lay prone behind a tree with his revolver drawn and aimed at the station. Apart from the overhead street light outside the railway station it was pitch black. Hard to see anything or anyone moving outside of the dull artificial light.

Sid Hadley and Bruce Lowe took opposite sides of the trainline, moving quickly east towards the High Street railway bridge. As Bruce moved down the trainline he considered his options if he saw the gunman. Would he shoot first before giving him a chance? The revolvers that the police had were grossly inadequate against military and semi-automatic rifles. When it seemed that they were going into a black void, they turned back and each took up a position on either side of the booking office.

It occurred to Rick McIntosh that perhaps the gunman or gunmen would try what bushranger Ned Kelly and his gang had failed to achieve under a full moon at Glenrowan in 1880. Kelly had intended to derail the special police train that ran on Sunday nights, and shoot any survivors.

On the high-bank side of the Merri Creek near Rushall Railway Station stood the Old Colonists' Retirement Village. The cottages were well over 100 years old and had originally provided homes for aged actors and entertainers who had fallen on hard times. There was a rattle at the main door; someone was trying to open it. Jenny Horman, a nurse, had been watching television and had seen the news flash. She stood behind a corner wall and remained quiet as she heard someone run along McKean Street.

Graham Larchin told Robert Kovacs to remain behind the brick wall until he gave him the signal. As the man got closer Graham sensed he was not the gunman. It was just a feeling he had, one that most police possessed or developed, like an instinct. Graham noticed that the man was wearing an overcoat. "Halt! Police! Put your hands up!" Graham yelled. John Watson threw his hands up into the air and kept running, almost tripping over his feet. He cried out that someone was trying to shoot him. Graham yelled, "React!" and Robert Kovacs stepped out from behind the wall and brought John to the ground, dragging him behind the brick wall and searching him. Graham lowered his revolver.

Susan Middelhuis, a dental nurse, was driving her husband Paul and a friend, Jenny Owen, south-east along Rushall Crescent in a Ford Fairlane. When they were about thirty metres north of McKean Street, Susan and Jenny saw the gunman running crouched and flat out, along the nature strip, the rifle slung over his shoulder. He came from their left in McKean Street, beside the Old Colonists' Retirement Village, and ran in front of their car. Momentarily he lost balance, falling almost to his knees and putting out his hands to break the fall. Susan braked as the gunman regained his footing and continued running down McKean Street.

"I wonder what's going on?" Susan asked.

No one in the car was aware of what had been happening. She drove down to Queens Parade hoping to find some police to report the incident to.

17

10.12 p.m.

For a moment, John Delahunty had been stunned at the realisation that the police helicopter had been forced to land. He struggled to understand what type of person would cause the death and injury that was around him. What type of firearm would force the helicopter to land? For the first time John felt intimidated by the fire power of the enemy. If the weapons could move a helicopter, what chance did he have of surviving a gunshot blast? Other police and ambulance officers felt the same way. They were hopelessly out-powered and vulnerable. John snapped out of his daze when he felt a whack on his arm.

"There he goes," Ralph Lockman said pointing north-west into Rushall Crescent where he had seen the gunman running. He saw the gunman run crouched, diagonally across Rushall Crescent and into McKean Street, rifle slung over a shoulder. John turned around and caught a fleeting glimpse of the gunman.

"Let's go!" he yelled, running to the police car some ten metres behind them. Files and other loose paper flew everywhere as John tossed his equipment from the front passenger seat into the back. He slammed his foot on the accelerator and roared into Rushall Crescent. Ralph took the radio transmitter and tried to get through to D24 calling, "Urgent!"

John told him the street names as he accelerated, the tyres squealing and the car almost fish-tailing as it entered McKean Street. From the grey outer area of the headlights he saw the running gunman about fifteen metres ahead, on the right-hand side of the footpath. Then he lost sight of him among the parked cars.

"There he goes," Ralph said pointing at movement at the front of a house two doors from a lane, situated between 239 and 241 McKean Street.

10.13 p.m.

John turned the steering wheel to the right and pulled out the handbrake. The brakes locked, the tyres screeched and the high-beam headlights tore into the lane, illuminating an ivy-covered fence, light pole and trees. Ralph tried again to give their position to D24. "Fitzroy 213. Urgent, we're in McKean Street," Ralph said.

He felt like throwing the radio transmitter through the windscreen. His attempt to relay an urgent message was overridden by other police. He continued to try and contact D24 while in his right hand he had a firm grip on his .38 revolver.

A blue Dolphin lantern torch was on the floor. It jolted towards his feet then back under the seat. Ralph bent down to retrieve the torch just as the police car came to a sudden stop and several rounds from an M14 military rifle, burst into the car. John, who was still holding the handbrake, saw a huge flash to his right and was almost deafened by the noise. It shocked him; it was so loud. He felt a hard slap across the right side of his head and severe pain in his left hand. He threw himself towards Ralph who was wiping blood from his face and hands.

In that split second of gunfire many things raced through John Delahunty's mind. At first he thought that he had been killed and then, when he realised he wasn't dead, he was sure that he was about to be. The adrenalin surged through his body, it gave him a kick as endomorphins reacted to the threat. He felt terrified and exhilarated all at once. On the floor near the centre console was a fired M14 bullet jacket.

Susan Middelhuis stopped her Ford Fairlane behind the police car and yelled that there was someone in the street behind with a rifle. Graham Larchin made to run back up to Rushall Crescent but was ordered back by Inspector Fyfe. He argued with the Inspector as he felt that they were committing suicide confronting the gunman in a police car. It went against all the principles of his army training. Inspector Fyfe yelled at Graham to get in. Robert Kovacs accelerated towards the Terminus Hotel as Graham shut the door behind him.

John Delahunty scrambled out of the driver's door. His body had taken charge, he seemed to act without conscious thought. Using his elbows he dragged himself to the back of the police car as another burst of gunfire deafened him. He heard a spent shell ricochet against the bluestone fence and felt the gunman was coming after him, almost standing over him. He had to get to safety.

He crawled under the police car behind the rear wheel. Another burst of gunfire. As he dragged himself along the ground, under the car boot, he felt a bullet part his hair. He saw the flashes and knew that the gunman was near the front of the police car. He saw the partial silhouette of the gunman's head in the light from the flash. He was behind the brick wall near the lane.

John scrambled to his feet. Standing straight up and with both hands holding the .38 Smith and Wesson he pointed in the direction of where he had seen the head of the gunman. He squeezed the trigger once. He saw the man fall backwards and to the right, and then out of sight. Still standing upright with the revolver in both hands, John thought he had shot him.

"Don't shoot! Don't shoot!" the voice screamed, high pitched, scared.

"Get out! Get out! Throw the gun out!" John screamed back.

He remained standing, partly covered by the boot, his revolver trained on the gunman whose hands were reaching for the moon. So outstretched were his arms that the sleeves of his denim jacket rolled down to the elbows. The palms of his hands stretched wide and outward towards the two officers. Neither believed that he was on his own and both waited for him to make a sudden attack. It just seemed too easy, too simple.

"He's already thrown it out, it's on the ground," Ralph Lockman said. He had seen the rifle as it was tossed onto the bluestone, sliding towards the road.

"Don't shoot, I'm unarmed. Don't shoot, I'm unarmed. Don't shoot, I'm unarmed," the gunman screamed.

"Get out, get under the fuckin' light, cunt!" Ralph Lockman ordered, standing up now from his crouched position behind the passenger door. He could see the white of the gunman's forearms, but his head was still in darkness. Ralph trained his revolver on the gunman. After the first burst of gunfire, Ralph had no idea where John was, and thought that they were both about to be murdered. So loud had the gunfire been that it felt as if the gunman had been right next to the driver's door, ready to pick them off.

It sounded like a machine gun, the two rapid bursts of gunfire. Rick McIntosh was outside the Old Colonists' Retirement Village. He limped as quickly as he could into McKean Street feeling that he had a greater chance of survival away from the confines of a motor vehicle.

10.14 p.m.

The gunman stepped out, and under Ralph Lockman's directions, put his hands behind his head, then lay prone on the ground – his feet towards the lane and his head towards the police car.

Ralph yelled to John Delahunty for their location. He tried D24 again, repeating, "Urgent. Fitzroy 213 in McKean Street."

Mick Hogan was engaged in transmission with Northcote 303. Ralph repeated his call ending with the word, "Urgent." Gary Ricardo cut across Hogan's transmission with the Northcote van.

"We've got an offender here," Ralph said.

It was suddenly very quiet at D24. The speakers in the room were on high volume, and everyone's attention was focused on them or on Mick Hogan and Gary Ricardo. Police officers from adjoining rooms came in. Everyone was stunned, and relieved, and happy.

"The unit with the 'offender here' just give your call sign and your location," Gary Ricardo said.

"Fitzroy 213. We're just off where you turn left to go to Rushall Station. I'm not too sure, it's thirty metres east of the railway bridge," Ralph Lockman said.

Mick Hogan checked his Melway.

"VKC for a unit to attend in Brennand Street ..."

Tim Edgeworth ran over to Peter Butts who was standing near the Ramsden Street railway-crossing gates and signal box. He told Peter about the bodies on the eastern side of Hoddle Street and that one of them was still alive, that he had seen an arm rise and drop.

"Where's the fuckin' car?" Butts asked.

Tim ran back across to the other side of Hoddle Street and met Peter again, this time, standing barefoot in the middle of the intersection. He had taken off his brand new Adidas runners because of the reflector strip. He jumped into the front and lowered himself under the dashboard.

Donna Randall, who had lost sight of her partners, rushed over to the car. She wanted to be with people she knew, her work colleagues, and she tried to open the driver's-side passenger door but it was locked.

The car started to move forward. Donna rushed behind a police car on the south-west corner of the intersection and watched as Tim drove almost blind across the south-bound lanes, peering over the dash every half second. The car mounted the gutter then turned left travelling slowly over the footpath and the grass towards the three bodies, thirty metres away. Tim and Peter passed the Stubby and the Black Sorrows billboard conscious that it was here that the slaughter had originated. Tim drove towards the lightpole on the edge of the footpath bordering the grass strip, as he knew the bodies were directly under its light. As they got closer he steered completely off the footpath and onto the grass to avoid running over the bodies, then, when the front passenger wheel was parallel to the lightpole, he turned the steering wheel hard left. Tim felt more vulnerable than before as his side of the car was in view of the gunmen. There was no engine block to deflect any bullets, just the thin metal skin of the door. The front wheels of the police car dropped off the footpath and onto the road. With the bodies now protected by the length of the car Tim applied the handbrake, pushing in the end button to ensure that the ratchet made no noise. Then he turned off the engine.

Peter scrambled out quickly, grabbing his runners as he went. With a lot of broken glass spread about he did not want to cut his feet. He decided to risk the reflector strip. Tim followed almost on top of his sergeant. They knew that if they got shot now, they would be regarded as idiots.

John Delahunty was screaming at the gunman for information about his accomplice. Told that he was on his own John screamed back at him, "That's bullshit!"

From the driver's-side door John ran towards the gunman. Fearing that it was a set up Ralph Lockman yelled out, "Come back John!"

"I was only going to see my girlfriend," said the gunman, still prone on the ground.

Ralph was staggered by the comment. It seemed so flippant – as if he thought it were a satisfactory explanation.

Ralph, who was standing next to the passenger side door of the police car, covered his partner. He was certain it was a set up, with a second gunman ready to pick them both off. John thrust his revolver hard into the back of the gunman's head, as he continued to plead for his life at the top of his voice.

"Don't shoot me! Don't kill me," he screamed.

John could smell a faint odour of beer on the man's breath. He was not drunk – his speech was not slurred and he was too controlled. John grabbed at his hair but it was short like newly-cut lawn.

"Don't move or I'll blow your fuckin' brains out," John screamed.

"Okay, okay, okay, okay."

John took hold of the denim-jacket collar and, half pushing, half lifting, dragged the sweating, tense gunman over to the bonnet of the police car and pushed him down hard. Ralph had already left the side of the car still covering John and still convinced that they were about to be ambushed. Ralph could smell the sweat and fear of the gunman as he ran to the police car and helped pin the gunman down over the bonnet. When he told John that he was unsure of their location, John released his grip and ran back to the police car.

10.15 p.m.

"Fitzroy 213. Urgent. I've been shot," John Delahunty said. He was puffing, trying to catch his breath.

"The unit 213, urgent," Mick Hogan said pressing his foot down on the transmitter.

"213. We're off Rushall Crescent, about two hundred metres to the left."

John could hardly talk, he was gasping for breath. His heart was pounding out of his chest, up into his throat. He pressed the transmission button, "We have an offender and a weapon."

"You have the offender?" Mick Hogan asked.

"I've been shot, it's a bloody automatic weapon."

John paused to catch his breath then continued, "We've got one offender and we've got one weapon."

"Fitzroy 213, has a member been shot or has the offender been shot?" Gary Ricardo asked.

It was quiet at D24; everyone was listening to the monitor. Having to repeat everything irritated John Delahunty. It made him more anxious and concerned for his safety. He still worried that a second offender could shoot them.

"213. I've got blood on me. I don't know where it's from, all right?"

John dropped the transmitter and searched for his handcuffs on the back seat among the litter he had earlier created.

"Roger 213. You've got the situation contained there at this stage?" Gary Ricardo asked.

John ran back to Ralph Lockman with his handcuffs. There was silence on the police radio for two seconds. It seemed like two hours at D24.

"That's them gone (sic)," Mick Hogan said.

Greg Splatt watched his sergeant dry swallow and momentarily drop his head. Mick Hogan's right foot pressed down on the floor pedal.

"VKC to a unit that can come down to Rushall Crescent," he said in despair.

It was just never ending.

Tim Edgeworth knew that Robert Mitchell and Vesna Markovska were dead by their injuries, but still he checked for pulse. He crawled over to Gina Papaioannou who was on her back looking up at the sky, eyes blinking. She had what looked like a shark bite to her side and Tim yelled to Peter Butts to get an ambulance.

"She's still alive!"

John Delahunty ran back to Ralph Lockman as other police arrived on foot and in cars. Graham Larchin had jumped out of Inspector Fyfe's car before it had stopped. Graham saw the M14 in the lane and was surprised as he thought a shotgun had been used. He was convinced there was a second offender.

Some other police were yelling out, "Kill the fucker!"

The gunman said his name was Julian Knight.

Robert Kovacs and John Delahunty secured the handcuffs behind his back.

18

10.16 p.m.

Peter Butts, who had been covering Tim Edgeworth from the passenger-side wheel arch of the police car, reached inside the car. He tried to get through to D24 but he was not heard. He went back to the wheel arch then minutes later returned to the radio to overhear St Kilda 500 and Russell Street 500 advise Mick Hogan that they were approaching the arrest scene.

Mick Hogan tried again for Fitzroy 213. There was no response.

"Prahran 452," Peter Butts called.

"Stand-by 452," Mick Hogan said, then repeated his call for Fitzroy 213.

Inspector Pat Murtagh called from a portable radio. His transmission was a sea of waves and distorted sounds. Gary Ricardo advised him that he was unreadable and was cutting off other police trying to communicate with D24. Gary tried again for Fitzroy 213. He wanted to hear from any unit that was in Rushall Crescent.

"Prahran 452," Peter Butts said again.

"Prahran 452 have you located Fitzroy 213 yet?"

Gary Ricardo's voice was urgent but hopeful.

"Negative. I realise the urgency of the situation. We are with two code thirty-threes and one other, totally seriously injured. If we can get some urgent medical help opposite the railway station. We are here with them."

"On the eastern side of the railway station?"

"I can see an ambulance opposite, about twenty metres north of Ramsden where we are. There is one here urgently requiring medical assistance. We've got cover at this stage," Peter said, looking about the police car and further north in Hoddle Street.

Mick Hogan advised he would arrange an ambulance immediately. He was still concerned about John Delahunty and Ralph Lockman. Where were they? Why hadn't they responded to calls?

Closing In

"VKC to Fitzroy 213," Mick Hogan said. He was certain he was calling to dead men.

Peter ran across Hoddle Street over to Turnbull Street where ambulance vehicles and their crews were positioned. Unable to get any equipment, he took an overcoat from Glen Sheluchin and Phil Bradley and covered the bodies of Robert Mitchell and Vesna Markovska with one. He then crawled over to Gina and covered her with the second overcoat and held her to him. She told him that she had got out of her car to help Robert and Vesna. Peter told her that she had been brave, and they talked about their lives and families. He watched as Donna Randall crawled along the footpath towards them.

"When this is all over we'll have a drink together," Gina said.

Peter moved one of the bodies away from her to make her more comfortable. He believed that out of this tragedy he had made a friend. He held her hand tightly.

"You'll be all right," he said. "You'll be all right."

"Who else is with you?" Graham Larchin asked.

"I'm on my own. I've had military training," Knight said.

"What?" Ralph Lockman asked.

It was such a shock to Ralph and it seemed to him that Knight was telling everybody that they were of the same standard. To Ralph, Knight was a coward. Apart from the haircut he did not look like a soldier. To Ralph he looked more like a chinless twelve-year-old boy. The soldiers Ralph knew would not kill and injure unarmed civilians, and ambush the innocent. No soldier he knew would give up on the first return of fire. Ralph burned with anger and drew back his fist. He wanted to punch Knight as hard as he could.

A detective put his hand up and shook his head. Ralph dropped his fist. Inspector Fyfe approached saying, "Don't touch him."

Tim Edgeworth was disturbed by the headlights. They lit up the area where he, Peter Butts, Donna Randall and Gina Papaioannou were imprisoned by circumstance. He edged quickly to the cars, crouched like a monkey, his hands almost scraping the ground. At any moment he thought he would be cut down by a sniper's bullet, but he had to go on. He reached inside the Gemini that Zoran Trajceski had driven and turned the headlights off. He edged over to the Toyota that Vesna Markovska had driven but was unable to find the light switch. Using the butt of his revolver he smashed the headlight lens but the filament still gave light. He smashed that with the butt too, then moved to the other headlight and did the same again, then ran back to Peter, Donna and Gina who were now not so obvious.

"Are you all right?" asked Rick McIntosh of Knight.

"Yeah."

"Are you injured?"

"No."

"You are under arrest for murder. You are not obliged to say anything but whatever you say may be given in evidence."

"Yeah."

"Do you understand that?"

"Yeah."

"Where's the other bloke?"

"There's no one else, only me."

"Are you sure?"

"Yeah."

"It is very important."

"Only me."

"We don't want anyone else hurt."

"No, it's only me, believe me."

Rick turned Knight in the direction of the lane and pointed at the rifle.

"Is that your firearm?"

"Yeah."

"What is it?"

"7.62 M14."

Inside the Mobil Service Station, Kevin Farmer was angry. The uniformed police tried to calm him but he wanted no part of their pacifist talk.

"Give me your gun! Give me your gun! I'll shoot the bastard!" he yelled.

Noel Shiels looked all around him. There were no John Wayne characters among the police and ambulance officers. Everyone was shit-scared and still trying to do his or her job. While he treated the injured he still could not believe that it was really happening. He could see that he was doing what was expected of him, doing what he was trained to do, but it seemed unreal. The yellow street lights made it surreal. There were times during the night when shots were fired and he felt terrified. No one knew where the shots were coming from, or going to. He just wanted to crawl under the ambulance and wait for everything to return to normal. He and Peter Collins looked across to the eastern side of Hoddle Street and discussed how to give assistance to Gina Papaioannou. They had been told by the police that she was the only survivor. Noel wanted to run across to her but the risk was too great. If he was shot then further strain would be placed on the ambulance crews. There would be one less ambulance officer available to treat the wounded.

Terry Howard and Dennis Harnetty ran through Mayors Park, taking cover behind trees, then ran crouched onto Turnbull Street where they holstered their revolvers. Terry revealed that Gina Papaioannou would die if she did not receive urgent medical treatment. He told them that he believed the gunmen were of the type who would kill the wounded rather than give them an opportunity to live. He offered to drive the ambulance if Peter Collins and Noel Shiels would come with him. Darrell Rintoule advised them that they were not obliged to go as it was still unsafe. A dead ambulance officer was no good to a victim. It was up to them.

"Were you shooting at people over in Hoddle Street with that gun?"

"Yeah, I've had military training. I've had military training."

"Why did you do it?" Rick continued.

"I don't know, I don't know."

19

Terry Howard manoeuvred the MICA ambulance around in Turnbull Street so that he could reverse rather than drive forward. They would be provided greater protection that way. Dennis Harnetty tried to find the interior light switch in the roof visor. He flicked a switch and the whole interior was illuminated. Everyone shouted at him and he flicked another switch and the ambulance was in darkness. With the ambulance turned around Terry quickly reversed east along Turnbull Street mounting the north-west corner kerb. Equipment in the overhead shelves spilled out, showering Peter Collins and Noel Shiels who were on the floor. The two ambulance officers looked at each other, they would have to clean up the mess.

Dennis Harnetty held his own revolver in one hand and Terry Howard's in the other. Terry had reasoned that he could not drive and defend himself at the same time. This way they had twelve rounds in the front and, with Paul

Storey covering the ambulance officers in the back, another six. They all felt that they carried insufficient ammunition and were inadequately armed. What they had was nothing compared with the infinite arsenal the gunmen seemed to have.

Donna Randall was with Gina Papaioannou, stroking her hair and talking to her, telling her that she was safe and that she was going to make it. Peter Butts was beside the wheel arch of the DSG vehicle listening to the radio.

"God it hurts," Gina said.

The MICA ambulance bounced off the footpath and onto Hoddle Street, then hard over the centre concrete strip which emptied whatever was left in the overhead cupboards and drawers onto Paul Storey and Dennis Harnetty who had moved to the back to give better directions. Terry, who had driven bulldozers, earth moving equipment and articulated vehicles in previous occupations, had never before driven an ambulance.

Terry checked the side mirrors and followed the directions given by Dennis Harnetty. Running behind the ambulance was John Anderson, the driver of City West 203 and partner of Paul Storey. John ran, crouched, with his revolver sweeping across Hoddle Street and into the darkness of the park and bushes. A sniper could be hiding anywhere. Donna Randall moved away from Gina and directed her revolver towards the railway station.

"Just remember, he could be waiting for us," Terry said as he stopped the ambulance.

Noel Shiels and Peter Collins lifted the hatch and clambered out after Dennis and Paul. Paul and John covered them from the side of the police car. Noel pointed to the bodies of Robert Mitchell and Vesna Markovska.

"What about them?"

"No, they're thirty-threes," Tim Edgeworth said.

Mick Hogan again asked for any police who had sighted Fitzroy 213. A detective from Russell Street 500 advised that Fitzroy 213 was outside 243 McKean Street with one offender, one automatic rifle. The offender said that he was by himself. Both members looked okay. Mick Hogan drew a sigh of relief, and repeated the news to Inspector Pat Murtagh.

Noel Shiels did not know what thirty-threes meant but assumed that it was police speak for dead bodies. He and Peter attended to Gina immediately. She followed them with her eyes as they took out their equipment. The two ambulance officers were taken aback by the ferocity of her injuries. In their combined twenty-three years experience they had never seen such a severe gunshot wound. Noel applied padding to the gaping hole in her left side and together they fought hard to find a vein.

"What's your name?" Noel asked.

"Gina," she said in a very weak voice.

"Can you tell me your surname?"

Gina shook her head. Noel felt her forehead and it was very cold. Her face was white. He checked her pulse which was rapid and thready, but could not get a reading on her blood pressure. Noel tried to insert an IV but was not successful. Then Peter suggested placing a Military Anti-Shock Trouser suit under her which enabled him to insert an IV and get a drip flowing. The two MICA officers climbed back inside the ambulance and received Gina's stretcher from Dennis Harnetty and Terry Howard. They closed the hatch behind them while Gina continued to try to talk. She whispered to Noel, "I jush got out to help."

Noel told her that she would be all right, that everything was OK. At that moment, he felt foolish as he looked out of the ambulance at the dead, the wounded, the shattered glass everywhere, and the bullet holes in car bodies and windscreens. He looked at the police who were seemingly powerless to do anything other than contain the area and at the ambulance officers who struggled to do their work properly for fear of being the next target. Gina seemed to want to talk some more, to tell what had happened but she was too weak to go on. They closed the back hatch and Paul Storey, who, like Terry Howard, had never driven an ambulance before, started the drive to the Alfred Hospital with Donna Randall ready to take Gina's dying declaration statement.

The volley of shots sounded like the opening of the duck-shooting season to Bruce Lowe. He was unable to work out where the shots originated, from his position at the Rushall Railway Station. He walked out of the carpark and caught a lift in a marked police car to Queens Parade. They travelled into Hoddle Street but the abandoned Northcote police car blocked further passage. They tried to cross over to the west-bound lane of Hoddle but the vehicle became stuck on the median strip. Bruce and two others pushed the police car off the median strip then Bruce crossed over to the other side and walked back along the train line. He saw a man lying flat on his stomach beneath the overpass. Bruce levelled his revolver at the man, telling him to remain still and searched him. Each was as scared as the other.

1. Tracey Farmer

2. Dusan Flajnik

3. Vesna Markovska

4. Robert Mitchell

5. John Muscat

6. Gina Papaioannou

7. Shane Stanton

8. 　　　　　　　　Julian Knight in the custody of Detective Graham Kent
　　　　　　　　　　　　　　　　　　　　　　　　(Photo Herald Sun)

9. 　　　　　⋮ Knights House　　　　　⋮ Signal Box

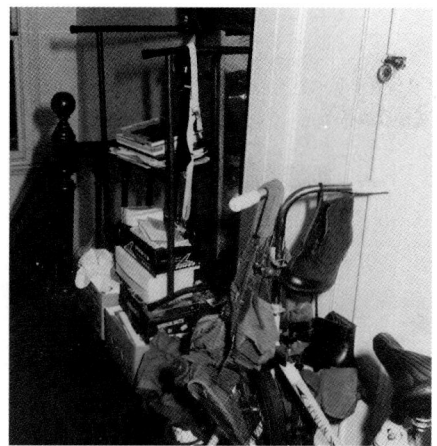

10. Knight's army equipment on the landing of the Ramsden Street house, at the foot of the stairs

11. The rifle bag and boxes behind the couch in the lounge room, bedroom

12. Knight's bedroom, the lounge room

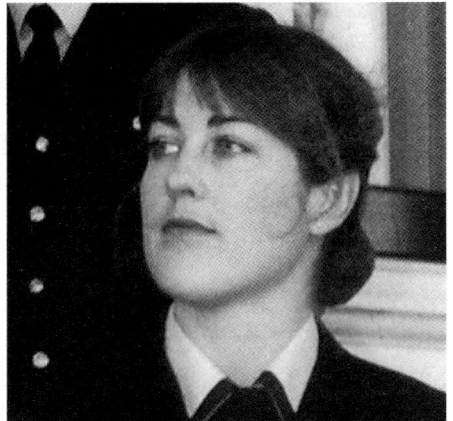

13. Belinda Bourchier

14. Glen Sheluchin

15. Hoddle Street at Ramsden street intersection

16. Hoddle Street looking north from Ramsden Street

17. North along Hoddle Street

19.   Dianne Fitzpatrick

18.   Alan Jury
(photo Herald Sun)

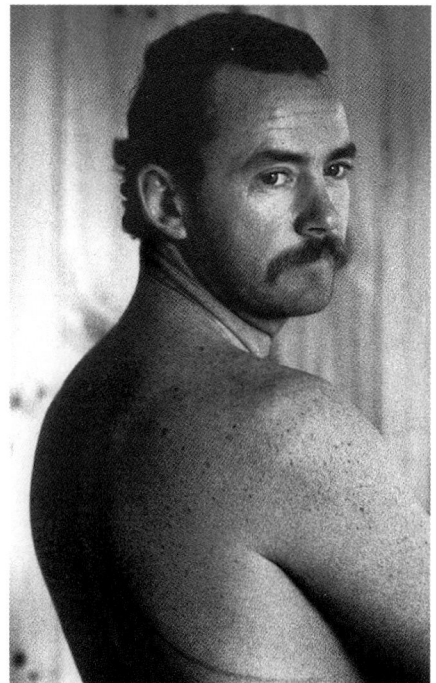

20.   Steve Wight
(photo Herald Sun)

21. Zoran Trajceski's car   Gina Papaioannou's car   Police Car
        Vensna Markovska's car   Robert Mitchell's car

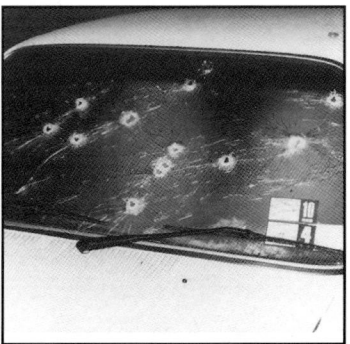

22. The wind screen of the car driven by Zoran Trajceski, peppered by 12 gauge S.G. 00 buck shot cartridges

23. The car Vesna Markovska was driving

24. Darrell Rintoule, Noel Shiels, Graham Ryan (Communications) and Peter Collins. Commendation from ambulance services

25. Bruce Lowe

26. Dusan Flajnik's car and the damage to it caused by the M14 rifle

27. Clifton Hill railway station Shane Stantons motor cycle

28. Constable Domenic Cannizzaro's police car and the Ford driven by Dimitrios Collyvas. Looking south along Hoddle Street

29. Damage to concrete kerb in Hoddle Street caused by the M14

30. Shane Stanton's motor cycle

31. Damage to Shane Stanton's motor cycle

32. Adrian Fyfe

33. Betty Roberts

34. Graham Larchin

35. Domenic Cannizzaro

36. Domenic Cannizzaro's police car

37. Dimitrios Collyvas' car

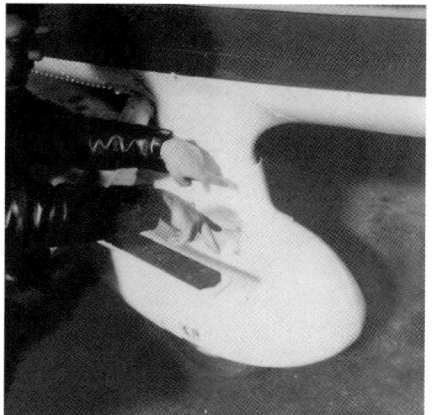

38. Damage to Air 495

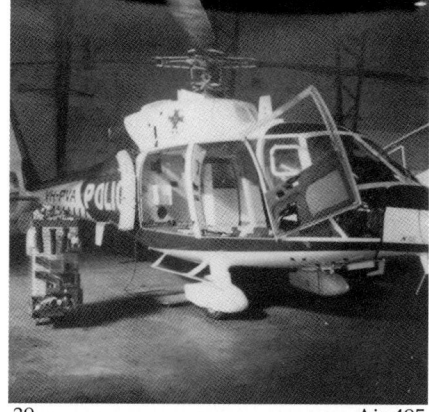

39. Air 495

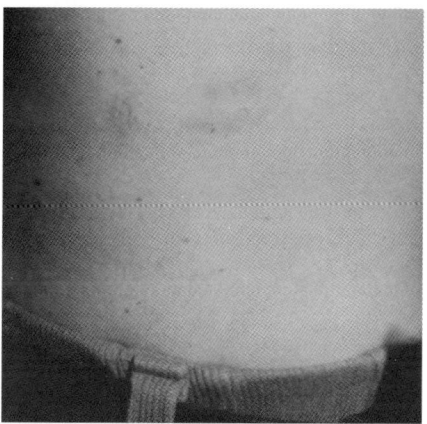

40. Constable Colin Chambers and his fricton burn from the M14 round

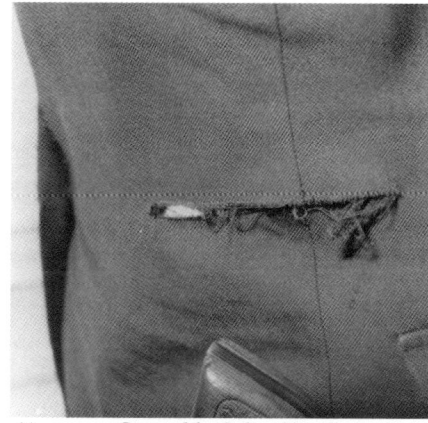

41. Constable Colin Chambers tunic damaged by an M14 round

42. Intersection of Hoddle Street and Queens Parade

43. Mckean St, Nth Fitzroy - the lane where police arrested Knight after a brief exchange of shots

44. Detectives inspecting the scence in Mc Kean St, Fitzroy with the M14 rifle, the last gun used on the evening

45. Constable John Delahunty

46. Chief Commissioner Sinclair 'Mick' Miller presenting Valour Award to Constable Ralph Lockman

47. Julian Knight, Detectives Senior Sergeant Brian McCarthy and Senior Constable Graham Kent - during a re-enactment

48. Interior damage to the police car in which Police Officers John Delahunty and Ralph Lockman were ambushed

49. The police car in which Constable John Delahunty and Ralph Lockman were ambushed as they faced the lane off McKean Street

50. Julian Knight's message to a former school mate as drawn in a 1985 Melbourne High Year Book

51. Knight (second left, back row) during scouts

THE INVESTIGATION

20

When the online supervisor from D24 paged Detective Senior Sergeant Brian McCarthy, he almost jumped out of bed in shock. He turned off the pager, saying to his wife of thirty-two years, "Shit! I wonder what job it is this time?"

Brian rang D24 and was told of a shooting in Hoddle Street and that his instructions were to go straight to the office. He was not to go direct to the scene. He rang Graham Kent.

Suddenly it was daylight, blinding daylight. Dennis Harnetty felt like he was on stage as the cameraman's spotlight followed him towards the Ramsden Street signal box. He felt his hamstring tear as he ran harder to get away from the spotlight. Max Drake covered him from the signal-box landing as he limped up the stairs.

"Turn it off! Turn the fuckin' thing off!" Dennis yelled.

"I'll shoot you if you don't," Max said, turning his revolver in the direction of the cameraman. They could not see because of the intense lighting.

As the area returned to darkness, save for the yellow glow of the street lighting, Max stood back to allow Dennis room to kick open the door. The door burst open and Dennis went in crouched, and searched the office area. Another police officer followed him and together they searched inside the signal box. Dennis switched on the lights then said, "Clear."

Dennis went down the stairs still carrying his revolver, while Max allowed the other police officer to go past him. It was time he needed, time to regain his breath. Dennis turned around to see where Max was. Max walked down the stairs, grasping the banister rail.

Graham Kent was reading a book when the telephone rang. He was unaware of events taking place outside, television did not interest him. He picked up the phone and recognised the voice straight away.

"Squirty, we've got a job," said Brian McCarthy.

Graham's father, a policeman for twenty-six years in country Victoria, would probably not have named him Graham had he had the foresight to know that his son would be given the same nickname as a Melbourne 'career' criminal. But he would have understood. You couldn't escape the black humour of the police force. When he left school, Graham was torn between being a teacher and a detective. His father, who had worked primarily in one-man stations, encouraged him to join the police force.

As a police cadet, Graham was still undecided so he spent his first lot of leave at teachers college. After several weeks, his mind was made up. He knew he was better suited to being a police officer. But not just any police officer. From the first day of recruit training through transfers to Russell Street, South Melbourne, St Kilda and St Kilda CIB, his one ambition was to be an Armed Robbery Squad detective.

He spent four years in the Armed Robbery Squad and he enjoyed the challenge of solving difficult crimes and apprehending some of the State's most dangerous criminals. He was persistent and relentless in his quest to arrest criminals who had committed crimes of violence. To help identify one offender he conducted a line-up parade which consisted entirely of overcoats. Other detectives laughed at the unusual line-up but when his witnesses selected the offender's overcoat he had his arrest, and had set a standard for other detectives.

Apart from hard work, he had luck on his side when he stepped outside the Melbourne Magistrate's Court on 27 March 1986 as car bombs exploded outside the Russell Street Police Station. He was not injured but several others were. Constable Angela Taylor died less than a month later from her injuries.

Brian McCarthy told Graham that one person was dead and eight or nine were injured, that there could be more involved. They talked for a few minutes as Graham wrote down the details.

"Get in there as quickly as you can," Brian said.

Graham rang the Sexual Offences Squad and waited the fifteen minutes for his wife to come home so that he could leave.

Graham Larchin, the Northcote Sergeant, holstered his own revolver and took John Delahunty's as a precaution against Knight suddenly taking it. Graham checked the revolver and saw that one round had been discharged. He put the weapon in his pocket and checked the shrapnel wound on John's left hand. It was bleeding but he reassured John that he would be all right, that he was not seriously injured.

Graham felt ill at the sight of Knight. To look at him made him want to vomit. He said to someone that Knight had small-man's disease and needed firearms to have people take notice of him. He put his hand to his mouth to suppress the volcano that was forcing its way up his throat. He rushed away to the end of the street.

"Why didn't you kill the bastard?" someone shouted.

Paul Storey glanced at the speedometer as the MICA ambulance screamed down Hoddle Street. It was reading 140 kilometres per hour. He looked at the red traffic light at the Johnston Street intersection and anticipated that it would change to green by the time they reached it. It didn't and he braked heavily, tossing Noel Shiels and Peter Collins, who were already surfing in the back, forwards.

"I think we can cut the rush down a little bit," Peter said.

Terry Howard peeked around the edge of the booking office wall while Peter Butts covered him with his revolver. Terry then moved quickly towards the waiting room, his back against the wall and revolver held with both hands. Peter moved out towards the edge of the platform, revolver aimed at the open doorway, as Terry looked inside.

"Clear," Terry said.

Peter ran past him training his revolver into the waiting room, looking in and then out along the train tracks. The area of the railway station seemed clear but they were still wary.

Keith Stewart landed Air 495 on Knott Reserve. With the blades still rotating Daryl Jones elected to check for body damage, while the others remained in their seats anxious to be airborne again. Daryl crawled underneath the Dauphin and saw an oval hole from which clear liquid was dripping. He wiped some on his finger and tasted it. He crawled back out and went to the front of the aircraft indicating to Stewart, with a cut-throat signal, to shut down the engine. As the helicopter began to shut down, he plugged into an intercom lead and told Keith Stewart that aircraft fuel was leaking from the second engine. There was a concern that the helicopter might catch fire or even explode.

In the darkness they felt their lives were at risk. They were still within the vicinity of Hoddle Street and being unarmed made them feel extremely vulnerable. Alan Scott, the ambulance officer, gathered as much medical equipment as he could and radioed for transport to take him back to Hoddle Street. He jumped out of the helicopter and rushed to Heidelberg Road. A police car collected Keith Stewart and Trevor Wilson and took them to the police air wing at Essendon Airport. They intended to go up in another helicopter, but the nightshift crew had already left for Hoddle Street. Daryl remained with the helicopter and took cover behind a semi-trailer. This was the second time that he had been shot at and he was not taking any chances. Seven years earlier, in South Melbourne, a bullet flew past his head while he was searching for an armed robber. He vowed, in future, to always carry a revolver. You were not safe, not even in a helicopter several hundred feet above the ground.

Domenic Cannizzaro remained by the Hoddle Street entrance ramp near the Clifton Hill Railway Station. Cars were lined up behind his and the red car which had crashed into it. He heard running and looked towards the High-Street end of Hoddle where he saw a man approaching. Domenic drew his revolver and directed it at the runner, ordering him to stop, but he kept running.

"Stop and identify yourself!"

The runner could be one of the gunmen and Domenic had no intention of being killed like those around him. When the runner was within five metres he yelled out again.

"Stop!"

Bruce Lowe stopped, saying, "I'm in the job."

"You deserve to die!" Domenic said lowering his revolver.

It did not occur to Bruce that he would not be recognised as a plain clothes police officer. He took out his freddy and showed it to Domenic then continued on his way towards Ramsden Street. He was running on nervous energy and felt almost robotic. Domenic was too upset, his heart thumped too hard for him to think about what would have happened had Bruce been running with a revolver in his hand.

Detectives Rick McIntosh and Kim Cox led Knight away and placed him in the back of the St Kilda CIB car. Robert Kovacs got in beside Knight while the two detectives returned to the scene. Ralph Lockman walked away and stopped other vehicles from entering the street. Later, when other police took over from him, Ralph knocked on doors in McKean Street and took brief details from those who had witnessed anything, for follow up by the Homicide Squad.

"I've never heard such crass language before in my life," said a woman – a resident of McKean Street – referring to John Delahunty and Ralph Lockman.

John Delahunty walked over to a fence and sat down, examining his injuries and reflecting on what had happened. His left hand was shaking and he felt a pain in the wrist. He wondered if he was alive and yet he knew. It seemed stupid to think that way when his heart was pounding a million beats a second.

The Investigation

Everything was like a dream.

People were coming out of their houses and John felt for a moment that his bullet may have shot one of them or there was someone lying injured or dead inside their house, as Knight was not injured. He tried to see if there were any holes in a window, a door or a wall where he had aimed, but there was nothing. Across the road at 244 McKean Street, a double-storey terrace house, there was bullet damage to the ground-floor window ledge. On the ground beneath the window were the remains of an M14 bullet.

It upset John Delahunty to think that he may have shot someone and his only thought was to find out. He approached a number of people and asking if they were all right. His right eye troubled him, it hurt and the eyelid felt heavy. He wiped his head and felt something embedded in the eyelid. There were pieces of shrapnel and splinters from the interior of the police car in his hair and some of it was embedded in his scalp. One man whose health he inquired about looked at John with concern, responding with, "I'm fine, but are you okay?"

Simon Black lay with his back against the side of the divisional van. He looked along the footpath towards Ramsden Street then back towards the railway station. There was something moving in the bushes, it was long and black. Terrified, he ran towards the railway station then towards the long black object, his revolver drawn, shouting, "Don't move! Don't move!"

As he got closer, he saw that the long black object was a telephoto camera lens and a photographer behind the cyclone fence.

"Fuck off, idiot!" Simon screamed.

Rick McIntosh had a brief conversation with Inspector Adrian Fyfe. They had known each other for years from the days when the Inspector had been a sergeant and Rick a constable at Fitzroy.

"Fuck! You're still here." Rick said.

Rick hobbled back to the police car where Knight was being held, trying to avoid aggravating his back pain any more than was necessary. No matter how he walked the pain was still present. He looked at his watch and realised that time was slipping away. They had less than six hours to interview and charge the offender unless he consented to an extension, before a magistrate.

Inspector Pat Murtagh remained crouched beside the police car opposite the Clifton Hill Railway Station and tried to get through to Mick Hogan on the portable radio. Everything he said was distorted and while he was trying to transmit, communication for other police was not possible. He felt like throwing the radio away.

Max Drake and Dennis Harnetty heard crunching behind them. It was coming from the train lines. They turned and saw the silhouette of men heading towards the Ramsden Street railway crossing. The two police officers aimed their revolvers at the approaching men, taking cover behind a police car. Max had his finger around the trigger ready to pull it back just that little bit further, when Dennis said, "They're in the job."

The three police officers, from another district support group, each carried a revolver. Dennis had momentarily caught sight of a police badge hanging from the jeans waistband of one of them although his waterproof jacket partly obscured the badge as he ran. Max and Dennis lowered their revolvers as one of the men said, "We're in the job."

Constable Anita Adair parked the divisional van in Ramsden Street. She and David Depyle walked up to 6 Ramsden Street and went inside. Outside, the media with their cameras and microphones, preyed on the occupants. Anita introduced herself to Pamela Knight, the adoptive mother of the offender, and to his fifteen-year-old sister, Sarah. Pamela offered them something to drink while they talked about what had happened. Both mother and daughter were extremely upset. Pamela was distraught that it was her son who had been responsible. She could not think of any reason for his actions, but Sarah mentioned that at his grandmother's house he had seemed preoccupied – sitting on a chair, and staring into space. Julian tended to keep things to himself and not to discuss his problems.

Sarah took Anita to her bedroom and showed her from where she had seen her brother going along the railway line. She said that even though it was dark, she knew it was him by the silhouette and the way he walked. Sarah could not say why, but deep down she knew it was her brother.

"You can use the phone if you like," Pamela said. Anita picked up the phone and dialled her fiancé. He was unaware of what had happened, and she felt silly for having woken him.

A resident in Delbridge Street, North Fitzroy reported to D24 that dogs were barking in the backyard of a house two doors up from McKean Street.

Tim Edgeworth, Bruce Lowe and Peter Butts covered one another as they conducted a line search down Hoddle Street. Opposite the pedestrian crossing, under the bushes, they found eleven fired .22 cartridge cases and a magazine for a Ruger .22 rifle. Seventeen metres south of where lay the bodies of Robert Mitchell and Vesna Markovska, they located seventeen fired .22 cartridge cases and two magazines for a Ruger .22 rifle. Opposite the Gemini that Zoran Trajceski had been driving, on the grass, was a ten-shot self-loading .22 Ruger rifle.

Further north were four fired .308 cartridge cases and eight fired S.G. 00 buckshot cartridge cases. Below the billboard advertising the Honda Accord were eight fired twelve-gauge S.G. 00 buckshot cartridge cases and three fired .308 cartridge cases. Behind the billboard were two fired twelve-gauge S.G. 00 buckshot cartridge cases and a fired .308 cartridge.

Between the Honda billboard and the next, advertising Invicta, under some bushes, was a Winchester cartridge box for twelve-gauge S.G. 00 buckshot cartridges. Then there was a Winchester packet for centre-fire rifle cartridges, a .308 cartridge packet flap, a polystyrene .308 cartridge insert holder, seven fired .308 cartridge cases and one unfired .308 cartridge. Under the Invicta sign, they located four fired .308 cartridge cases. Then they found a Mossberg 500A twelve-gauge, slide-action shotgun and seven fired twelve-gauge S.G. 00 buckshot cartridge cases.

On the ground between the Coke billboard and the start of the railway-station building were fourteen fired .308 cartridge cases.

"We picked a bad day to give up cocaine," Peter Butts joked with Tim Edgeworth.

Julian Knight sat between Kim Cox and Robert Kovacs as the detectives' car travelled to 412 St Kilda Road, Melbourne. Rick McIntosh had told Knight that he would not be asked any further questions until they arrived. There was silence in the car as it travelled briskly through the streets of Melbourne. Knight seemed unemotional, cold, as if dissociated from everything that had happened during the evening. It was as if he had been watching a film on TV.

21

Fraud Squad Detective, Sergeant Noel McCrohan, had been watching television at home when the news flash interrupted the film. He rang Northcote Police Station, where he had previously worked, and was told that Knight had been arrested and that a Bruce Powell was thought by the police to be the other offender. Noel, who had been an operational police officer throughout his career, knew Powell so decided to go to the police station and lend a hand. As he travelled along High Street, Northcote, he felt a thud against the side of his unmarked car. Bruce Powell had thrown a cricket bat at the car.

As Noel got out of his car, two other men appeared from out of the shadows. Noel returned to his car and reversed away from Powell and his associates. He took some side streets but was stopped at Westbourne Grove by a white Ford sedan which suddenly blocked his path. Powell got out of the Ford and rushed at him, swinging the bat against the bonnet of his car, smashing the passenger-side headlight. Noel reversed down a lane but stopped when he reached a dead end. Powell and his two associates came rushing toward him, armed with cricket bats and, what appeared to be, a rifle. Noel opened his boot and took out his shotgun. He levelled it at the three men, telling them he was a police officer. They ran off in different directions while Noel got back in his car and drove quickly to the Northcote Police Station.

A resident rang D24 to say that someone was in their Rushall Crescent backyard.

Assistant Commissioner Vaughan Werner crouched beside Inspector Pat Murtagh and looked across Hoddle Street towards the railway station.

"Why are you hiding? The offender's been caught," the Assistant Commissioner said.

"Same reason you are," replied the Inspector.

There was a struggle as Bruce Powell came into the Northcote Police Station with Detective Sergeant Noel McCrohan and other police from Northcote. Betty Roberts came out of the locker room to see what the commotion was about. She knew Powell was thought to be the second gunman. He could have been shooting at her in Hoddle Street. She rushed at him as he struggled against the others. Screaming loudly, she tried to punch him. She was restrained by another police officer as Powell was led into the interview room asking, "What's wrong with her?"

After several hours of questioning by Noel McCrohan, Powell was charged with criminal damage and assault offences. Detectives from Hawthorn and Fitzroy charged him with burglaries and with receiving stolen property. Sergeant Mark Stella of Heidelberg charged Powell with several counts of criminal damage and theft arising from the incidents in Heidelberg and Preston earlier that night when he was thought to be in possession of a firearm. Detectives from the major crime squad, later that morning, exonerated Powell from involvement in the Hoddle Street murders.

John Delahunty had been in the casualty waiting room at Prince Henry's Hospital for what seemed like hours. He paced around the waiting area, sitting down occasionally then getting up and pacing again. A hospital security guard tried to persuade him to sit and rest, but he was too edgy. A journalist approached him and asked about Hoddle Street, but before he was able to answer an orderly interrupted.

"He's here for security."

John could see doctors working on a body in a theatre room. He walked in and watched as the doctors tried to revive a man who looked as if he had been involved in a motor vehicle accident. Then he saw the gunshot wounds. When the medical staff left the room John paused and took one last look at John Muscat.

Detective Senior Constable Rod McDonald came into the waiting room and sat with John talking to him about Knight and his arrest. John was comforted with the knowledge that Rod had been through a similar experience – he too had been ambushed and been shot by Mad Max Clarke on 25 February 1986. Clarke had been killed in a shoot-out with Rod and another detective, Sergeant John Kapetanovski. Rod stayed with John until it was his turn for medical treatment. The doctor gave John an injection and x-rayed his hand.

"It looks just like the milky way," the doctor said holding the film against the light. There were more than thirty, white splinters and dots in Delahunty's left hand.

Peter Butts and Bruce Lowe followed the trainline north, past the Clifton Hill Railway Station. They covered each other, alert to the slightest movement. They moved from tree to tree believing that at any moment a rifle would be aimed in their direction, the trigger squeezed and they would be dead. Without a portable radio they were unable to communicate with D24 and receive any updates on the offenders' location. When they could not see more than a few metres ahead, they turned back.

Flemington 250 had advised that the second offender might be in the train that was stopped at Rushall Railway Station. Inspector Pat Murtagh cautioned that it was a containment situation and directed that the Special Operations Group sweep the train.

Some two hundred metres south of Ramsden Street, Constable Glen Sheluchin directed traffic at the intersection of Hoddle Street and Roseneath Street. He wanted to be back where it had been happening, to see it through to the end. After all he had been one of the first police officers to attend the incident. But orders were orders. He had gone from being an active participant to being nothing more than a spectator.

He did not feel the cold even though he was wearing a short-sleeved shirt and his cap was in the van where it had been from the beginning. He signalled cars to turn right, left or make a U-turn. Some motorists argued with him and others wanted to know why, before they would give some consideration to his hand signals.

"Because you can't go through!" he yelled.

He was not normally so aggressive with the public, but they annoyed him by wanting to argue, by asking questions and by trying to push past in their cars. Everywhere he looked he saw the dead and injured. The headlights from the traffic made him feel vulnerable and edgy. He indicated for a woman driver to turn left into South Terrace but she refused to move. She wanted to continue travelling north along Hoddle Street.

"I always go this way," she said.

"You bloody well can't! Now do as you're bloody told!"

Glen banged the side of her car door and pointed to where he wanted her to go.

There was someone running across the roof of 242 McKean Street, North Fitzroy.

"Where's your cap?" Assistant Commissioner Vaughan Werner asked the constable, who had been there from the start.

"How do I know where the fuck it is!"

Rick McIntosh parked the CIB car and led the others to the lift. On the sixth floor, Knight was led into an interview room where a dual tape deck was in position. Neither of the detectives was familiar with the taping process, it was part of a pilot program being tested at St Kilda Road Police Station. Rick and Kim Cox were acutely aware that if any evidence was to be gained from Knight it had to be obtained within six hours of his arrest in McKean Street. To interview him with a typed record of interview would be long and drawn out, and if Knight objected to going past the six hours, then under Victorian State law, no further questions could be put to him. It would be quicker using the tape recorder but having never used it before, neither officer was comfortable with it. Sergeant Frank Smith, who was stationed at St Kilda Road, came into the room and showed the detectives how to operate the recording facilities.

Rick looked at his watch. It was 10.55 p.m. He asked the questions while Kim wrote down everything that was being said in his folder pad. This was a precaution in case the tapes were faulty or certain words or phrases were indecipherable.

Rick was polite and friendly to Knight, gently probing into the background to the shootings. He asked Knight how he felt, was he ill, would he like something to drink, where did he fire the M14 rifle, where had he been – times and places.

Knight snivelled as he answered, revealing that he had been depressed in the morning. Rick felt he was dealing with a spoilt child rather than the sort of criminal he had become accustomed to during his thirteen years of police service.

"What were you depressed about?"

Knight considered the question for almost ten seconds then said, "Nothing in particular, I just ... "

Rick could tell that Knight was on the verge of breaking down and was trying to hold back the tears. He waited fifteen seconds for Knight to continue his answer but nothing was forthcoming.

"Can you tell me what it was that depressed you?"

"It wasn't anything in particular."

"Was it a number of things?"

Rick waited a further fifteen seconds then offered Knight his handkerchief to wipe his nose and eyes.

"I'm not sure," Knight said and he began to cry.

"What do you mean you're not sure what worried you?" Rick asked in a paternal manner.

"I don't know," he cried.

Kim Cox offered Knight a glass of water but this was declined. The detectives then left the room for a minute to give Knight time to regain his composure.

When they returned, Rick continued the questioning, gently asking Knight about his movements during the day. Knight sniffled and tried to contain his emotions. He had drunk two cans of beer at his grandmother's house in Hawthorn. He spelt out the name of her street. He had been bored so went there with his sister and left with her. He then went to the Royal Hotel where he had a pot of beer. After that, he drove to Clifton Hill to give a *Choice* magazine to a girl named Lisa Ellison. The magazine featured an article on travel to Bali and Lisa was going there for a holiday with her boyfriend. He mentioned that on the way home his Torana got stuck in second gear. At home, he had a can of Victoria Bitter beer. Then he went back to the Royal Hotel with $45 in his wallet and consumed fifteen pots of beer, although he lost count, it could have been twenty pots. Rick counted $34 in notes and two dollars in coins. With pots of beer costing $1.10 Rick calculated that Knight had bought closer to ten pots of beer.

"I'm not sure, like I said, I'd lost count. I don't remember."

Knight said that he drank six or seven pots of beer every night after work. He left the Royal Hotel feeling depressed.

"You were depressed were you? What was depressing you?"

"I don't know. The car, and having to leave the army."

Knight said he had joined the army on 11 January that year.

"Why did you have to leave the army?"

"They said to get out or we'll (sic) throw you out."

Knight's voice wavered as he spoke about it.

He said that he had stabbed his Cadet Sergeant Major, Mongo Reid. Rick again told Knight of his rights. He was not obliged to answer any further questions as anything he said might be given in evidence.

"Do you fully understand that?"

"Yes."

Knight was sobbing and the detectives knew that it was pointless interviewing him any further while he was so depressed. Despite wanting to continue, the detectives left the room at 11.26 p.m. They returned at 11.34 p.m. and took him upstairs to the Homicide Squad office on the tenth floor. It was going to be a long and uncomfortable day for Rick. He wanted to change out of his suit and get something to relieve his back pain.

City West 253 reported that they had been told by a man that two persons, wearing army-type uniforms and carrying rifles, had been seen going into the Clifton Hill Railway Station at the time that the shooting started.

Detective Senior Sergeant John Hill of Homicide walked carefully along Hoddle Street while Bruce Lowe sketched the crime scene. Bruce tried not to look closely at the bodies and the cars as he sketched their position in his folder.

Domenic Cannizzaro explained to Graham Larchin that the red Ford had reversed into his police car. With the number of high ranking officers at the scene and more on the way, Domenic took his cap out of the car, but held it under his arm as his sergeant did not have a cap at all. Domenic was concerned that he would lose his police driving authority. Graham reassured him and together they walked along Hoddle Street dazed, yet with a heightened sense of reality. They noticed the slightest sound, the slightest movement. Graham told Domenic not to worry about the damage to the police car, it could be replaced, unlike those bodies they saw in cars and on the footpath.

The Investigation

Deputy Commissioner Kel Glare approached them and told Domenic to put on his cap.

"I've just got it out of the car, sir," Domenic said.

Graham Larchin was incensed. The Deputy Commissioner was wearing a suit, he was less of a target than they were.

"We've just been involved in a shooting," Graham answered aggressively.

"Where's your cap Sergeant?" the Deputy Commissioner asked, turning his attention to Graham.

"It's in the police car where I left it when I got ambushed."

"It's over now and I want you both to put your caps on."

Graham shook his head in disbelief, then walked away, muttering, "Get fucked". It seemed that the only thing the officers in the police force were concerned with was how their subordinates were dressed. They did not seem to care if they were all right, whether they were injured or distressed. Even though Knight was in custody, wearing a white cap was like wearing a flashing neon sign on your head.

Constable Phil Bradley was standing guard outside the crime-scene tape at the Ramsden Street intersection, when an officer approached and asked him where his cap was, where his jacket was. It was a good question, one that Phil was unable to answer. He knew his overcoat was covering the bodies of Vesna Markovska and Robert Mitchell.

When told that he had no idea of the whereabouts of his attire, the officer asked, "Have you been here from the start?"

"I have sir."

The officer opened his mouth to say something then walked away. Minutes later Belinda Bourchier gave Phil one of the jackets she had taken from the Collingwood Police Station. He put it on over the long sleeved jumper he had worn all night and made a joke about it belonging to Charlie Chaplin. Its sleeves were half-mast and he had trouble zipping it closed.

Detective Sergeant Peter Spence was taking Ralph Lockman's statement in the main office of the Major Crime Squad. Ralph leaned forward and related his observations as Peter took him carefully through the incident. They were absorbed in making the statement when there was a sudden loud bang behind Ralph. Another detective picked up the brief book he had dropped and apologised. Ralph casually turned around to see what had caused the noise.

"Well, you're not gun shy," said Peter Spence.

Constable Michelle Young drove the unmarked police car to the Russell Street Community Policing Office. Beside her was Sergeant Judy Cousins who had been with her to 6 Ramsden Street to take over from Anita Adair and David Depyle. The policewomen had been instructed by the District Superintendent, Barry Phelan, to take Pamela and Sarah Knight from their house, while forensic and video-operations personnel went through it. Judy chatted with Pamela, who seemed guarded.

Senior Constable Henry Glaser and Sergeant Hubert Peters, of the crime scene section of the Forensic Science Laboratory, carefully checked each room of 6 Ramsden Street, Clifton Hill. In a corner of the lounge room they found a packing box for a Mossberg Model 500 slide-action shotgun. Behind an armchair they located a box which carried rifle cleaning equipment and a 7.62, 51 millimetre, Nato 308 Winchester calibre-proving dummy cartridge. There was a rifle bag behind the box. Behind the settee and behind a wooden chest, they found a military ammunition box containing firearm accessories and ammunition.

They then went upstairs to Pamela Knight's bedroom. At the foot of the double bed they located, in a firearm packing box, a .177 calibre Daisy air rifle. Under the bed in another packing box was a .177 calibre Crosman air rifle and a Chinese Pioneer .177 air rifle with a home-made bayonet attachment.

On top of the wardrobe was rifle-cleaning equipment and a telescopic sight.

Phil Bradley did not want the media around. He stood in the way of photographers hoping that their film would be unusable because of his foreground presence. Although he knew that they had a job to do, quite often, they didn't like it any more than he did, he still felt that at times like this, the photographers, television crews and journalists were parasites.

After making a statement at the Major Crime Squad office at 412 St Kilda Road, John Delahunty was driven to the Fitzroy Police Station. He did not want to be alone and he did not want to go home. As he went up the steps and through the swing doors he was aware that there was an unusual amount of activity for this time of the morning. On nightshift there would normally be a handful of police on duty, now there seemed to be a hundred. There were officers he had previously seen only on television, and detectives and other police from just about every branch and station in metropolitan Melbourne.

"What's the quickest way to get to Northcote?" asked someone in the watchhouse.

"Dunno," said someone else.

"Shoot down Hoddle Street," was the answer.

The Investigation

The black humour of police was not always appreciated by others but it was a safety valve for those in the front line. John grinned at the joke then went upstairs with some others, where they found a spare room. They shut the door and opened some cans of beer. As the sun was rising he was driven home to Flemington where he fell asleep immediately. He needed some rest as the Chief Commissioner wanted to see him.

Pamela and Sarah Knight, Michelle Young and Judy Cousins sat around the mess table at the Russell Street Community Policing Office drinking coffee. Michelle Young talked about her no-win situation with her parents. They had blasted her the year before, for not ringing them after the Russell Street bombing, believing she might have been hurt. She had been at home listening to music. This time, when she did ring them, they blasted her for ringing at three in the morning. She told them about Hoddle Street but they had been unaware of the incident. Michelle grinned at the irony and sipped at her coffee. She would have preferred something stronger.

Sarah Knight was very quiet. She seemed meek and confused, sitting at the table with her arms crossed. She talked of how Julian had had a fight with his former girlfriend, Renee Cross. He had been really mad with her. Then he was really mad about his car, his pride and joy, which had blown up.

She said that Julian was not enjoying his job. He felt that everyone was turning against him.

"How many has he killed?" Pamela asked, almost afraid to ask and afraid of the answer.

"I don't know," she was told, even though both police officers knew the answer. They had been instructed not to say anything about Hoddle Street. Michelle wanted to yell out loudly to Pamela, "He's friggin killed six!"

She checked herself and felt guilty for thinking the way she did. She knew these two women were not responsible for what he had done. They were just as upset as everyone else.

Pamela said that Julian wanted to be like his father and that was why he went to Duntroon. He had an obsession with war and had always wanted to be in the army. Julian had stabbed a sergeant at Duntroon. Pamela said that he was angry with his father, upset that his parents had separated.

"Do you want to ring your ex-husband?" Michelle asked.

"No, no. How on earth am I going to go back into my street?" Pamela asked.

In Turnbull Street, Darrell Rintoule had only two words to say to his district superintendent, who had asked, "Where's your reflectorised (sic) vest?"

The two words were, "Get fucked!"

22

Brian McCarthy had a wash, splashed aftershave on his face and used plenty of deodorant. Experience had taught him that it could be a while before his next shower. While he changed into his work suit – one of two that he possessed – Betty packed a Pritikin meal for him. He hugged his wife then went outside to the CIB car parked in the driveway.

"I'll see you when I see you next," he said to Betty.

As he drove slowly through the fog, Brian contacted D24 and asked for an update. The operator was unable to elaborate any further so he travelled to Melbourne, at least an hour away under the conditions. He had little knowledge of what lay before him. It puzzled him that he was to go direct to the Homicide office and not visit the crime scene first. Whatever the reason he hoped that this investigation would not be as strenuous or time consuming as the Mildura murder inquiry. He realised the importance of giving evidence at a trial and to do so when you're lacking sleep and fatigued, is risking months, sometimes years, of work. He had gone to court in just that manner many times but he did not like it. To lose a murder trial because of a slip up due entirely to lack of sleep was not something he wanted to live with.

Graham Kent caught the lift to the sixth floor of the St Kilda Road CIB offices and spoke to detectives Rick McIntosh and Kim Cox. Rick briefly explained that the scene in Hoddle Street was hectic with at least five dead, and he believed that Knight had acted alone.

Vaughan Werner, the Assistant Commissioner for Crime, told Graham that it was a Homicide job and that he was to "take over till Brian gets in."

While Knight was being examined by the police surgeon, Graham caught the lift up to the ninth floor and unlocked the Homicide Squad offices. He could hear the phones ringing as he opened the door. It was going to be a long shift. It was not unusual for Homicide detectives to work ten to twelve hours a day, and when taking over a murder enquiry, to work at least twenty hours straight. Quite often, it was forty hours without a break, without sleep, before they could go home. The adrenalin kept you going. While there were people to interview and evidence to gather, the first weeks meant little rest.

The police surgeon, Dr Stephen Jelbart, had been with Knight since 11.00 p.m. and took samples of his blood and made a physical examination. Dr Jelbart observed that Knight smelt of alcohol but was steady on his feet and spoke coherently, calmly, and without affect to his speech. The only injury to Knight was a one-centimetre graze on his left elbow, and his eyes were bloodshot. He found that Knight was fit enough to be interviewed.

At 11.35 p.m. Graham Kent went with the Officer in Charge of the Homicide Squad, Detective Chief Inspector Brendan Cole, into the interview room.

"I only want to know one thing for the moment and it is most important. Was there anyone else with you tonight?" the Chief Inspector asked.

"No sir," Knight replied.

"Are you absolutely sure?" asked Cole.

It was an important question, as the police were still not convinced that he had acted alone. Clifton Hill, Fitzroy, and surrounding suburbs were still being searched for a possible accomplice.

Graham Kent's first impression was that Knight was like a young kid who had been on an adventure and had been caught doing something naughty. He seemed to be interested in what was happening to him, but not concerned. For a nineteen-year-old, he seemed very immature.

Graham escorted Knight up to the Homicide office with Inspector Fyfe's driver, Robert Kovacs. They stopped at the toilet where Knight gave a urine sample. He was then taken to the interview room where Robert Kovacs sat with him. Graham, who had been taking notes of everything connected with the inquiry so far, was aware that time was running out. The clock began to tick from the moment Knight was arrested in North Fitzroy some three hours earlier. Anything Knight said outside of those six hours was not admissible evidence. Even worse was the fact that the six hours included the time required to have him appear before a magistrate or court registrar and formally agree to an extension of time. Brian McCarthy had yet to arrive from his home and Graham wanted to find out more of what had occurred in Hoddle Street. He felt at some disadvantage in not having attended the scene as was the usual procedure. Getting accurate information was important.

At 12.10 a.m. Peter Ross, a scientist from the State Forensic Science Laboratory, entered the interview room. It was explained to Knight that the scientist wanted to take swabs from his hands, to check for firearm residue. Knight consented to the swabs and once these were taken he sat waiting with Robert Kovacs.

Brian McCarthy parked the CIB car outside the St Kilda Road police complex and raced inside the building. He looked at his watch and saw that there was little time to properly investigate the offence with the suspect if he refused to cooperate. It was legislation that hampered rather than aided police in their inquiries, particularly with major criminal offences. Career and other opportunistic criminals had used the legislation to their advantage. Often, by the time police had interviewed suspects for one offence out of several, sometimes including murders and armed robberies, the six hours had passed. The investigating police would then be frustrated when the magistrate asked the suspect if he consented to an extension of the interview. Invariably the suspect said no and he had to be freed from the interview room. There had been occasions when detectives had charged an offender with one crime, such as murder, when there were several other like offences that needed to be discussed. The opportunity was lost once time ran out. Raymond "Mr Stinky" Edmunds was one such case. He was charged with two murders, but other murders that he was believed to have been involved in were not put to him. The police just ran out of time.

Outside the interview room Brian McCarthy discussed what had taken place with Brendan Cole and the other detectives who had had any involvement with the offender.

"How long has he been in custody?" McCarthy asked one of the detectives.

It was the most important thing to him at the moment. He removed his suit jacket and put it over his chair.

Brian McCarthy and Graham Kent entered the interview room feeling they knew less about the case than any other police on duty at the time, and they felt hampered by not having visited the crime scene. They had less than four hours to interview the killer of six people. Ten days later that number would be seven.

They entered the interview room and went to the back where there was a mirror window, facing the door. Knight sat near the door and facing the mirror window. Sitting opposite Knight, Brian opened his black spring-back folder to a page where he had made some notes. Knight was crossing and uncrossing his legs. Graham sat to the right of his senior sergeant and took notes.

"Goodday, how are you?" Brian said.

He spoke in a conversational style designed to gain Knight's confidence. Brian believed a good investigator did not need to yell and scream, or resort to sarcasm. It was all about psychology, getting the suspect to feel comfortable and open up. Brian felt that while Knight wanted to talk they should interview him immediately, even if they did not have a lot of facts and were ill prepared.

"Julian, I have been introduced already. My name is Graham Kent, Detective Senior Constable. This is Detective Senior Sergeant McCarthy.

"We're both from the Homicide Squad," Brian added and continued the conversation with Knight. He obtained the basic details such as his name, his address, who he lived with and if he was married. Knight spelt his surname and his street name. Brian then cautioned Knight, telling him that he was not obliged to say anything, and that anything he did say was being recorded and might be given as evidence."

"Do you understand that?"

"Yes."

"Okay, would you start off with (sic) telling me what caused this thing tonight?"

"I dunno."

Brian continued to question Knight in an almost priest-like manner. It was generally a successful tactic that he had employed throughout his years in the police service. It had earned him the nickname, Father Confessor. As much as he loathed certain offenders he knew that by talking to them in a non-threatening way, like a friend, he was more likely to gain their cooperation. He did not know if Knight was telling the truth but at least he was cooperative. He directed Knight back to the beginning, to what he was doing prior to the shooting.

Knight said that he had slept that night at home and had got up at 11.30 on Sunday morning feeling somewhat hung over from a drinking binge the previous night. Knight showered and dressed in black shoes, socks and trousers, with a blue shirt and black tie. From home, he and his sister went to his grandmother's house in Hawthorn, arriving at about 1.30 p.m. His mother and brother, Matthew, were already there. Family and friends gathered to celebrate his mother's birthday, which had been on the previous Wednesday. After lunch and two cans of beer, Knight, and his sister, Sarah, left the party at about 4.00 p.m. He dropped his sister off at their home in Ramsden Street, then drove to the Royal Hotel in Spensley Street, Clifton Hill. He had a pot of beer at the Royal Hotel then drove to a nearby block of flats. He spoke to Lisa Ellison, a friend he had known from Fitzroy High School and gave her a copy of *Choice* magazine which he had borrowed from his grandmother.

A child care worker in Fitzroy, nineteen-year-old Lisa Ellison was outside her first-floor flat cleaning her bicycle when Knight parked his car opposite her block. It was about 5.00 p.m. She worked part-time at the Royal Hotel and it was there that Knight and their mutual friends would meet on Friday nights. Knight gave her the magazine and told her where he had been. He complained that the party for his mother had been boring.

"We all have to go to those sort of things," she joked.

She told him how snappy he looked and he replied that he just wanted to get into his jeans. To Lisa he seemed to be in a happy, jovial mood, not influenced by alcohol. On the night before, Saturday night, when she had seen him at the Royal Hotel, he had been upset at not being invited to a party put on by his former girlfriend, Renee Cross. Lisa thought that when she saw him on Sunday, he was over the snub.

"What did you do then?" Brian McCarthy asked.

He studied Knight's every mannerism – how he crossed his legs, looked down at his feet, moved about in the chair, how he tilted his head against the wall. Apart from his crimes there was nothing significant about him.

Knight replied that he had returned home and changed his clothes, apart from his shirt, and then returned to the Royal Hotel where he stayed till about 8.30 p.m.

"How many pots do you think you had?"

"I'm not sure. I think about fifteen."

Knight explained that he had been drinking on his own in the public bar. Brian asked Knight about the bar staff who served him.

"There was a girl, I don't know her name. And there was Jim the barman."

"Can you describe the girl?"

"About five foot nine, slim, long black hair. She had a prominent scar on her chin and down the left-hand side of her face."

"Were you conversing with her while you were drinking?"

"No."

Karlina Byers had worked as a barmaid all over Australia for ten years, when she began work that Sunday for the first time at the Royal Hotel. The left side of her face down to her chin was scarred. At about 6.00 p.m., she had noticed him sitting on a bar stool near the bottle shop and the Berry Street entrance, drinking with another patron. She felt uncomfortable as she felt his eyes follow her every move. She thought that he was strange. She served him a pot of beer.

"Have you been knifed?" Knight asked her.

She told him she had been in a car accident and then tried to ignore him.

"I'm fascinated by scars. I've got them all over my body," he said, and then he told her that he was fascinated by her scar.

Karlina moved away and served someone else. Twenty minutes later, when she returned, Knight told her, "I'm sorry that I offended you. I didn't mean to upset you."

He repeated this several times. She moved away and ignored him.

"Did you have a conversation with anyone in particular?"

"Yes, I had a conversation with a friend of a friend – I don't know his first name. He bought me a couple of drinks, and an old German bloke called Karl, and he bought me a few drinks."

"Were you short of money?"

"No."

"You went shout-for-shout or something like that or what?"

"Ah, I was shout (sic) – I bought this bloke who is a friend of a friend – bought him a couple and he bought me a couple."

"Uh huh."

"The German bloke bought me about three beers and that wasn't in shouts, that was ..."

Lindsay Lockett, an apprentice sheet-metal worker, was wearing a Carlton football jumper underneath a denim jacket, covered all over its back with AC/DC patches, when he came down to the bar of the Royal Hotel. He lived on the premises and would be eighteen in September. He had a meal in the bar sitting at a table next to a space invader machine, then he went over to Knight whom he had known for seven weeks. They discussed the football and how Essendon, the team that Knight supported, had been involved in some close matches with Carlton over the last five years.

Lindsay shouted Knight a pot of beer while Knight talked about the trouble with his Torana, how it stuck in second gear and was costing a lot to run. He was still paying off the car and intended to sell it as soon as he had the gear box repaired.

Noticing the motifs on Lindsay's jacket, Knight told him that, in Laverton, where he had been based in the army, if you didn't like AC/DC or The Angels you were no one. Knight shouted Lindsay a pot and talked of his time in the army. It was easier living in the army, according to Knight.

"They take $40 a week out of your wage and that pays your board and bills," he said.

He told Lindsay that he had been a marksman and had signed for three years but had only served two.

"It's a cunt of a life," Knight had said of the army. He told Lindsay that he wouldn't mind being a jackaroo.

Lindsay went up to his room to watch television but returned soon after. He and Knight continued to shout each other beers. Knight talked about the split-up with Renee, his girlfriend of two years, in January. He had seen her in the hotel days earlier and had tried making small talk, but she virtually ignored him. She had told him that college was all right, and that was it. Girls were easier to get in Canberra, he had said. In seven months there, he had had five girlfriends.

Near closing time, Karlina Byers noticed Knight sitting on his own when Karl Klug, a wood turner, sat next to him. Karl who had seen Knight in the hotel regularly over the past two years, watching him play pool or mix with his friends in the lounge area, asked Knight to make room for him so that he could buy some beer. Karl noticed that Knight had an empty glass and paid for a refill. Knight smiled and thanked Karl.

At 8 o'clock, Karlina saw that Knight was holding an empty glass. She gave him a pot on the house and continued to clean up the bar area. It was closing time. She noticed that Knight had gone by 8.15 p.m.

"Did you have any difficulty in walking?"

"I was staggering about."

The licensee of the Royal Hotel, Luigi Gudic, knew Knight to "sit on his beer" and play the pool table with his friends who either came with him to the hotel or who would meet him there. James Coulston, who had worked as a barman for twelve years, served Knight four pots during the evening and also knew him to be a slow drinker. In the six months James had worked at the Royal hotel he had seen Knight come into the hotel every fortnight. But in the preceding ten days the pattern had changed. Knight had come every evening, arriving about 8.00 p.m., drinking between four and six pots of beer, and then leaving at closing time. It was always beer, never spirits. Like the other bar staff at the Royal Hotel that evening, he believed that Knight was unaffected by the alcohol he had consumed. He seemed a little depressed, but sober.

"All right, when you got home what did you do?"

"I went upstairs and got the firearms from underneath my mother's bed and the ammunition out of the cupboard."

"Why were they under her bed and in her cupboard?"

"I used to keep them in my own room which is now the lounge room. When I went to the army, she ... all my stuff was moved out and it was turned into a lounge room."

"What firearms did she have under her bed, of yours?"

"Three air rifles and a Ruger 10/22, .22 rifle."

"A Ruger .22 rifle?"

"Yes, a Mossberg ... "

"Sorry to interrupt you. The Ruger .22 is that a single shot or a ... "

"Ten-shot rotary magazine semi-automatic."

"Right, okay. What was the other one?"

"There's a Mossberg pump action, eight shot, twelve gauge."

"Right, okay. And you took both those firearms?"

"And a 7.62 rifle, M14."

"Right, so you had three firearms?"

"Three rifle firearms."

"And ammunition for all of them?"

"Yes, I had three ten-round rotary magazines for the Ruger. I had the belt of twenty-five rounds for the shotgun. I had one magazine for the rifle and about sixty rounds."

"Why did you go and get these firearms out, and ammunition?"

Brian looked at Knight, who for the first time since Brian had been interviewing him, faltered in making a direct response. The seconds seemed like hours. When Knight did answer his words were more deliberate and hesitant.

"'Cause I was going to go out with them. Out into the street."

"Why did you want to do that?"

Again, Brian noticed the delay in answering.

"I wanted to see what it was like to kill someone and I wanted ... " Knight paused before continuing.

Brian believed that this part of Knight's answer was truthful and the words exact, and their significance stayed with him long after he had retired from the police service.

Brian thought that Knight seemed to bite his tongue at this point, and then continue, as if what was to follow was an explanation that wasn't what he really felt but that would make him appear to be less culpable, less criminal.

"I knew soon as, I knew soon as I killed someone that the um, police would arrive, and then SOG would arrive and then they would finish me off."

"Right. Did you want to be finished off?"

"Yes."

"Why?"

Knight paused, becoming emotional and silent. Brian thought it strange that one who wanted to kill and then be killed would act this way. He was aware that Knight had already cried when interviewed by other detectives soon after his arrest and he assumed that the emotion would have, by this time, been drained from him. Finally, Knight answered, struggling to hold back his tears. "I don't know."

Knight began to sob, telling Brian that he had been thinking for years, about what it would be like to kill and be killed. He said that he had started thinking this way from the age of sixteen or seventeen.

"What started you thinking about it?"

"I don't know, I always wanted to join the army but ... "

Brian continued with the questions, gently probing, conscious of the time and wanting to get the fundamental proofs – the elements necessary to prove that the interviewee was guilty – answered before the six hours were up.

"Did you have some disappointment in your life that made you think that way or is it something that came into your head?"

"I dunno. I always wanted to join the army," Knight said. He wanted to be like his father, who was an officer.

"Is this feeling that you had of wanting to kill someone, is that in any way connected to your father?"

"I dunno," Knight cried, almost hoarse with emotion.

"When you got the guns from under your mother's bed and ammunition out of the wardrobe, your intention was to go and kill someone. Is that right?"

Unable to answer verbally, Knight nodded his head. By this time, he was coughing and spluttering, and crying and sniffling.

"Were you only going to kill one person or was it your intention to kill more than one?"

"I was just, I was just going to keep on shooting until I ran out."

"Yes."

Knight continued to cry, his sentences broken by sobbing.

"And before I left, had one round for the rifle and, I put it in me pocket – and that was for meself (sic). But when I got into McKean Street, and I only had about ten rounds left and the police arrived, I let loose with them and I was looking for that last round and I couldn't find it."

"So what you are saying is your intention was to commit suicide?"

Sobbing, Knight said, "I was, I was going to keep on shooting until I ran out and that last one I kept, I was going to use on myself."

Brian kept probing, Knight telling him that he intended to shoot at anyone.

"Was it your intention to kill them when you shot at them?"

"Yes."

"How many people did you intend to kill?"

"I didn't, I didn't intend on (sic) any number."

Brian paused briefly, allowing Knight time to regain his composure and wipe his face. Referring to the firearms he asked, "How did you carry them all?"

"The M14 I had slung, and the shotgun and the .22 I carried in either hand."

"And were all the firearms loaded when you left home?"

"Yes."

Knight revealed that he went on foot onto the Clifton Hill railway line and hid among the hedges growing beside the train tracks on the east-side of Hoddle Street.

"Were you just going to shoot at the cars or at the people in them?"

"The people in them."

"And which firearm did you intend to use?"

"I started with the .22."

23

Senior Constable Henry Glaser carefully searched the ground outside 241 McKean Street, North Fitzroy. He and his Sergeant, Hubert Peters, took measurements and sketched the scene. The Fitzroy police car was still where John Delahunty and Ralph Lockman had left it, the 7.62, 51 millimetre Nato M14, self-loading rifle was on the pavement and the breech was open. Henry counted ten, fired M14 rounds on the ground and noted their position.

As Brian McCarthy continued his questioning, Knight became more composed. Apart from a runny nose he again displayed no emotion, speaking matter-of-factly about what he had done. His manner was no different than if he had been giving directions to someone wanting to go to the Melbourne Cricket Ground.

"And do you know whether you hit any of these people in the cars?"

"No."

"How many cars did you shoot at?"

"All told?"

"Yes."

"About a dozen, including one motorcycle."

"Did you shoot at the motorcycle or at the person on the motorcycle?"

"The person on the motorcycle."

"What happened when you hit him?"

"He downed (sic) and I let off another three rounds – I hit him and he started screaming out and he hit the ground and he was still screaming so, um, I didn't want to keep him in any other ... in any more agony, so I let off another three rounds until he stopped screaming."

"Were you shooting at him?" Brian asked.

It was a question to which he already knew the answer, but he needed to be specific. In the Supreme Court such questions and the answers given would be vitally important. A good barrister could make a big deal about questions that were not asked and, what happened in court was infinitely more important than what happened in the interview room. In Knight's matter-of-fact manner, he simply said, "Yes."

"Do you think you hit him?"

"Yes."

Knight told how he reloaded the rifle and shot at two more cars. Having fired the forty rounds of ammunition for the Ruger, he left the weapon in the hedges where he had been hiding. He then jumped the fence onto the railway station platform, carrying the shotgun in his hands. At a vantage point at the other end of the platform Knight fired at the cars that travelled along Hoddle Street.

"Were you firing at the cars or the people in the cars?"

"The people in them."

"And how many cars do you think you hit?"

"About six."

"Did any of these cars stop?"

"About four and I think two reversed."

When he had run out of ammunition for the shotgun, Knight left the firearm where he had been taking aim, in the hedges. In the interview room Knight still wore the shotgun cartridge belt around his waist. He said he then started to use the semi-automatic M14 which he had loaded with twenty rounds in his mother's bedroom.

"And how many rounds of ammunition did you have for it?"

"Approximately sixty."

Moments later, he was more specific when he told the detectives that he had carried eighteen rounds in his denim jacket and another forty rounds in an old, shotgun-cartridge box that he kept down the front of his jacket.

"What was your intent when you were firing at them?"

"Kill them."

"What was your intent when you were firing the shotgun at the people in the cars?"

"Kill them."

"What was your intent when you were firing the .22 rifle at the people?"

"Kill them."

Brian thought about an important aspect that needed to be proved in a murder case – intent: intent to kill. Knight's answers left no doubt as to his intention. Brian liked interviews of suspects being recorded on tape. It removed much of the argument that arose from type-written interviews, and, more importantly, the jury could hear the voice of the offender. Type-written records of interview would, traditionally, be read aloud to the court by a detective, generally in a dull, flat, monotone. The impact on the jury was reduced and they gained less of an understanding of the offender. Brian felt confident Knight's lack of feeling, let alone what he said, would make it difficult for a jury to consider anything other than a guilty verdict.

"Did you hit anyone with the M14?"

"Yes, think so. Cars would stop by the side of the road and someone got out (sic) ... and fired a shot and saw him drop."

"How many people did you see drop?"

"I saw one then I moved on to another fire position."

Robert Kovacs knocked on the interview room door. He told the detectives that it was urgent, that Homicide Chief Inspector Brendan Cole, was on the telephone. Knight asked to smoke; the two detectives left the room, irritated at the interruption. Once an interview was interrupted it was often difficult to resume in the same manner, to have the same rapport with the offender. They returned three minutes later and Brian explained why the interview had been interrupted.

"Our Chief Inspector said that there are, as far as he can tell at this time, six people dead and thirteen wounded, and it appears they were all people who were in Hoddle Street where you say you were firing your guns."

Knight made no answer, choosing instead to look down at the floor. McCarthy had to get the rhythm back into the interview.

"We got, from memory, I think we got to the stage where you were firing your M14?"

"Yes," answered Knight, barely audible.

Knight then explained that he had fired thirty rounds in Hoddle Street, at three or four cars and the motor cyclist. Brian was confused. He believed that, initially, Knight had said that he had shot the motorcyclist with the .22 Ruger.

"Was there only one motor cyclist that you fired at?"

"Yes."

"When we were talking before, it appeared as though you did that with your Ruger .22."

"No, it was with the M14."

Knight said that he saw a person drop to the ground outside his car after being shot with the M14. At this stage, Brian decided to go back to another point which he had felt was not the truth. If Knight had changed his mind on who was shot with the Ruger, then maybe he would say something different again.

"You said before that you had one round for the M14 in your pocket. You thought?"

"I definitely put it there."

"Did you?" Brian asked.

There was no immediate response and rather than upset the flow of questions again, he moved on. He felt at a decided disadvantage because of the six hour time limit. Brian asked Knight what happened then.

Knight explained that during a break in the shooting, someone fired a single shot from a handgun in his direction, "But it didn't come anywhere near me so I kept on firing. I just moved fire position and kept on firing."

Knight moved ten metres further along the railway line among the hedges. He reloaded and could see someone lying on the ground so he fired more shots at him. He stopped firing and then the shot was returned. Knight could see the flashing lights from police vehicles and assumed the shot came from them. He shot the motorcyclist, then fired at two cars and then jumped the fence of the railway station.

"I ran along the platform and kept going."

At this stage Knight believed he had approximately 25-30 rounds for the M14. He ran along the railway line and stopped under the Heidelberg Road bridge as the train had stopped on it.

"The train had its lights on me so I ... I think there was a power station house or something. It wasn't very ... red brick ... (sic) in the fork of the track and it sheltered me from the lights of the train."

Knight moved along the sloping side of the embankment and saw a police vehicle. He described a divisional van. He fired shots at the vehicle but was unable to see if any police were inside. He then moved parallel along the Epping train tracks and hid under the shelter of trees.

"I had a cigarette there, and waited and listened."

Knight finished his cigarette and crawled through the grass from where he saw two police cars parked by the side of the road near the High Street bridge.

He waited, and not seeing any police, he ran across the road. He saw the search lights of the police helicopter and fired three shots at it from the west side of High Street. Then he ran along the railway line towards Rushall Railway Station.

"I decided that I'd go to my ex-girlfriend's place in McKean Street and get her to ring you to hand myself in."

Knight ran along the fenceline parallel to the Old Colonist's Home in Rushall Crescent, North Fitzroy. He traced where he ran on the interview table, with his hands. He dropped to the ground and saw the police vehicle. While lying prone, another car, travelling in the opposite direction, swept its headlights over him. He thought he had been seen. With cars everywhere, he said, "I ran as fast as I could to my ex-girlfriend's place." Knight then hid in the lane nearby. Just as he thought the police might not have seen him, a police vehicle screeched to a halt just before the entrance to the lane, its headlights illuminating part of it.

"I realised I only had eight or nine shots left, and I still thought I had the one left in my pocket. I was behind the wall and they started yelling out. I could barely understand them. They were words to the effect to come out and put your hands up. I just popped up and let off what was left in the magazine."

"Where were you firing at?"

"At the police, at the actual van. I couldn't see the actual police, it was more or less covering fire just to keep their heads down. And then I popped back down and looked for the last round and couldn't find it. And that's when I put the rifle out into the beams of the headlight."

Knight demonstrated with his right arm outstretched how he had held the rifle by the breech.

"They were yelling to come out and put your hands up. I said, okay okay I'm coming out. Here's the rifle and ... "

With his mouth, Knight made a noise that resembled spitting. His outstretched hand released the grip of the imaginary rifle.

" ... dropped it in the alley and put my hands above my head. I was still shielded by the wall."

He demonstrated how he had placed his hands flat on top of his head and then gradually raises his hands above his head, palms open facing the detectives.

"I popped up and got about chest high above the wall with my hands in the lights of the car, and one of the policemen fired a shot so I quickly popped back down and said don't shoot, I'm coming out. I rose back up really slowly 'cause I thought they were going to have another shot, then the policeman came over and dragged me to the van and threw me on the bonnet."

"And do you know where that last round went to?"

"No."

"You haven't worked out where it went to?"

"No."

Knight wiped his nose and looked at the back of his right hand for a moment.

"Which pocket did you have it in?"

He said that the last round had been in the left pocket of his jeans. Brian asked to see the pocket and Knight turned slightly in his chair to show him. Brian was not convinced, but went on with the interview.

"You said that earlier in your life you had a desire to kill someone to see what it was like, or words to that effect. Is that true?"

"Yes. In combat."

Knight explained that he tried to emigrate to South Africa with the intention of joining the army there. At sixteen, he had written to the South African embassy. In answer to further questions, he said that his earliest desire to kill someone had been at the age of sixteen. He did not know why he wanted to kill. He had a desire to go where there was fighting – Central America, Afghanistan, the Middle East or South Africa. He wanted to go there to be in the fighting.

Knight explained that his father was a teacher in the army and had never had combat experience. His mother disliked the army and firearms.

"You are in the army now?"

"No. I was discharged about a month ago."

"Why was that?"

"Stabbed my company sergeant major – senior cadet, not a regular sergeant major."

He explained that he had spent twelve months in the army reserve before undertaking six months of officer training at Duntroon. He had had personality conflicts with the senior cadets and had clashed with instructing staff. They did not like him.

"Did you like them?"

"Not particularly. I got along with the system quite well, it was just certain people I didn't get on with."

At 4.30 a.m. Pamela and Sarah Knight were moved to the Townhouse Hotel in Swanston Street, Carlton, where they went to a room and waited for members of the Major Crime Squad to arrive. They took the opportunity to have the stiff drink that they each had wanted and Pamela talked about her dislike of Julian's fetish for guns. She believed that his guns were always loaded. She was unable to understand why he had flipped, as nothing untoward had happened to him.

Knight told the detectives that the stabbing incident occurred as the result of a beating he had received at a Canberra night club from senior officer cadets, one of whom he would stab with a knife.

"I went back later and stabbed him."

Knight said that he was charged by the police with three offences – malicious wounding, assault occasioning actual bodily harm, and assault. He was to appear at the ACT Magistrates' Court on 10 November.

"That resulted in your discharge from the Army?"

"Get out or we throw you out."

Knight resigned. In answer to further questions, he talked about having to leave his girlfriend, Meg Rummery, a typist, in Canberra as it was not financially possible for him to live there. They were to live together in a flat but neither had the money. Renee Cross had been his girlfriend for almost two years but they split up when he joined the army. She did not like the army, and when he returned to Melbourne she did not want to resume the relationship.

Knight had been back in Melbourne for six weeks. He and Rummery had mutually agreed to end their relationship because of the distance involved, some 500 kilometres. They had both been upset about ending the relationship.

"Has this got any bearing on this incident tonight?"

"No."

"The stabbing incident. Has that got anything to do with tonight?"

"No."

During the shooting, Knight explained that he could not see his victims in the car clearly, but he could see them. He said that he was greatly affected by alcohol and had had trouble changing magazines. He could not see the sights of his rifles due to the dark and the effect of the alcohol. He fell over many times and had found focusing difficult. Knight explained that he took aim using "natural alignment", a term used to describe taking aim using the natural alignment of the eye and the barrel of the rifle.

"Have you been trained to do this?" asked McCarthy.

"Yes."

In the army Knight had been trained to shoot in the dark and he had been trying to hit targets in Hoddle Street. He knew that he had shot some people in the street.

"Are you sorry that it's happened?"

"Yes," Knight said quietly.

Graham Kent turned another A4 page over and looked at Knight for a moment before continuing to write.

"I'm sorry SOG didn't get to me first," he added.

"That's what I was just about going to ask you. You said before you wanted to shoot yourself, commit suicide or ... "

"I'd prefer SOG to take me out."

"Would you? Why is that?"

"Better to die in combat than to take your own (sic)."

"Why is that?"

"Thing of honour, I suppose."

"Pardon?"

"Thing of honour," Knight repeated. "The last round was ... I thought the SOG would be there quicker (sic). When I started shooting at the helicopter, at the chopper, I thought there would be an SOG marksman in the chopper. I was practically staring in the searchlight waiting for it."

"So you really wanted to die?"

"Didn't bother me, hasn't bothered me for a couple of years now... I'm over-violent."

"How do you know that?" Brian asked, his arms loosely folded in his lap.

Knight paused.

"Being upset and having a few too many drinks. It's (sic) always ended up with violence. You can contain it to a point."

Knight explained that he had been upset about his car, financial troubles and ex-girlfriends.

"So that, associated with the alcohol you had, you think, triggered the situation off? (sic)"

"Mm."

"Do you think if you had not been drinking today it would have happened?"

"If I hadn't have been drinking it wouldn't have happened."

"Pardon?"

"If I hadn't have been drinking it would've happened."

"It would've?"

Knight's voice faltered, "Wouldn't have."

"You lost control of your emotions or..."

"I lost control altogether."

Knight added that he had not wanted to kill anyone until he had started to drink that Sunday. He had formed the idea for the first time about half-an-hour before he had left the Royal Hotel.

"I decided that I'd go home and get my weapons and start shooting. But at that stage I had no intention to kill anyone."

"When did you form the intention to kill anyone?"

"When they got in my sights."

"Apart from wanting to die did you have any other reason for wanting to kill these people?"

"No."

"Why didn't you just generally fire around the place, not dangerously ... "

"I wanted to see what it was like to kill someone," Knight interrupted.

"You wanted to see what it was like to kill someone?"

"Once the first windscreen smashed I just kept going."

"How did you feel when you knew you had killed someone?"

"I wasn't sure," Knight said.

Until Brian had told him that there were six dead, he was unaware of the number of people he had killed.

"The one I dropped, I thought I'd pretty well got him, and the motorcyclist, I thought I'd pretty well got him too."

"How did you feel then?"

"Didn't bother me," Knight answered.

Then, almost as if it was an after thought, he said, "Throughout the whole incident I thought, SOG would be here soon."

"Did you have some satisfaction from thinking that you would have killed or might have killed these people?"

"Once I heard what I thought was someone returning fire then I gained satisfaction from that 'cause I knew the gunfight was on then. And I knew there'd be rounds starting to come my way. The only fear I had was getting wounded and not being able to return fire because then they would just patch me up and I'd be stuck in a courtroom."

Graham Kent stretched across to Brian McCarthy's folder and wrote re-enactment. This prompted Brian to mention this to Knight who agreed to participate in a re-enactment. Brian then advised Knight that they had to appear before an authorised officer before the six-hour interview ended and get Knight's permission to interview him further.

"No problem," Knight said.

Brian was pleased to hear this as it gave them an opportunity to properly investigate the incident. Knight slouched in the chair, resting his head against the wall. Graham Kent lit him a cigarette and then took his foam cup outside to make him a coffee.

"White and one."

Knight asked to see his former girlfriend, Renee Cross. He did not want to see anyone else till then and he gave Brian her address and phone number. It would interfere with the investigation at this stage, Brian thought, and asked Knight if they could arrange it later that day. Knight agreed and they left him alone in the interview room while paper work was prepared in relation to an extension of the six-hour limit.

Rick McIntosh and Graham Kent walked Knight down the steps of the St Kilda Road police complex with Knight to the waiting CIB car parked around the corner. As they made their way to the car, a group of aggressive-looking men walked towards them. The detectives braced themselves but the men walked past them. The detectives looked at one another and inwardly breathed a sigh of relief.

At 2.05 a.m., Knight, Brian McCarthy and Graham Kent had carried out a video re-enactment in Hoddle Street, before getting an extension of interview time from the Melbourne Magistrates' Court. In the dark of Hoddle Street, Knight matter-of-factly explained what he had done. He had been firing at a rapid rate, then reloading and firing again, all the time moving quickly along the hedges and billboards. He had been lying prone on the grass when he shot at many of his victims, and was in such a position when a police officer fired a shot in return. He thought it had come from the vicinity of the swimming pool. Knight said that he ran "full pelt" along the platform.

"What was your intention when you were walking, running along here?" Brian McCarthy asked.

"Evade the police."

Brian McCarthy was intrigued.

"As soon as I heard that shot I thought the police were on to me..." Knight said. Part of his military training involved tactics of escape and evasion.

"Can't shoot you if they can't find you," Knight continued.

"You told us before that you had a desire to be shot," McCarthy said.

"Yeah. I still had ammo though."

"So you weren't prepared to be shot until you ran out of ammunition?"

Knight paused for a moment then said, "Oh, that's (sic), I wanted to keep on going until I ran out of ammo."

At 6.28 a.m., the two homicide detectives re-entered the interview room. Knight sat dragging on a cigarette waiting for them to return. Graham Kent went outside to get Knight a cup of water. Knight finished the cigarette and stubbed it in the bin. Brian McCarthy wanted to establish exactly how much alcohol he had been drinking. Police had been to the Royal Hotel where the licensee had said that he believed that Knight had drunk five pots of beer. This conflicted with Knights claim of fifteen pots.

"Karl bought me at least three, the other bloke-friend – bought me two, on top of what I spent there."

Knight, under further questioning, said that he had two cans of Foster's beer at his grandmother's house, a pot of beer at the Royal Hotel, a can of beer at his house, and fifteen pots of beer at the hotel when he returned a second time.

"Some of our men have spoken to your sister and she said you got home about nine o'clock and she saw and spoke to you. Is that right?"

"Yes."

"She said she's seen you drunk before and that you didn't appear to be drunk on this occasion. Would that be a fair assessment of your sobriety?"

"No. She only saw me briefly."

"She said that you appeared to be in a weird mood, not happy but not drunk."

"Drunk."

"How drunk do you think you were?"

Knight did not answer for what seemed a long time. He sat with his left hand in the palm of his right staring at the table, towards the notepad Graham Kent was using to write.

"Drunk enough to lose co-ordination of movements. Like bumping into walls."

Knight told Brian that he wanted to see a psychiatrist about his violent temper when he was still with Renee Cross the year before. Knight had stabbed his company sergeant major and had beaten Cross on one occasion.

"She was aggravating me and I lost my temper."

On both occasions Knight claimed to have been drinking heavily.

At 6.55 a.m. Brian McCarthy asked Knight if he felt that it was abnormal or unnatural to have the desire to kill people.

"I'd say unusual but not abnormal," Knight said.

He spoke as if he was chatting with two friends. He sat with his back and head up against the corner wall, his legs outstretched.

"Not everyone wants to do it but I don't think it's abnormal to have (sic)," Knight added.

There was a brief pause in the interview while Brian took stock. He wanted to make sure there was nothing he had omitted. Graham lifted his head from his notes and looked at Knight.

"Just along that line," Graham began, "Are you influenced by anything such as books or movies (sic) that you've seen or read?"

"No."

"Is it just something you developed yourself, is it?"

"Yeah. If I see, say, a documentary on, say, Angola or South-West Africa, then I know it boosts up that feeling. But seeing a movie like *The Wild Geese*, it's just a movie."

"Have you got any feelings of regret over these people dying?" Brian McCarthy asked.

"Yeah." Knight looked away from the detectives and along the pale wall.

"What do you think about it then?"

"I regret that it had to be civilians and I regret that I was captured rather than killed."

"Did you want to die yourself? Why didn't you then just go and commit suicide?"

"I wanted someone else to put the bullet through my head."

"Why?"

"I'd rather go down in a blaze of fire than do it myself."

"Why do you think that way?"

"More honourable to get killed in combat than to take your own life."

"Did you regard this as being combat tonight?"

"With the police, yes. When I shot at the helicopter I expected a return of fire because I thought there'd be an SOG marksman in there. I was disappointed when nothing came except it just flew off and came back."

"If you just wanted to die in combat with police why did you fire at civilians?"

"That's how it started off."

"Couldn't you have just fired a few shots around somewhere without hurting anyone and then attract the police that way?"

"Yeah I could have, in hindsight, but I didn't plan it. It wasn't a conscious thought, it was just a reaction. I walked out the front door into Hoddle Street and the first car I saw I started blasting away and I didn't stop."

Knight told the detectives that the only planning he did was for the Ruger to be used first. He saved the "larger stuff for later."

"More power, more fire power. A high rate of fire power," he said, referring to the shotgun and the M14.

"When you left home what was your plan of action?"

"I didn't have one," Knight said.

Knight picked up the white plastic cup and sipped at it, then replaced it on the table. Brian asked about the motor cyclist who had been shot and lay injured on the road. Why did he want to "finish him off" as Knight had put it?

Knight did not answer straight away. With his finger he picked at the corner of his right eye and looked across at the other wall, away from the detectives.

"It was always impressed on me it's better to be killed than to be seriously wounded, and this bloke sounded seriously wounded."

"So you thought he was better off dead?" asked McCarthy.

Knight barely nodded.

"And the persons on the footpath, the two of them, did the same apply to them?"

"Yes."

At 7.00 a.m., Detective Senior Sergeant Brian McCarthy suspended the interview to make some enquiries and advised Knight that he hoped to return to Hoddle Street to get a daylight re-enactment. He asked if Knight

wanted anything to eat or drink.

"No."

"You're right? You're happy?" Brian asked, as he rose to leave the interview room.

Brian placed his pen as a type of book mark in his folder, and closed it. He turned when Knight asked if he could have a newspaper to read.

"What do you want the newspaper for?"

"To see how this things been written up."

"Why do you want to do that?"

"I just want to see what the press, what the press have made of it."

Graham Kent continued to write notes while his senior sergeant left the room. Knight asked Graham for a light for his cigarette as Brian returned with the first and second editions of *The Sun*. Knight sucked on his unlit cigarette and moved the white cup aside for the newspapers. Brian talked to him about what he was going to do, but realised that Knight was focused on the newspapers, and was unaware that Brian had spoken to him and had left the room.

"Dressed in army clothes," Knight said.

Then, moments later, "In Ramsden Street as well, eh?"

"Shooting at ambulances too. Jeez they're good."

Knight dropped *The Sun*, as if in disgust, but before the newspaper hit the laminated desk his eyes swooped on it again. The newspaper had barely touched the table when he was hunched, absorbed over it again. Graham Kent watched from the other side of the table. He had not seen behaviour like this before.

"What do you think? Is that how it happened?" Graham asked Knight.

Knight straightened up in his chair shaking his head, his eyes still on the newspaper.

"I don't fuckin' believe these cunts. An M14 machine gun, pump-action shot gun, another shotgun," he said, incredulous that a second shotgun had been mentioned. "And a .22 rifle."

Graham continued to make notes and watch Knight as he read the newspaper. Knight turned the page and drank from his cup, his eyes never leaving the newsprint. He brought to Graham's mind a vulture picking at the carcass of a new-born lamb.

"Two at the railway station and two outside a nearby hotel," Knight said, referring to where four of his victims were reported to have been located.

"Two men were dressed in army-style uniforms. Did you ever get them? Or was that a goose chase?"

Graham looked up from his notes. He had not quite heard what Knight had said.

"Sorry?"

"The two dressed in army-style uniforms."

"No. This is something obviously the press have picked up as best as they can from what they overhear," Graham explained.

"M14 rifle and M14 machine gun is totally different," Knight argued.

"Have you read the headlines?" Brian McCarthy asked as he returned to the interview room. "What's your reaction to what they wrote?"

Knight shook his head taking his hand away from the unlit cigarette dangling between his lips.

"Cunts write the biggest load of shit. I dunno where they get all this crap from."

He spoke with venom, an anger that surprised the detectives.

"What are they saying?" Brian asked.

"Oh," Knight began, turning back to the front, his eyes still yet to leave the pages, "The whole thing is just – a lot of it is made up. Gets into shooting at ambulances, M14 machine gun. Pump-action shotgun, another shotgun and a .22 rifle. Two people found dead at Clifton Hill Railway Station, another two outside a nearby hotel."

Knight turned the first page, "Two men dressed in army-style uniforms."

Brian read a note left for him by his partner, placing it inside his black folder. He formally suspended the interview and asked Knight about extending the interview period, once again. He cautioned him, and Knight agreed to a further extension past ten that morning. The two detectives left the interview room while Knight continued to read the newspaper, dangling the unlit cigarette between his lips. As they were leaving the interview room Graham lit Knight's cigarette. Outside, Brian discussed the note that had been passed to him. Graham wanted to ask Knight some questions which he felt were important to the case.

"When you pulled the trigger, you say that's when you formed the intent. Does that apply to each car that you were shooting at or to the first time that you pulled the trigger?"

"The first time."

"You stopped and you've reloaded (sic) so that if you formed the intent the first time when you pulled the trigger, what was your intent the next time when you reloaded the magazine and aimed at a different car?"

"Same thing ... shoot at the people in the cars."

"By shooting at them, was it your intention to kill them?"

"Yeah."

"Does that apply to each time that you aimed your weapon at the car?"

"A lot of them were not well-aimed shots."

"The ones that were well-aimed shots, does that apply to them in that situation?"

"The only well-aimed shots were the two people I shot on the pavement and the motorcyclist. All the rest were just rapid-rate into the car."

"With your knowledge of firearms and your training, would you expect that, by firing into a motorcar the way you did ... "

"At a rapid rate," interrupted Knight.

"At a rapid rate – what sort of injury would you expect to inflict on someone being struck by a bullet, and what sort of nature?"

"A minor flesh wound. A .22, I doubt, would be lucky to go further than the panels. A shotgun might go through. An M14 would go right through."

"So when you were firing an M14 you'd certainly expect more than a minor flesh wound wouldn't you?"

"Mm, although it's surprising what the body can take."

"You'd certainly expect to injure someone, wouldn't you, if you fired at a rapid rate, a number of rounds into their car?"

"Yeah."

"And certainly the people who you were firing at, the ones on the footpath, when you were firing at them, did you have any doubt as to what would happen to them once you shot at them, if you struck them?"

"No. The first shot I fired I had doubt, but as soon as it hit its target ... "

"With your first shot, what was your intent?"

"There was no intent as such," Knight said taking his time to answer.

He shrugged his shoulders as if to indicate that it was just something he did, without thinking about it. He demonstrated the actions with his right hand which still held the cigarette between his fingers. "It was just sights, target, bang."

"The following shots, after you'd wounded the people – what was your intent with the shots that followed?"

"After I dropped them?"

"Yes."

"To finish them off."

"To kill them?"

"Yes."

"Anything else?" Graham asked Brian.

"Did you in fact know how many people you had hit in the cars?"

"No. The only people I knew I hit were those three."

In answer to Brian McCarthy's questions, Knight said that he had not seen anyone else in military clothing and that he had heard only two shots fired by others. He had not seen anyone wearing clothing like that of the Special Operations Group.

"Did you count the number of shots you fired just before you were arrested?"

"At that last incident in the lane?"

"Yes."

Brian was not convinced by Knight's explanation in relation to the spare round and his intent to suicide. There were many things which did not add up.

"No but...," Knight sighed then tilted his head back against the wall and looked up to the ceiling, " ... thinking back on it, probably about nine rounds."

Brian looked down at the desk and asked Knight if he fired the nine rounds at the police car. Knight said yes, and lit another cigarette.

He had fired at the two constables just as he had at all the others. At a rapid rate. He could not see where they were due to the muzzle flash, he had just fired in the direction of the police car. He believed that Delahunty and Lockman were hiding behind the doors of the police car on the road.

"Firing at such a rapid rate, the muzzle flash blocks everything out of view," Knight explained.

He used his right hand to demonstrate the rapid use of his trigger finger, the muzzle flash.

"I could hardly see, I just fired in their direction. Nine rounds took about two seconds to get rid of."

"Was it your intent to shoot the policemen to kill them?"

"No."

The two detectives looked up at Knight. It was an unexpected answer.

"What was your intent when you were firing at them?"

"I thought that they'd shoot back."

Knight said it would not have surprised him if he had killed the constables, given the close range and the fact that he was armed with an M14.

"So you were shooting recklessly as to the consequences (sic)?"

"Yeah." Then, almost as an after thought, he added, "I stood up in plain view."

"What was your purpose in standing up in full view?"

"They'd return fire. They'd let off enough shots." Knight rubbed his shin as he spoke. "They'd easily put two to three rounds into me. It was one of the reasons I wanted SOG to come because I didn't particularly want to lie bleeding in the gutter with a .38 slug in my heart, coughing blood up. I'd prefer SOG to take my head right off. Like I said, it is better to be killed outright than to lie bleeding, wounded."

The two detectives left the interview room and Knight went back to reading *The Sun*. He drew on his cigarette and hunched over the paper studying every word, every photograph.

At one point he picked up the newspaper and knocked on the interview room door, which was ajar. Graham Kent met him as he began to open the door. Knight showed him an article in the newspaper which carried a photograph of a sheath knife similar to the one that he had used at the nightclub on the senior-officer cadet.

In Queens Parade, Henry Glaser examined the walls of the Terminus Hotel. He found bullet damage on the north wall of the hotel and, on the ground, located fragments of an M14 bullet. Judging by the point of entry to the wall he reasoned that the bullet had been fired from the railway line along the Merri Creek, 120 metres further north.

26

It had been daylight for about an hour and Michelle Young had dozed off in her chair while Sarah Knight was having her statement taken by a Major Crime Squad detective. She started when she heard laughter.

"You were snoring," Sarah said, and she giggled, probably for the only time that day.

Michelle had worked seventeen hours straight and was to remain on duty for another three-and-a-half hours before she and her sergeant, Judy Cousins, could go home. They returned to Russell Street where Pamela Knight was met by her brother, Graham. While Michelle watched Julian Knight's relatives leave, she thought it interesting that, in the whole time she had been with the mother and daughter, there had been no hugging or other sign of affection or comfort. Pamela seemed to be on auto-pilot. Michelle thought that perhaps that is how most people would react in the same situation but for Michelle Young, at twenty-one and with less than two years service in the police force, it was unexpected.

It was daylight during the second re-enactment. The two homicide detectives and Knight started filming outside Knight's home, 6 Ramsden Street, Clifton Hill. The porch light was still on. Knight was told of his rights, something the detectives did at almost every break. If it could be shown that any evidence was obtained without Knight being fully aware, at all times, of his rights, then that evidence, no matter how valuable, could be omitted by the judge. Evidence which could mean the difference between a conviction and an acquittal.

The two detectives and Knight, hand-cuffed, walked through the crime scene. The air was cold so that little puffs of cloud could be seen as they spoke. Knight went over his actions, again, with Brian McCarthy. He could have been talking about the weather or the results of the weekend football matches, so casual was his manner. Graham Kent took notes of everything that was said. Brian was again concerned that the video recorder would not pick up their voices. They moved around the scene without entering the areas which had been roped off with crime-scene tape.

Knight would point to where he had secreted himself in bushes and to where he had seen his victims for the first time. He talked about what had happened to them when they had been shot. Standing on the footpath, opposite the body of the motorcyclist, Shane Stanton, Knight said, "He was moaning in agony and so I put another two rounds into him."

"What was the purpose in doing that?" Brian asked, just as he had in the interview room.

"To finish him off."

Knight pointed out where he had jumped over the cyclone fence and onto the railway-station platform. They walked to the main entrance of the railway station, where trains were still operating. Other police moved the waiting passengers away while Brian answered his pager and rang the homicide office. When he returned, he told Knight that his blood alcohol content had been analysed at .08 per cent. "Would you care to comment on that?"

"Sounds accurate," Knight said.

"It appears, from that reading you wouldn't have had the fifteen or sixteen pots and three cans that you said you had. Would you care to comment on that?"

"I recollect as having fifteen pots to the best of my memory."

They walked along to the northern end of the platform as a train pulled into the station. When it left Knight explained how he had jumped off the platform and run along a track on the west side of the train line. Knight said that he bruised his hip, which was sore, when he bumped it scrambling around an embankment. He was not sure where he had hurt himself. He had run along the track past the signal box and under the Heidelberg-Road overpass, then across the train tracks to the eastern side of the line, and then back across the tracks to where the Epping and Heidelberg lines separate. He had fired two shots at a police car which had entered Hoddle Street from High Street. Knight pointed out two cartridge cases from the M14, on the ground and between the tracks. He had reloaded behind a concrete block then raced to trees running alongside the Epping line – the detectives could see the downtrodden grass. Knight said that he had stopped to have a cigarette before crawling under a small channel fence, down towards the Merri Creek where he ran through some small trees.

Brian directed that they walk around this area. He was careful not to disturb anything. Knight stopped before the bridge showing them where he had run across the creek, over rocks, and up the embankment and under the bridge to the other side. Then up to the footpath at the top of the bridge where he had fired a shot at another police car. He had then run back down along the embankment to the creek, where he crossed the water once more, near the Rushall Railway Station.

Knight took them to the embankment where he had seen the police helicopter circling above. He had fired three shots at it while kneeling in grass on the eastern side of the tracks, while hidden among the trees. He had run along the worn track towards the railway station. He did not think that shooting at the helicopter would "bring it down." He realised that he had only nine or ten rounds left after that, and he had felt confused.

"I thought I'd go to ... I'd kind of half decided I'd go to my ex-girlfriend's place ... Renee in McKean Street, and hand myself in, and I was half thinking to shoot it out with the last ammo that I had."

He showed the detectives where he had crossed the tracks. He hadn't seen anyone. He followed the shared bicycle/foot path to the corner of the Old Colonist's Village. He had halted when he saw a police car in Queens Parade. He then ran between the row of trees and the fence and stopped at Rushall Crescent, where he could see two cars approaching on his right. On his left were the flashing lights of a police car in Queens Parade. Another car was approaching from Michael Street. It turned left into Rushall. When the two cars on his right passed, Knight ran across the road and into McKean Street where he ran along the footpath. He could hear the police car behind him travelling "at some speed."

Knight took cover in a lane and saw the police car screech to a halt. He saw the car doors fly open and he stood up and opened fire with the M14. The rounds would have gone straight through the doors. Knight said that the constables had no chance.

Knight demonstrated how he had bent down, his back against the fence and his body side-on to the police, how he had removed the magazine from the M14, and how he had searched for the round in his jeans pocket. He had refitted the empty magazine into the M14 and, in response to orders from the police, had stretched out his arms showing the rifle then resting it, butt-end down, on the ground. He then let it drop. He heard them scream at him to put his hands up in the air, to come out. Knight demonstrated how he had risen and then ducked when a shot was fired at him. He said that the police yelled at him again and he asked them not to shoot. Knight then indicated where he had walked out of the lane and to the edge of the footpath, where he was arrested.

"You've got a fairly good recollection of the events that happened. Do you agree with that?" McCarthy asked Knight.

"Yes."

"If you were extremely affected by alcohol you probably wouldn't have this recollection. Would you agree with that?"

Knight explained that in the past when he had been drunk he could still always remember what he had done, but that his co-ordination was affected by the alcohol.

"Is this the situation with last night?"

"A lot of things are just blanks. I can't remember where I came out or what direction I took."

In an office of the City Watchhouse in Russell Street, Knight was introduced to a criminal psychiatrist. Dr Allen Bartholomew had worked for many years at Pentridge Prison and was now in private practice. Knight spoke with Dr Bartholomew for an hour, commenting that he felt it was "too short."

Initially, Knight was charged with one murder – the murder of John Muscat – whose identity had been confirmed. He would receive further charges when the identity of the other victims had been established.

THE AFTERMATH

Noel Shiels

Paramedic Noel Shiels was one of the first ambulance officers to arrive at Hoddle Street. At great risk to himself and his partner, Peter Collins, he assisted in the rescue of several people, including Gina Papaioannou.

Noel Shiels went to the back of the bus where it was quiet and where he could gather his thoughts. The sun was bright and traffic was building as the bus travelled towards Elwood. Children on their way to school were giggling, talking loudly and laughing. Men and women on their way to work read newspapers or looked out of the windows. Nobody seemed to realise that things were different. He wanted to ask them, "Don't any of you realise what's happened? That things have changed?" Melbourne was no longer the Melbourne that he knew. It was now like New York or Chicago.

His thoughts returned to Gina Papaioannou as he had tended to her severe injuries, in the back of the ambulance. She told him that she had left her car to help. Outside the resuscitation cubicle he met Donna Randall, from the Prahran DSG, who was sitting by herself, crying. Donna said one word to him. "Why?"

He shook his head in disbelief, as if what he had been through had all been a dream. Three kilometres away people were acting as if nothing had happened yet he felt that all of Melbourne should be in mourning.

As soon as he could get to a phone he rang his wife Sally, in case she had been watching the TV or had heard about Hoddle Street on the radio. She had been asleep so he down-played the tragedy by saying there had been a small incident in Clifton Hill. He did not want to worry her, but the media was a concern. It exaggerated things and he did not want his wife and children to be alarmed.

Noel put down the phone and went to his ambulance, opening the hatch. Everything was a mess and he had no idea where to start. As he began cleaning up the back of the ambulance his pager, which he had lost somewhere in Hoddle Street, went off. He found it clipped to the side of the stretcher bed. It was 11.20 p.m. and he answered a call, a man had had an acute asthma attack. The controller wanted to know how soon they could be operational again.

Five minutes later, they raced toward Flemington to pick up the asthma patient. Noel tried to push everything about Hoddle Street out of his system. He found it difficult to remain focused, as all he could see were dead and dying bodies. He felt that he needed time to put the incident aside before attending any other jobs. He thought about his courage, and the fear that he had felt. Ambulance officers were not supposed to feel scared, they were tough, nothing should bother them. But he had been scared. He and Peter Collins did not talk about Hoddle Street. They were still in shock.

They went to Prince Henry's Hospital, where Noel learned that John Muscat had died. Then they returned to the ambulance depot, where Noel tried to sleep. As the day shift crews arrived he felt unable to talk and gave one- or two-word answers to their questions. A station officer, John Andrews, asked him if he was all right. He responded affirmatively but he was not feeling all right. Everything around him seemed to be unreal.

When Noel arrived home, his two children were watching cartoons while having breakfast. He was glad to be home but he couldn't say anything to anyone. He was tired, physically and mentally, and felt unable to tell Sally in any detail what had happened. He took the phone off the hook and went to bed where he tossed and turned. Just after midday he got up and put the phone back on the cradle. It rang almost immediately – a station officer asking about Hoddle Street, and how he was coping. Noel said that he was having four days off and would be fine.

Then the Public Relations Department rang and asked him to talk to the media but he refused, feeling that the ambulance service was more interested in good public relations than in the welfare of its officers. The phone rang with more requests from newspapers, radio and television. He declined them all and, in an effort to escape the calls, took his wife and children to Flinders beach.

By Wednesday, Noel felt that he was going insane. His body shook and twitched. He rang crisis counselling at the ambulance depot and was told his reactions were normal, that it would take time. He came home with his family and, on Friday, returned to work.

Other ambulance officers asked him why the police did not kill Knight. They said that they would not have let him get away with what he had done. They would have killed him. This was how Noel felt, yet if he had been violent, he would be stooping to the same level as Knight, and that thought was repugnant to him.

At the end of 1987, Noel qualified as a Mobile Intensive Care Ambulance Officer – a paramedic. It was as high as you could go in the ambulance service. Before he went on a month's leave he attended a call where a ten-year-old boy had shot dead another youth, using his father's rifle which had a bullet up the spout. When he returned from leave he resigned from the MICA unit. He had had enough and was taking to alcohol.

Despite regular counselling he still suffered flashbacks. He could not talk to other ambulance officers, as they believed that Hoddle Street was no different from any other shooting, except that it was on a bigger scale. Sally had to deal with his fallout and she gave him as much support as he would allow. He was placed on reserve and then in the roster office, losing several thousand dollars in salary and the prestige that goes with being the best. After a year he became a radio operator. It felt good to be able to get away from everything as he struggled to come to terms with his own mortality. Some time later he resumed duties on a standard ambulance unit and then he returned to the MICA section.

At the Royal Humane Society presentation ceremony, Noel looked around. Where were the John Waynes? They were just ordinary people who had been caught up in extraordinary circumstances. As he accepted his medal Noel felt humbled and unworthy. He felt that he could have done more and that he should not have been scared.

His nightmares are less frequent now. Noel believes that something inside him changed at Hoddle Street. It had to do with staring death in the face. He often wonders how he would behave if he was faced with a similar situation. There is no *Rocky* music in the background when people are confronting their fears.

Jenenne Stiles

Jenenne Stiles was one of the first police to attend the scene.

The divisional van pulled up outside the block of flats in John Street, Clifton Hill. It was the day after Hoddle Street and Jenenne Stiles was back on patrol. She looked across to Hoddle Street and saw the crime scene tape, and forensic police still in attendance. The cars were still there and the bodies were being removed to the Coroner's Court. She flashed back to the incident only twelve hours earlier. It had seemed to go on and on, you had time to get scared.

She asked the little girl if she had called the police and was told that she had called an ambulance. The girl was agitated and led Jenenne into a small flat where an old man lay dead on the floor. His eyes were glazed. She felt his pulse and touched his face which was cold and stiff. There seemed to be no escape from death and she felt the room close in around her, with people screaming and crying.

"Do something. Do something!" a woman pleaded.

Jenenne put her mouth close to the old man and feigned mouth-to-mouth resuscitation. The thought of putting her lips to a corpse made her feel unwell. She pressed down on his chest as she had been trained to do. She jumped at the sound of his ribs cracking, and stopped. She tried to get through to D24 on the portable radio but the battery was flat. All the batteries were being recharged at Collingwood, but she had hoped that there was enough life in her radio. Her partner, Rod Keuris, came in and pushed her aside to attend the old man, before, he too, realised that nothing could be done. While they waited for the ambulance, Jenenne took down the details of the old man in her folder. It was her first Form 83, a Report of Death, and she understood when his wife said that he had been frightened to death by what had happened the night before. She said that her husband was another victim of Hoddle Street. During the shooting he had been lying on the floor to avoid being shot.

Jenenne needed air and went outside where she removed her jacket and tie.

In the van she wanted to talk to Rod about how she felt, but took it no further when he seemed not to be listening. She put her head down and wrote up the running sheet, feeling an urgent need to talk to someone, but who was there to talk to? She wanted to speak to someone who knew about life, who knew about death. Someone who would understand from personal experience not just from reading text books.

She rang her sister-in-law and they met in a hospital carpark, where they talked. She kept hearing the old man's ribs crack, and worried that she was responsible for his death. She broke down and cried. She wondered if the police force was really for her. From the age of thirteen she had been obsessed with being a police officer, regularly visiting their careers office until she left school and joined at eighteen. The excitement and the variety were the attractions, not the salary or the security. Her sister-in-law reassured her that the old man was already dead, that she had not killed him.

Belinda Bourchier

As the Collingwood 303 team, Belinda Bourchier and her partner, Glen Sheluchin, were the first police to arrive at the scene. Using the divisional van to block the northbound lanes of Hoddle Street, they prevented an even greater loss of lives. Belinda struggled with Zoran Trajceski when he wanted her revolver to pursue the gunman.

It was all over but still everyone was on edge. Belinda had taken two lots of witnesses to Fitzroy Police Station. They all felt lucky to be alive. She grabbed overcoats from the police station and gave them out to those police who were inadequately dressed for the cold, night air. When she had the chance she sat in the police car and lit up a cigarette. If someone was to chip her about it, she wouldn't care. What was a cigarette after what she had been through?

She took the Coroner, Hal Hallenstein, and the Assistant Commissioner, Vaughan Werner, through the crime scene and watched the Coroner checking his watch as the doctor examined each body and certified it as being deceased. At 2.00 a.m. she returned to the Collingwood Police Station and drank some warm wine in the mess room to help her relax. There was a buzz about the police station, everyone was high on adrenaline.

The next day, Monday, Belinda was sent to a demonstration where she was pushed and prodded. She felt ill. Whatever she drank she brought up, and she just wanted to go home. Her mind was full of Hoddle Street. She felt that she could have done more, that she would do things differently if in a similar situation. She had received counselling from a police psychologist but felt that talking it over with her work mates was more useful.

She was having nightmares and would jump at the sound of a car backfiring. When someone came to her door she would panic, believing that she was going to be attacked.

In her nightmares she shoots Knight then finds that he is still alive. In one of her nightmares Knight wears a pinafore and is chasing her with a rifle.

She remembered Shane Stanton: seeing him die and being unable to help. She felt guilty for not having pursued Knight and her confidence sagged, making her feel that no one at her police station wanted to work with her. Even when the Divisional Chief Inspector shook her hand and congratulated her on the work she had done at Hoddle Street, she still felt that she had been inadequate. When she returned to work after the night shift six days off, she continued working the divisional van for another three weeks, until the pressure became too great. She took another week off. She questioned her commitment to the police force. She felt that her work was not important anymore whereas before Hoddle Street it was the most important thing in her life.

Bill Willis, the Senior Sergeant at Collingwood, tried to help her. He took her off operational duties and made her the Collator. Then his sub-charge asked her to leave the police station and to transfer somewhere else. She moved to Mt Waverley where there were ten incidents involving firearms within five months. At the last incident the offender was keeping the police at bay in a house. She gave another police officer, a trainee, a direction which he ignored, and she felt that his actions put her life and the lives of everyone else in danger. The reckless attitude of the trainee was the straw that broke her back. In 1991 Belinda Bourchier resigned from the Victoria Police Force.

Glen Sheluchin

Glen Sheluchin was the driver of the Collingwood divisional van, which was the first on the scene. Against the billboards he saw the silhouette of someone he thought was the gunman but, because he was unsure, he did not shoot at him.

As he pulled into the driveway of his Nunawading home, the lights were out. The house was in darkness and he wished that he had his service revolver with him. For a moment he thought he would be ambushed again and he rushed inside locking the front door behind him. He listened for any noise outside and then went to the bedroom and woke his wife. He told her briefly what had happened on Hoddle Street then snapped at her when she struggled to comprehend what he had experienced.

"You don't understand," he said.

He would not discuss Hoddle Street with his wife or with anyone else who had not been through the same or a similar experience. Only those who had been through life threatening situations could know what he had experienced. He felt that he had not benefited from seeing the police psychologist.

Some time later, he was home on holidays when he heard a loud bang. He took cover inside his house and watched the back flap of the tip truck slam against the tray as it delivered sand to his neighbour. His heart was beating fast and he wondered if he would ever escape Hoddle Street.

Glen Sheluchin has since resigned from the Victoria Police and lives in country Victoria.

Dianne Fitzpatrick

Dianne Fitzpatrick was one of the first victims. A .22 bullet was caught in the weave of her jumper without actually penetrating her back. She escaped the scene by heeding an inner "voice", which led her to safety.

Thinking that Dianne had been shot in the grounds of the MacLeod Repatriation Hospital, staff secured the doors and rang for the police. The switchboard at D24 began to erupt with calls from Clifton Hill, West Heidelberg, Preston and now MacLeod. All were reports of shots being fired.

Dianne Fitzpatrick was taken to the Heidelberg Repatriation Hospital by ambulance. When Resident Medical Officer, Dr Anthony Stubbs examined her, he found a bullet entwined in her jumper. The bullet had penetrated the flesh leaving a hole in the right shoulder blade. There was massive bruising around the wound. The x-rays revealed that no bullet fragments had entered her body. To be certain that the x-ray had not missed anything, the Surgical Registrar, Dr Manolas, explored the wound down to the muscle, then cleaned and packed the injury. Shortly afterwards, Dianne regained consciousness. The first sound she heard was a rattling noise and she felt the bed shake. She realised it was her teeth chattering and her body shaking.

She tried to get up but her legs would not give any support. A nurse tried to help but she brushed the nurse away.

"I can walk," she said, but the nurse grabbed her before she fell to the floor.

Dianne's daughter, Dawn, accepted the reverse charge call and knew immediately who it was. She had had a restless night worried that something had happened to her mother, and when she saw the morning papers she knew her mother had been at Hoddle Street.

The first thing she said to her mother was, "You've been shot haven't you?"

Dawn arrived at the nurse's home before 10.00 a.m., and was overjoyed to see her mother.

After several hours of fielding calls from the media Dawn decided that, in order to give her mother some rest, they would grant one interview.

The Age newspaper agreed to the conditions. The journalist and photographer were given ten minutes and published the article on Tuesday, 11 August.

Depressed and upset, Dianne wanted to be left alone but the media continued to harass her over the next four days. They all wanted the exclusive interview with pictures of her lying in bed, displaying her wound. By Friday Dianne was well enough to travel home to Rye, where it was peaceful, and where her address was unknown to the media.

Friends, clubs and organisations that she belonged to, even people she didn't know, sent Dianne flowers, telegrams and cards. Dianne was more relaxed at home but at the same time she was a prisoner. She was too frightened to go outside.

The charges laid against Knight required that victims' injuries be photographed. So, shortly after returning to Rye, Dianne had had to make the ninety-minute trip to the St Kilda Road Police Complex. The experience was another ordeal. The humiliation of being partially undressed and having to remove the bandage to be photographed was only made worse by the knowledge that Knight would receive copies of her photographs.

It took seven weeks for Dianne's wound to heal. Her wound became infected and she took anti-biotics but it was four months before the constant pain left her. Almost worse than the physical pain, however, was the pain of not being able to pick up her grandchildren. Even the simplest things, like making her bed or washing the dishes, became an effort. She became forgetful and lacked concentration and her blood pressure, previously low, fluctuated continually between high and low.

Community Services Victoria arranged for Dianne to see a psychologist. She was sent to Sandringham, more than an hour's drive from home, but kept only one appointment when told she was coping quite well.

On 8 December 1987 Dianne was at Northland Shopping Centre in Preston when the muzak was interrupted by a news flash. Eight people had been murdered in Queen Street, Melbourne. For weeks Hoddle Street returned to haunt her with almost the same intensity as it had four months earlier.

Dianne felt incapable of returning to work, but after four months, her leave entitlements were exhausted. She had taken half-pay to give herself time to fully recover, but when that ran out she had no choice but to return to work. The Crimes Compensation Tribunal awarded her $11,000 and it seemed that her age was against her. Other victims, including those who had not been shot, received $20,000 – but they were younger – in their teens or early twenties. She was sixty.

The superannuation fund that she belonged to would not allow her to retire and receive a pension.

Before she could return to work, Dianne Fitzpatrick had to retrieve her car from the Forensic Science Laboratory. They had had the vehicle for several months and when it was returned it had to be repaired. For much of the time that Dianne was without her car, Dawn provided the transport. Then, when Dawn's own car was involved in an accident, Dianne had to use taxis.

When Dianne returned to work in December 1987, it was an ordeal. To drive her car from the south-east to the north of Melbourne had become daunting. She felt that she would be shot again. By the time she had parked her car she would be sweating, and breathing heavily. Her hands would be damp and she could feel her heart thumping against her chest.

Dianne Fitzpatrick had intended to retire at 65 but she felt that she would not last the distance. She tired quickly and was always nervous. She kept feeling that something was about to happen to her, it affected her work performance. She had always enjoyed being a nurse and helping others but now it was a relief to go home. Well-meaning staff introduced her to others as "the lady who was in Hoddle Street".

On New Year's Day, 1988, Dianne was driving through Clayton. She turned from Heatherton into Clayton Road when a shot was fired across the front of her car. The feeling of being hunted returned but she continued on, driving to work where she quickly went inside. She was in a lather of sweat. The thought of ringing the police made her feel worse. She could not go through the process of being an official victim again, even though she knew it was the proper thing to do.

Dianne loved fishing and would often fish with the Rye RSL Fishing Club, but she could not go out after Hoddle Street. For twenty-five years she had played golf with the La Trobe Golf Club, but for two years she stopped playing. When she began to feel better and more in control of her life she returned to golf, but then someone would make some comment about Hoddle Street and she would lose her concentration.

Dianne's experience at Hoddle Street strengthened her faith in God. She believed that the voice that she had heard and followed had saved her life. Before Hoddle Street, she had feared death but she is no longer scared of dying. Dianne Fitzpatrick retired at 62.

Phil Bradley

One of the first police to arrive at the scene, Phil Bradley crawled on his stomach towards the victims lying near the railway station with detective Rick McIntosh. He also assisted in the rescue of Steve Wight, John Muscat and Peter Gauci.

Phil Bradley was supposed to sleep over at Russell Street Police Station as he was supposed to start at 7.00 a.m. that morning, but all he wanted to do was go home and be with his wife and family. The night shift senior sergeant Bob Leviere, asked him and his partner Gary Maddern, to clean the blood and dirt that covered them from carrying the injured, and from being on their hands and knees. He suggested they write down what had happened in case they forgot, so after changing their uniforms, the two made brief notes. They were released from their next shift and went home.

Inside his house his wife and children were sleeping. The house was in darkness and he turned on the kitchen lights and took out a bottle of scotch from the liquor cabinet. His wife approached cautiously, not expecting him home.

"What's wrong?" she asked, seeing his state.

Phil broke down and cried like he had as a small boy. Between sobs he told his wife what he had been through. All the while she listened and held him to her. It was the first time that he had ever spoken of his experiences at work. He had been to two cot deaths and several fatal accidents, which she knew nothing about. It was not the done thing among some police officers to tell your partner what you had experienced at work. The only other time he could remember crying as an adult, was when his sister lost one of her children to cot death. Phil showered and went to bed but did not sleep.

At work the following day, a police officer joked about getting blood under your finger nails. Phil exploded, calling him a fucking idiot – he had not been at Hoddle Street – and for a moment things were tense between the two. Phil left the room before he did something that he would regret.

At the end of his shift he hurried home, as that was the only place he wanted to be. He found his wife in tears. She had been watching news and current affair programs. Phil's photograph was on the front page of *The Sun* newspaper and his wife was upset. Now it was his turn to comfort her. His sister was also distressed and Phil started to feel that he was losing control of his life. He took the rest of the week off from work and remained home with his family.

His wife rang 3AW and spoke on talk back about the lack of support offered to her husband by the police force. Within days there was a debriefing at the St Kilda Road Police Complex but there was an attitude among police officers that seeing the psychologist was a sign of weakness. Instead Phil saw the police chaplain and felt better at having done so.

He had nightmares of Hoddle Street. He likened them to a video continually playing for there was no stop button. He would wake screaming, and shouting and would break down, crying. Then just as he would feel he was getting better, there would be an article and photographs of Julian Knight in the media, and everything would happen all over again. When the Queen Street mass murders occurred, they brought everything back.

His relationship with his wife began to go downhill. She was frightened that he would not come home one day, that she would be a widow.

Before Hoddle Street, Phil was a social drinker. He would drink, at the most, two stubbies a week, but now he drank every day to try to relax, to feel numb. As Christmas 1987 approached he knew that he was drinking too much, but didn't care. His attitude to life was more reckless.

He regularly thought of Gina Papaioannou. He could have picked her up and carried her to the ambulances on the other side of the road. He had read in the newspapers that Gina had gone to help Vesna Markovska and Zoran Trajceski and yet felt that he lacked the guts to help her. At the time, Phil had believed that if he and Rick McIntosh had gone any further they would have been killed. Yet in hindsight, he believes that he could have done more to help Gina.

In 1990 his marriage broke up. Hoddle Street was not the reason for the divorce but it was a major contributing factor, together with his job as a police officer.

He believes all firearms should be banned and, after Hoddle Street, disposed of his own .22 rifle and shotgun. He spent six years in the Royal Engineers of the Army Reserve, and gained a lot of firearm experience in that time. Phil is now an instructor in firearms and critical incident management with the Victoria Police.

Peter Collins

Peter Collins was a paramedic whose partner was Noel Shiels. At personal risk he rendered assistance to several of the injured, including Gina Papaioannou.

As Noel Shiels left for home, Peter remained behind and watched the morning news on television. He was too hyped up to go home just yet. He hadn't been scared at Hoddle Street, he had felt a sense of exhilaration rather than fear and he was conscious of being in a leadership role. He couldn't let the others in the ambulance branch down. He listened to the radio, channel hopping between 3LO and 3AW, to get more background information. As he drove towards his home in the outer reaches of Melbourne he felt reality starting to set in. He was coming down from the adrenalin rush and he began to feel a sense of disbelief about what he had been through. This was Melbourne, not Chicago. Such events happened to other people, in other countries – not to Peter Collins in Melbourne.

Over the next few days, Peter talked constantly with his wife, Kerry, about Hoddle Street. He felt it was good to talk about it as there was no counselling available to ambulance officers at the time.

On the Friday after Hoddle Street he was asked to attend a debriefing. A crisis counselling unit had been set up to deal with trauma experienced by ambulance officers. It took a while for the ambulance officers to open up and talk frankly, but Peter had left the meeting feeling that it helped to share the experience.

On 28 August, Peter went to the Homicide Squad offices to make a statement and as he looked at photographs of the crime scene, the severity of the incident really hit him. He felt worse leaving the office than when he was leaving the scene itself.

He agreed to help the producers of a television documentary about Hoddle Street believing that it would be a factual, behind-the-scenes account. Peter was angry with the finished product. It seemed to focus on the gruesome. It was the Julian Knight show with flashing lights and bells.

He was asleep in December 1987 when he felt Kerry shaking him awake.

"It's happened again," she said to him.

He found it difficult to comprehend another mass murder. He felt that the whole fabric of society was falling apart, that Melbourne was no longer innocent. He had attended at the bombing of the Russell Street Police Station, an incident he considered to be the first terrorist attack in the State. He wondered where society was heading.

At times, as he drives down Hoddle Street, he relieves the tension by pretending to duck under the dashboard and joking about it happening again. He feels contempt, anger and disgust for Julian Knight.

Margaret Kidd

Margaret Kidd was working at the watch-house counter at Fitzroy Police Station.

Margaret Kidd had been fielding continual complaints about the helicopters' noise or lights when she heard that John Delahunty had arrested Knight, and had been hurt and taken to hospital. Margaret felt bad about John being hurt as she had sent him out when he should have been on his way home.

After a sleepless night, she arrived for duty at the Fitzroy Police Station at 3.00 p.m. the following day. She needed someone to ask if she was okay. But no one seemed to understand that she had been involved and she was rostered to work the divisional van, which surprised her. Going out on the streets made her feel vulnerable. She believed that if she had been at Hoddle Street itself she would have resigned that day.

She saw John in the police station the following day. She saw his shrapnel wounds and she felt even more guilty about sending him out on the job. She had heard other police criticise John, behind his back, for missing, not killing Knight. John never spoke about Hoddle Street.

Margaret went to the Police Academy and watched John Delahunty and Ralph Lockman receive their bravery awards. After John had been presented with the Valour Award from Chief Commissioner Sinclair 'Mick' Miller, she kissed John on the cheek but felt uncomfortable being near him and felt even greater guilt when she saw the scabs on the back of his hand.

Margaret had joined the police force for life. A police officer was all she had ever wanted to be. Hoddle Street was the beginning of the end of her career. In 1994, when she was first approached to discuss her experiences of Hoddle Street, she broke down and cried. It was the first time anyone had ever considered her a victim of Hoddle Street. She continued to work in the police force for some time then became ill and has not returned to police duty.

Adrian Fyfe

Adrian Fyfe was one of two officers at the scene. He was on his way home when he took charge of the scene from Queens Parade.

Everyone was concerned not to make a mistake with Knight. There was not to be any chance that he would escape conviction because of a technicality. Whenever a police officer spoke to Knight, his or her first words were, "You are not obliged to answer any questions, as anything you do say will be taken down in evidence."

Inspector Adrian Fyfe organised traffic control around the arrest scene then went to the Clifton Hill divisional inspector's office, where, with other officers, he helped coordinate the police role at Hoddle Street. At 5.30 a.m. he left for home. He was due back at work at 1.00 p.m.

His wife knew not to expect him home on time. After seventeen years of marriage she knew that if the telephone did not ring it meant that he was delayed by some unfinished business. It was difficult to keep appointments and commitments. Adrian got home, feeling on a high, and told his wife what had happened. He tried to slow down but it was difficult. They placed a call to his wife's parents, who lived near the street where Knight was arrested, just to ensure that they were safe. Adrian went to bed but had trouble sleeping. He kept seeing the bodies; the cars in Hoddle Street. People laying in gutters, or slumped over steering wheels. He kept remembering the nagging fear that there may have been a second offender, and the feeling of being powerless to talk, uninterrupted, with D24.

For six months, he wrestled with the thoughts of Hoddle Street and believes that he eventually overcame them with the support of his wife, by not becoming too emotionally involved and by continuing his work with the Scouts and other community projects.

In the first week after Hoddle Street, Adrian forwarded a report through police channels recommending that various police officers be recognised for their bravery and actions at Hoddle Street. He submitted a separate report recommending Valour Awards for John Delahunty and Ralph Lockman. Later that year, he made inquiries as to what had happened to his reports and was shocked to learn that, apart from the report on John Delahunty and Ralph Lockman, his recommendations had gone missing. He was pleased that the Royal Humane Society recognised police and ambulance officers, and members of the public, in 1991, although he believes several deserving police officers were not recognised at all.

On 8 December 1987 Adrian Fyfe found himself in charge of another mass-murder incident. He was on duty during the Queen Street massacre and soon acquired the nickname of Disaster 150.

He considers Julian Knight a coward. He shot indiscriminately at innocent people but as soon as gunfire was returned, he quickly surrendered. He was no hero.

Adrian Fyfe is a police superintendent in country Victoria.

Mick Hogan

Mick Hogan was the D24 radio communications operator throughout the course of the ambush.

He got up from behind his desk, his shirt saturated with sweat. He was exhausted and he held on to the side of the desk for a moment to keep his balance. His whole body ached and as he put the headset on the desk top he felt his mind go blank. An Officer asked him to complete the Log before he went home.

"Get fucked!" Mick said, and he staggered out of the control room. He went to the toilet and washed his face, hanging over the wash basin for a moment. He tried to keep calm but inside his head he felt to blame for the deaths in Hoddle Street. He had not allowed ambulance officers into the area. He thought of a million things that he should have done and he fought back tears. As he was leaving D24, the senior sergeant and an inspector told him that he had done a good job. They said that Deputy Commissioner Glare had passed similar comments about him. This meant nothing to Mick. He believed that six people were dead and many injured because of what he had not been able to do. Mick changed into casual clothes, then headed to a barbeque area in the grounds of the Royal Melbourne Institute of Technology. He took beer out of an esky he carried in the boot of his car and skulled the first can in seconds.

There were about thirty police there; most of them had been at Hoddle Street or were from D24. Someone said, "We're here!" and everyone cheered. Colin Chambers was with his wife Dianne Smith. He showed everyone his jacket which had been slashed by an M14 bullet.

As he drank another can of beer, Mick Hogan began to relax but his thoughts kept returning to Hoddle Street and the pleas for help. The screaming, the requests that he couldn't meet. He remembered ignoring one call sign for another. The calls that he had ignored could have been more important than the ones he had answered. He would never know.

When Mick arrived home just before 4.00 a.m., his wife Sharon was waiting up for him. She had seen the news flash but was unsure if Mick had been involved. She had expected him at least an hour earlier. She had thought that he was more likely to have been on his way home than to have been in the control room and she had been worried for his safety.

Mick just collapsed in her arms, and broke down and cried. He kept repeating that people had died and he couldn't let the ambulance crews through to save them. That it was his fault. Sharon tried to get him to elaborate but he wouldn't.

"You wouldn't understand, you weren't there!" he cried.

Sharon had never seen Mick so upset before, even during training, when he had come home from the mortuary where he had seen the bodies of small children. He had cried then, for their own children were around the same age as the bodies he had seen on the stainless-steel trolleys.

Mick had been unaware of the availability of any counselling or debriefing. He feels that he could have benefited.

In 1990 Mick Hogan resigned from the Victoria Police. He believes the massacre at Hoddle Street was one of the reasons that he left. He now runs a small business in country Victoria.

Nearly ten years later, Mick Hogan is still affected and breaks off this interview, his body heaving with sobs and his hands covering his face.

Bruce Lowe

Bruce Lowe attended the scene with other police officers from the Prahran District Support Group and searched for the gunman along the Rushall railway line. A police officer who did not recognise him and thought he may have been the gunman, almost shot him.

Bruce had been present during the re-enactment and felt uncomfortable that Knight seemed to relish the attention he was receiving from the police and the media. It seemed that he was almost gloating about what he had done. Bruce was also affected by Knight's comment that, given the choice of two paths to Renee Cross's house, he had considered taking the right before choosing the left. Bruce had been on the right-hand path.

His wife, Tracey, a police officer working from the Caulfield Community Policing Squad, woke at 6.30 a.m. and sensed that something was wrong. Bruce had yet to come home and he always rang to tell that he was going to be late. She went to work and everyone talked of Hoddle Street and still she did not know if he was safe. At 10.00 a.m. Bruce rang to tell her that he was okay. She broke down and cried.

When Bruce got home that night he and Tracey went for a walk with their dog. Bruce was hyped up and wanted to talk about Hoddle Street, whereas Tracey wanted to shut it all out and pretend that it had never happened. She felt inadequate in dealing with the situation as he had seemed immortal to her. All of a sudden Tracey felt vulnerable and, from that moment on, would always worry about him while he was at work.

For weeks, Bruce tossed and turned in bed replaying in his mind what would have happened had Knight turned right, rather than left. Would he have ambushed him or called out, "Police. Don't move!" thus giving Knight the opportunity to shoot him.

He went with Peter Butts to the hospital and sat for a long time holding Gina Papaioannou's hand. Bruce thought about Shane Stanton who had been at school in Shepparton with his brother. He felt personally connected to everyone who had been at Hoddle Street. When Gina died he was there at the hospital with her family and he felt that he had lost someone close to him. He became depressed, relying on more and more alcohol and he became security conscious. The windows and the doors were always locked and he slept with a baseball bat under the bed. He would wake up sweating several times during the night.

When Bruce and Tracey had children they decided not to have any firearms in the house. It was a big decision for Bruce as he had been a duck hunter and had been involved in clay target competitions since childhood.

Now he is a fisherman. You don't need guns to fish in the bay.

Tim Edgeworth

Tim Edgeworth drove an unmarked police car along the footpath to help Gina Papaioannou and, later, with other District Support Group police, located two of the weapons used by the gunman.

About two weeks after Hoddle Street, Tim experienced what he describes as a flash, making him feel that he was going to be shot. He was on leave, and maybe it was all the time that he had to himself that set things off. He had been a police officer for seven years and this was the first time he had ever had this thought.

Tim was in the toilet when the first flash occurred, and he felt very vulnerable. He imagined someone kicking open the door and shooting him. The flashes continued when he was driving his wife, or having a shower. He kept these feelings to himself as he didn't want to worry his wife, Virginia, and he felt that they would soon pass. He would lay awake waiting for someone to shoot him in his bed. He put a .22 rifle next to his bed, just to feel safe.

Tim began to dislike being on his own. It got so bad that if Virginia left the room he felt panic. He gave up walking his beloved dog. He gave up riding his motorcycle for fear of accidents. He stopped playing football which he had been doing since he was thirteen. He had been an active cricketer, golfer, and weight lifter. All this stopped and his weight went from 90kg to 107kg.

He contracted flu and experienced headaches. He saw a police psychologist, wishing that he had done this earlier, but there was a stigma attached. Even as he approached the psychologist's rooms and waited there, he was concerned that he might be seen by someone who knew him. You were considered weak if you saw a psychologist

He did feel significantly better after seeing psychologist Sue McNulte who gave him a two-page document to read on post-traumatic stress. However, he felt a constant pressure in his head and, for ten days, stayed in bed. He felt what seemed like a muscle spasm in his head and it began to alarm him. At night he slept with a walkman radio to keep his mind occupied. He took Serapax to help him sleep, although in the morning, the first thing that would enter his mind was the feeling that he was going to die.

Five weeks after Hoddle Street, Tim took his dog, Diesel, for a walk again.

Tim found it hard to remain still for more than a few seconds. He paced around and his fists were often clenched. There was tension between him and Virginia, and they had virtually no sex life, even though she was supportive and understanding of her husband.

He took up smoking roll-your-owns, smoking thirty a day. He carried the document Sue McNulte had given him everywhere he went. He turned to drinking heavily, and didn't like to leave the house.

When he left the DSG Tim returned to South Melbourne Police Station and to the divisional van. He couldn't shake the feeling that he was going to be shot, even when he was in the car with Virginia. Tim realised that his days as an operational police officer were numbered.

At one time Tim plotted revenge against Knight. He believes that Knight has no idea of the havoc that he has caused to the lives of his victims, their families and their friends.

When Tim had joined the police force he was admitted, during training, to the police hospital for an ankle injury. A 40-year-old police officer, a patient, had gone berserk while he was there. He warned Tim to get out of the police force while he had the chance. The job would send him crazy. Tim now knows what the police officer meant.

Tim transferred to Wangaratta Prosecutions, where he worked for several years, before returning to Melbourne. Eighteen months after transferring to Wangaratta Tim began to feel that he was finally moving towards recovery from Hoddle Street.

Donna Randall

A member of the Prahran District Support Group, Donna Randall attended to Gina Papaioannou and went with her in the ambulance.

At the Alfred Hospital Donna Randall had watched as medical staff attended to Gina Papaioannou. She went to a telephone and rang D24 advising them where she was and asking for an update on her partners. She told the operator that she was treating the hospital as a secondary crime scene. Donna had then checked the various departments at the hospital trying to account for every person who had been involved in Hoddle Street. She had seen blood on sheets and clothing and on people she did not know, and she tried her best not to be sick. The sight of blood had, in the past, caused her to faint.

She returned to Prahran Police Station where everyone wanted to ask her about Hoddle Street, but all she wanted was some space, to be left alone. She went to her flat where her boyfriend, Matthew, waited. She felt better after being comforted by him but still she had a restless night.

The following morning, Donna rang her father. He had not heard the news and she told him briefly what had happened, reassuring him that she was fine. He rang her back after getting the morning newspapers.

"You come home, little girl," he said, fighting back the tears.

Donna showered and went to her parents' house, two streets away. She told them that her love affair with the police force was over. From the age of six there had been no other job that she had wanted. It had been her life but suddenly Donna realised that she was no longer infallible. Her father cautioned her about making any rash decisions.

Donna was owed four rest days and went skiing at Mt Bulla. She was exhausted the first night and slept soundly. Then on the ski lift she suddenly felt scared and began to cry. A lift attendant came to her rescue helping her off when she could not move herself. Donna was scared of getting hurt. Nothing had frightened her until Hoddle Street, she was physically and mentally prepared for anything – or so she believed. She had been "a gym junkie", and she would run between three and five kilometres daily. She had coped with the heavy workload of the DSG – there was an arrest every day. And now she felt herself fall apart on a ski lift.

Donna made no arrests for two months when she returned from Mt Bulla. She had lost her drive and enthusiasm for police work.

She became aggressive and developed an explosive temper, when normally she was more controlled. In one incident, a man was urinating in the park. Donna called him to the van and he replied, "When I'm finished." He made a disrespectful remark which Donna couldn't recall. She went over to him and punched him in the face. Her partner was shocked and tried to calm her. Donna was also shocked. She could not believe what she had done.

Donna received messages to contact the police psychologist, but she ignored them. She was due to face a board, for entry into the Criminal Investigation Branch, and she felt that it might go against her if it was known that she had seen the psychologist. Donna asked to work the divisional van as often as possible. Even though she didn't want to make arrests, she needed the arrest figures to prove her worthiness as a detective.

When news of Gina's death reached her, Donna was devastated. She had visited Gina on two occasions and was confident that she was going to live. Gina was not supposed to die, she was not expected to die. She wanted to go to the funeral but there were commitments within the squad which had to be given priority.

After the CIB Board interview she saw Sue McNulte, a police psychologist, but Donna felt no improvement except relief that the messages to contact the psychologist stopped. She went to aerobic classes, and, instead of completing her usual two sets, she was unable to complete one. Hoddle Street kept reappearing in her mind. She felt guilty about being alive while others were dead.

Donna continued to have nightmares. One recurring dream took place in a department store. She was being shot at. Her mother was there too, but Donna was unable to help her.

Donna received an A rating from the CIB Board and in September 1988, transferred to Brighton CIB. Everyday she would drive for an hour to work, feeling that she would probably be killed on the way. There she was working with an all-male team who she felt were not really accepting of a female in their midst and her lack of previous detective experience was also a hindrance. She was always depressed and took to drinking alcohol.

When news of the Walsh Street murders reached Donna, she broke down and cried "like a big baby". It was particularly difficult for her as she had worked with both police officers. She started to feel responsible, as though she were the jinx, when police she knew were hurt or killed. She was referred to a psychiatrist and she saw him weekly for six months. During her first appointment, she cried for what seemed like hours.

She was given leave, placed on medication and diagnosed with post-traumatic stress. She felt a gradual improvement.

During the first four months, no one from the police force contacted Donna. Then she was visited by someone from the District office who told her to return to work, that there was nothing wrong with her. Donna had felt that because of the time lapse between Hoddle Street and when she stopped work that people thought she was malingering and making up her feelings of being unwell. She wanted to return to work. Sitting at home did not suit her.

Donna returned to work, completing detective training school, an intensive course of study over three months, which she struggled to pass. However, Donna asked to go back to the uniform branch, at Rosebud, close to home. She had, by this time, married Matthew, now a detective at Rosebud CIB, and she felt her life return to normal.

When Donna was pregnant with her first child she became the collator at Rosebud. She helped some victims of a shooting at Tootgarook and found it was good therapy. They respected her because they knew she had been a survivor from Hoddle Street.

Donna gave evidence at the Crimes Compensation Tribunal. She found the Tribunal intrusive, with such questions as how had Hoddle Street affected her love life? She received $7,000 in compensation.

It became clear to Donna that she could not stay in the police force. She had always known it since that night in Hoddle Street. On 12 August 1991 Donna resigned from the Victoria Police. It was a sad day.

Danielle Kissas

Danielle Kissas was with Alan Jury and Monica Vitelli when the gunman ambushed them.

Monica Vitelli and Danielle Kissas did not know the driver who had volunteered to take them to St Vincent's Hospital, and they were scared. The ambulances were transporting more urgent cases. Danielle worried that the driver might even be the gunman himself. Even at the hospital Danielle didn't feel safe.

Then a police officer sat beside Danielle and took her statement. She kept looking around the casualty section anticipating that the gunman would reappear and start shooting again. She smoked cigarette after cigarette and chewed the inside of her lips, then her fingernails. She rang Frances, her sister, and told her not to ask any questions when she got home, and to protect her from their father. He would not believe her story even if it was the truth.

She caught a taxi and lay, sobbing, across the back seat. The turbaned driver was reassuring and comforting as she told him that someone had been trying to shoot her. When the driver pulled up outside the Broadway Nightclub he declined the fare. Inside, she met her friend Avril and downed a whiskey and sat for the rest of the night by herself, talking to no one. There would be no dancing that night.

When Avril drove Danielle home, her father got up, angry that it was 4.00 a.m. and that she had broken her curfew. She tried to sleep but was terrified. She went to her sister's room and joined Frances in the single bed. Frances held her tight, reassuring her as she had done when they were small. Danielle went to sleep as the dawn was breaking.

Danielle's father did not believe that she had been involved in Hoddle Street, even after watching the news on television. He would not allow her out again but she sneaked out and caught a taxi to Carlton, where she was meeting Monica Vitelli and her parents. She lay across the back seat terrified that she would be shot at again. When a car backfired she felt that her worst fears were about to be realised.

At the restaurant they sat at the back, away from the windows. Alan Jury was there, and he and Monica discussed the interviews that they had given to the press. Danielle did not want to hear about it. When she returned home she knew that she could not sleep alone in her bedroom anymore. She shifted her bed back into Frances' room and felt safer.

She became moody and lacked patience. For the first time, she believed there was a God. There was something up there, something that made her shift her seat and sit behind Monica. If she had remained where she normally sat she would have been killed.

Alan and Monica encouraged her to appear in the ABC documentary on Hoddle Street. She was reluctant to participate and appeared before the cameras only after drinking too much.

She stopped seeing friends, becoming a loner and preferring to stay at home.

Danielle's attitude toward men changed. She found herself disliking men and she thought it was perhaps related to Knight.

Danielle is married, but separated, and has one child.

Steve Wight

The caretaker of the swimming pool opposite the railway station, Steve Wight called for police to attend, and was shot while going to help others already shot by the gunman.

Steve Wight tried to stay conscious and alert. He felt cold and alone despite the ambulance officers in the front and Peter Gauci beside him on another stretcher bed. He tried to talk but could only manage a whisper.

"I hope they shoot the bastard."

No matter what happened he could not, would not, unclench his fist. The pain in his body was immense, but his mind remained focused on his fist. He had to keep it closed tight.

At Prince Henry's Hospital, he sensed the urgency of the nurses as they cut off his clothes and covered him with a foil blanket designed to keep him warm. It was useless. He thought of his wife Lucy and his step-son Jesse, and he wondered if he would ever see them again. A nurse tried to unclench his fist but he resisted.

"The chlorine gas," he said, weakly. "It has to be switched off."

The nurse did not know what he meant and left him. A police officer heard her mention it to other nurses and knelt beside Steve asking about the gas. Before leaving the swimming pool he had turned on the chlorine gas which cleaned the water. If it was left on for more than an hour, swimmers would receive burns, and their hair and bathers would be bleached. Steve tried to say that he had the keys to the pool in his fist, but was unable to speak. He gradually relaxed his fist to expose the keys and managed to whisper who to contact. He also whispered his father's address. He wanted someone close to break the news to Lucy.

He could hear doctors in the next room working unsuccessfully on the body of John Muscat. His death made Steve feel distraught, at a loss to explain why innocent, unarmed people had been shot. He strained his neck, concerned to locate Peter Gauci. He was relieved to see him breathing.

Lucy reached Steve in the early hours of the morning and was shocked by what she saw. He had yet to be cleaned by medical staff and was covered in blood and had tubes attached to his body. Steve's parents arrived, and they comforted one another.

Steve felt intense pain but was unable to scream. Lucy was his only comfort as he lay on the hard mattress waiting for surgery. She clutched his hand.

Steve felt himself float near the ceiling as the thoracic surgeon repaired his wounds. He felt colder and colder as his body shut down. His lungs were reinflated and he felt pain down the full length of his spine. He was sure he was going the same way as John Muscat and he wanted to cry.

The long process of recovery began when he regained consciousness. A doctor told him that he had died on the operating table but his fitness, his twenty years of being a water-polo player (he had represented Victoria), had saved him. He had a bullet graze on the left side of his forehead where metal fragments were cleaned away, his right lung had been punctured and a rib had been fractured. The bullet had missed his heart by two centimetres but had embedded itself in shoulder muscle near his spine. The surgeon was unable to remove the bullet.

Steve's return home from hospital marked the beginning of the end of his marriage to Lucy. He became short tempered and aggressive. On one occasion he struck her. There was a constant high-pitched, whistling noise in his ears and he slept poorly. The hearing in his right ear had diminished 5 per cent.

In late 1987, as Wight was leaving for a tinnitus self-help-group meeting he witnessed a serious car accident outside his Coburg house. Instinctively he ran outside to give first aid to the injured pedestrian. He directed traffic away from the injured man. Lucy was already bitter that he had put himself at risk at Hoddle Street and this event caused the bitterness to erupt again.

In the area where the bullet had grazed his forehead he suffered from headaches which would last days at a time. Medication gave little relief. His right shoulder ached constantly. He would startle at any sudden, loud noise. When Jesse crept up behind him saying "Boo!" the child could not understand the hostile reaction from his stepfather.

Steve was depressed because he had survived the ambush while others had not. He felt guilt for exposing himself to danger that could have ruined his family's future. He wanted to work and provide for his family, and continue playing water polo, but felt uncertain that he could fulfil his responsibilities. He contemplated suicide. He contemplated taking his family's lives to rid them of the pain he was causing them. His weight rocketed from 85kg to 96kg.

During the immediate nine weeks he spent recovering from his injuries, Steve waited for WorkCare payments to come through. He arranged to have his mortgage payments suspended until he received the cheque and when it arrived, he immediately paid it into the bank. The manager advised that he had to pay interest because he had been unable to keep up the payments as required.

He had nightmares of being shot at. He left Lucy and moved in with his father because he feared he would harm his wife and children. Not with a rifle but in a car accident. He suffered mood swings and chest infections. When he went jogging he felt pains in his chest. He was always in pain. A year later, people thought that he should be over Hoddle Street. Steve felt frustrated that their reality seemed to be based on television or films where the victims don't suffer for long.

As part of the Memorial Service for Hoddle Street victims in November 1987, Steve Wight poured dirt over newly planted trees. He felt that it symbolised burying the past. It was time to get on with his life.

In 1989 he and his wife Lucy separated for good. Since 1993 Steve Wight has been living on WorkCover payments. In 1996 he enrolled at La Trobe University in an effort to improve his chances of rehabilitation. WorkCover declined to pay the fees incurred but reversed the decision. For Steve, it was a victory and he felt positive about his future. However the Dunblane and Port Arthur mass murders depressed him and he deferred his studies a year. He and his partner Julie have a daughter, Stephanie.

In 1991 Steve Wight was awarded the Bronze Medal of the Royal Humane Society of Australasia.

Alan Jury

Alan Jury was with Monica Vitelli and Danielle Kissas when the gunman ambushed them. He received minor wounds

Alan Jury returned to his mother's flat in Northcote, where he had been living, by taxi on Monday morning. The hospital had contacted his mother and told her not to come in and he found her in a state of shock. He had antiseptic bandages on his chest and neck wounds. The hospital required further x-rays so he went in again. The media contacted him and he was happy to talk to them. Weeks after Hoddle Street the reality started to hit him and he realised just how lucky he had been. He became less trusting and less caring of his friends. He felt lethargic, losing the will to work, and deciding that life had handed him a lousy deal. It would be so easy to die.

He moved to Perth. He contemplated suicide but caring too much for his family to carry it out, but still suffered anxiety about being shot while driving or in the bank.

Alan started a new job in which he was forced to go out and meet people. In this way, he began to recover from Hoddle Street and adopt a more positive outlook on life.

Giovanni Di Vincenzo

Giovanni Di Vincenzo was the stationmaster of the Clifton Hill railway station. He assisted Constable Domenic Cannizzaro during the ambush.

As he travelled home the incident replayed in Giovanni's mind every kilometre of the way. He thought of what could have happened if he had done things differently, if others had done things differently. Would it have made any difference to the numbers of people killed and injured?

At his home his distressed wife wanted to know what had happened. She made him tea and tried to comfort him but Giovanni could not relax. He paced up and down the corridor of his house and when it was daylight he went to a doctor for something to help him relax. He was required at work that afternoon and wanted to be able to perform to the best of his ability.

The telephone rang continually with journalists from all over Australia and New Zealand wanting his story. All he wanted to do was come to grips with what had happened. He politely declined all requests but there was no respite from the calls.

When Giovanni arrived at the Clifton Hill Railway Station for the afternoon shift he was met by a sea of TV, radio and newspaper reporters. Giovanni tried to get away from them but they persisted, wanting to know everything that had happened, but his mind was elsewhere. It was on World War II, when as a young boy living in Ubruzzo, Italy, he had witnessed his village being bombed by the Germans. Everything was destroyed but the church. He remembered seeing people killed and he felt a chill down his spine. It was the same chill that went down his spine in Hoddle Street.

His mother was the head of the family as his father was a prisoner of war in Africa. A drunken German soldier who was shooting wildly about his village, was killed by a partisan. The Germans marched everyone from his village into the snow and over a mountain. The villagers who did not die of exposure or hunger were shot. Giovanni saw his doctor again and was given time off. He took warm baths and listened to soft music, and the sleeping tablets seemed to be effective. He had never taken such medication before and at first they made him feel like he was drunk. But they gradually lost their impact. Giovanni would sleep for half an hour then wake up in a lather of sweat, unable to go back to sleep. For the first time in their married life, he and Lina argued. If she hadn't been so very understanding, Giovanni believes that their marriage would have been over. He used to play squash on a regular basis but could not get motivated to play again after Hoddle Street, even though he knew it was great for ridding his body and mind of tension. He cancelled their annual holiday and stopped playing golf at his club, where he had played weekly over several years. He returned to golf five years later. His mind wanders, his concentration span is weakened. At work when detonators are being used he is jumpy and nervous.

Paul McNichol

Paul McNichol was a Collingwood sergeant who pursued a vehicle thought to contain the gunman and who later assisted in taking charge of the scene at the Mobil service station.

When Paul McNichol came home on Monday morning he told his wife that he was a chicken. His training at the sub-officer course taught him to look after his subordinates and preserve the scene. But there had been nothing about being a target and going off in the pitch black after a gunman. When it was all over Paul ensured that the names of all the witnesses were obtained, that the traffic was diverted and that he had sufficient information to hand to the Homicide Squad. He walked up Hoddle Street to see what had taken place, leaving his cap in the car. It was a beacon to any other gunmen who might be out there. He sent a police car back to Collingwood to get overcoats for everyone. At first he hadn't felt the cold but with the adrenalin subsiding, it had started to affect him.

Back at Collingwood, upstairs in the mess room, the police officers were buoyant with the news that Knight had been arrested. Everyone was still high on adrenalin, laughing and joking. Paul thought back to Hoddle Street and immediately felt a sense of shame come over him. He was ashamed that he had not crawled on the ground, like Rick McIntosh did, to go after Knight and check on the casualties. It was then that he realised he was not a hero, and that he wasn't paid enough to get that close to getting killed. He also did not know the Clifton Hill area and felt that he would have been a liability to others if he had tried to do more. He had done the mundane things, like keeping traffic at bay and preserving the scene.

Paul submitted a report recommending that Belinda Bourchier and Glen Sheluchin be given a commendation for their efforts but he never received a reply. He believed that they prevented a lot of police charging off to almost certain death, by remaining at their vehicle and keeping D24 informed.

Kevin Farmer

Kevin Farmer was the husband of Tracey Farmer, who was murdered in their car as they drove along Hoddle Street.

The next day, Kevin Farmer went to the St Kilda Road Police Complex where he made a statement to Rick McIntosh. It was difficult for them both. Rick had never taken a statement from a man who had witnessed the murder of his wife and he led Kevin as tactfully as he could through the events.

When the statement was taken and signed, Kevin asked when the body of his wife could be given over to the family for the funeral? Graham Kent, the detective in charge of the case, rang the Coroner's office and was told that Tracey would have to be formally identified before her body could be released.

In 1987 the State Coroner was situated in the Flinders Street Extension, on the south side, over Spencer Street. It was a cream brick building covered in dirt and grime from years of neglect and pollution. The dilapidated building housed the Coroner, Hal Hallenstein, the courts, the mortuary, offices for the clerks, police, mortuary attendants and the viewing room. Every room seemed to carry the smell of preservatives, disinfectant and death.

Kevin approached David Stevens, the clerk, an efficient man with a gentle manner, and he was taken to the viewing room window. Inside the room, his wife's body lay covered with a sheet. The mortuary attendant waited for David to pull back the red curtain. Kevin Farmer did not want to see his wife as he had last seen her, and was stricken with grief. His knees buckled and tears streamed down his face. It was almost too much for him but he had to go on. David Stevens touched him on the shoulder. The curtain was drawn back and the sheet was removed gently from Tracey's head.

"That's her," Kevin gasped.

He was overcome with emotion and relief, grateful that the mortician had done his work with great skill and her body had been positioned to hide some of the damage. The attendant replaced the sheet and David Stevens closed the red curtain.

Almost a year later, Kevin Farmer returned to the Flinders Street Extension for the inquest into the death of his wife and six others. He watched as Knight sat, without apparent emotion, throughout the hearing. Reservist, Alice Cairns, sat beside Kevin, as she had heard that he wanted to kill Knight and she wanted to be there to comfort him.

When Knight's counsel, Richard Pirrie, said, "I am instructed that my client wishes to take this opportunity to express his deep regret to the relatives and next of kin of the deceased and all those affected by these insane and tragic acts," Kevin Farmer looked across at Knight, as did other survivors of Hoddle Street. There was still the same detached, emotionless expression on his face. The court was packed with detectives and police, there to protect Knight, but where, Kevin wondered, was the law when the public needed protection from Knight.

The Coroner found that Knight had contributed to the seven deaths. He could say no more as Knight was awaiting trial and he did not want to prejudice his fair trial.

Kevin and his brothers went to the Corner Hotel, in Richmond, a hotel which, ironically, was one that Knight frequented while a student at Melbourne High

School. They went into the bar and Kevin quickly got drunk. After several hours he could hardly walk and the barman asked them to leave. A fight ensued and the police were called and Kevin and his brothers were, after a struggle, placed in the Richmond divisional van. At the police station, Kevin wanted to continue fighting and tackled Senior Constable Leigh Wisbey, a three-time Asian and Australian powerlifting champion. It was the first time in his career that Leigh had been attacked. Kevin wanted a fight and spent the rest of the night in the cells. In the morning he revealed that he had acted out of frustration over his wife's murder and the seeming lack of justice in the world. Charges of assault were dropped.

Tracey Farmer's family
Val Corrigan

Val Corrigan was the mother of Tracey Farmer, who was murdered at Hoddle Street, and the grandmother of Adrian, 18 months, who survived.

Val Corrigan lay in her bed watching the 1988 Logies on television. There was something special about The Logies – seeing the actors, the producers and directors accepting their awards. It was for her, like most Australians, the closest she would get to experience the glitter, glamour and hype of Australia's equivalent to the Emmy Awards. During the nominations for the best news service of 1987 snippets were shown of various incidents that had occurred throughout the year. Suddenly, there on the screen, she saw Tracey, her daughter, slumped in the front passenger seat of her car in Hoddle Street.

Val Corrigan screamed, gasping for air, and ran out of the house barefoot and wearing only a nightie. She ran screaming down her street running in the direction of Bendigo Street, the studios of Channel 9. Then suddenly she changed direction and ran towards Bellevue Street where Tracey, Kevin and Adrian had lived. The neighbours who had been her watch dogs came out of their homes to see what was happening. One of them, Carol, ran to her and comforted her, persuading her to come inside where it was warm and they could have a cup of tea.

Val used Carol's phone to ring the television station, requesting that they not repeat the segment featuring her daughter. Val could not believe a television station could do such a thing. She was told it was not possible and during the weekend she stayed away from the TV for fear of seeing the segment repeated. On the Monday she contacted her local Member of Parliament, Theo Sidiropoulos. Soon after, the promo for Channel Seven News which won the Logie that year was dropped.

Tracey was brought up by her mother not to be pushed around. Some of her friends knew her as the angry ant because what she lacked in height she made up for in attitude. Tracey was six weeks old when her parents separated.

Kevin held Val to him and told her that Tracey, Val's four-foot eleven-inch bundle of dynamite, was dead. She could not believe her son-in-law and demanded to see Tracey. A nurse explained that it was impossible, that Tracey was still in Hoddle Street. She was taken to her grandson in the children's ward. Adrian ran to her and she hugged him desperately. She removed his blue skivvy, it was bloodied and stained. He had bits of shrapnel and windscreen glass embedded in his ears and on the left side of his head.

"Where's mummy?"

"In heaven, a bright star," Val said.

When Adrian was released from St Vincent's Hospital on the Tuesday morning after Hoddle Street, Val bathed him trying to remove shrapnel and glass fragments. Then suddenly she rushed from the bathroom to her bedroom. When Suzanne took over she understood what had caused her mother to break down. There was human tissue in Adrian's hair. For years Adrian would resist anyone touching, combing or washing his hair. Suzanne dried Adrian and he toddled around the house calling out "Mummy, mummy, mum."

On the day of Tracey's funeral there was no media in attendance as had been requested in the funeral notice.

At the wake at Val's house, a woman introduced herself as a great friend of Kevin and Tracey. When Kevin denied ever knowing the woman, she collapsed and Val put her to bed. Later, she persuaded Val to take her to the psychiatric ward of Prince Henry's Hospital where she was known to staff, and admitted as a patient. The woman pestered Val again telling whoever would notice that Val had raised her from childhood. Val kept her doors locked and for that first month felt a prisoner in her own home.

Adrian had bad dreams and troubled sleep and continued to look for his mother. On one occasion, while away with Val, he 'adopted' a woman who resembled his mother, following her and clinging to her. Val remembered once wearing a particular perfume, when Adrian smelled it he clung to her tightly, not wanting to be put down and kissing her. He said it was his mummy's smell.

Whenever Adrian stayed over with Val he asked to watch *Bell and Sebastian*, a video tape about a boy in search of his mother. Often, Adrian would make Val fast-forward the tape to where the boy finds her.

On the day Julian Knight was sentenced at the Melbourne Supreme Court, a reporter from Channel 10 came to Val's door with flowers. Val refused them, asking to be left alone. The reporter persisted saying that he had seen her on Channel 9 with reporter Sally Gluyas, so why not talk to him? As she slammed the door the telephone rang. Picking it up she heard another reporter asking how much she had been paid to appear on Channel 9. Could he have some photographs of Tracey? Val hung up. This harassment went on and on. On one occasion a journalist came to her door and asked what had she to be ashamed of? What was she trying to hide? At the end of their tether, Suzanne and Val stormed into Channel 9, interrupting a party for someone leaving the station. Suzanne threw a photograph of Tracey down onto a table saying, "Here's a photo of the girl who lost her face, now look at it because that's all you're going to get!" She gave them just sufficient time to look at the photograph, picked it up again and left.

Val went to most of the court hearings mistakenly believing that she was required to attend after receiving a Summons. She would look at Knight, to see if there were signs of remorse but there were none. It hurt her that he was given, as part of the hand-up brief, copies of all the police photographs including those of her daughter, before she was murdered, then in the state that she was found afterwards. It was a further intrusion.

She was grateful to Graham Kent for helping her leave the various courts unseen by the media. She recalls that, when he returned jewellery that belonged to Tracey, he broke down, telling Val that he had a boy just like Adrian.

Reporter Sally Gluyas visited Val's home. She wanted to speak about Knight's sentence and Val agreed. The interview lasted about an hour in which Val commented that she would pull the lever on Knight if capital punishment had been the penalty for murder. A ten second grab from the hour-long interview was all that was used on the news that night. It was her comment that he should be executed.

Sally Gluyas convinced Val to appear on *A Current Affair* and speak to Jana Wendt through a link-up with Sydney. Val could see Jana on a television monitor in the studio and was determined not to let the world see her cry. She felt that Jana was trying to get her to cry. At one point Jana commented that Knight was a young man of nineteen and had a minimum of twenty-seven years to serve. She remembers Jana saying, "Don't you think that's a long time for such a young man?"

"Don't you think my daughter was young too? She was only twenty-three and left behind a young son."

Jana commented that Val appeared to be a very bitter woman.

Val stood up and tried to remove the microphone from her clothing saying, "Of course I'm bitter, and lady you can get fucked!"

The prerecorded interview, was never shown. The segment was replaced with a story about motor-car racing.

On another occasion, a water rifle that a neighbour had brought back from the United States was shown to Adrian.

"This is the gun that killed your mum," the neighbour's boy said.

Adrian ran inside the house and asked Val if it was true. Val spoke to the boy's parents, who apologised, and took the rifle from their son.

Val rarely reads the newspapers in case she reads about her daughter's murderer. It seems that every year journalists would write about him, visit him in prison and quote him. There would be photographs of a seemingly smug individual who was famous for killing her daughter and six others, bringing untold misery to thousands of people.

"I feel I have been robbed of my daughter. Tracey and I were very close and we had a lot of fun together. On her wedding night she rang me four times to tell me about their room at the Hilton.

After Hoddle Street I'd sit in my lounge room and watch and wait for Tracey to visit me as she had done almost every day."

Suzanne

Suzanne was the sister of Tracey Farmer, who was murdered at Hoddle Street, and the aunt of Adrian Farmer.

"I need you. Your mum needs you. You've got to keep it together. Adrian needs you." Kevin was trying to pacify Suzanne. She remembers standing in St Vincent's Hospital helpless and angry, crying and screaming. She remembers the bewildered and frightened look on Adrian, his face marked with shrapnel, his mother – her sister – dead. Suzanne had separated from her husband and was having difficulty coping. Then to hear that her beloved sister was dead… it all seemed so unfair.

On the Monday following the murder Suzanne went to Tracey's to get clothing for Adrian. Notes and messages were stuffed under the door from the media. As she took bags of clothing out of the flat she heard a whirring noise. She looked along the street and saw a photographer, with a long-lens camera, sitting in a tree.

The family had been very upset by newspaper reports of Tracey as the woman who had her face shot off, that she had no face. When Suzanne and Kevin went to the mortuary to identify Tracey, they expected to identify her by her hands or feet. The attendant pulled back the sheet covering Tracey's head and it was such a relief to see her not, as the newspapers had reported, but with her face reconstructed. Suzanne could see stitching and pieces missing and she told the attendant that they had made her sister's face too fat, but, she went home happy and felt that perhaps even her mother would have come had she known about the reconstruction. Val had heard a news report that Tracey had been identified by dental records. Kevin and Suzanne were stunned and returned to the mortuary to see Tracey again and prove to themselves that the media had it wrong. Tracey looked like Tracey, or close enough.

When Adrian lived with Suzanne and her children in Braybrook he heard the other children call her mummy. When he called Suzanne mummy, four-year-old Rebecca angrily told Adrian that she was not his mother. His mother was dead.

No one had told him the truth about his mother. It was decided that he was too young to understand.

Suzanne felt depressed and suicidal. She became paranoid. She thought she or her children would be harmed. She became unable to work. She felt like a zombie taking various anti-depressants and drinking whiskey. When Tracey died Suzanne felt a part of herself had died too. Often she would pick up the phone and dial Tracey's number before realising that her sister wouldn't answer. Slowly she realised that she was becoming a junkie dependent on anti-depressants and sleeping pills and wasting her life.

It was one long nightmare where she battled to accept the death of her sister, then the media reports on how Tracey looked – that she had no face, and could only be identified by dental records. Suzanne would look at photographs of Tracey and see nothing but a blank. A second later she would see Tracey again in the mortuary. It hurt that the media continued to report that Tracey had been identified by dental records when it was untrue. The family wanted a funeral as soon as possible but it was unable to begin the process of recovery while the Coroner would not release Tracey's body.

Suzanne's eleven-year-old son, Stevan, had become difficult. He had been upset about his parents' separation and then his aunt had been murdered. He had been a good student but lost interest in his studies and became disruptive.

All the feelings Suzanne had begun to come to terms with returned with the mass murder in Queen Street. And again, a few months later with the Walsh Street killings.

"I feel a deep, deep disgust for Knight. I do hate him. I hate to hear his name. I hate the fact that he's going to school and demanding taxpayers' money. All he's lost is his freedom. It was so senseless. Why was it that this person, who could not make the grade as a soldier, be allowed to have such an arsenal of guns? I feel the Army should have kept an eye on him. Obviously they saw the disturbance in him. Given the chance I'd like to punch him with my bare fists, just to get rid of that anger. I feel that Knight should never be released, if he survives long enough.

"There should be a sort of dob-in line where you can point out someone you're worried about, who is strange. When things like Dunblane and Port Arthur happen, it brings back the memories. So many thousands of lives have been affected. It sickens me when I hear of these mass murders. You can only imagine the trauma that the survivors and their families go through. It gets easier with time but it never goes away."

Monica Vitelli

Monica Vitelli was with Alan Jury and Danielle Kissas when the gunman ambushed them. She was showered with windscreen glass.

Monica Vitelli lost trust in people after Hoddle Street. She found that she didn't like to drive at night. She avoids sitting next to windows. She cannot stop to help anyone in the street even though this makes her feel guilty.

In 1991 she saw a couple fall from their motor cycle. Other people went to help but Monica froze. Then there was the time in Doncaster where she witnessed a man having an epileptic fit on the footpath. She felt guilty about ignoring the man, he was thrashing about, but there was no way after her experience at Hoddle Street she was going to stop.

Max Drake

Max Drake came on duty early at Richmond Police Station in order to complete paper work, but found himself at Hoddle Street. He released a police officer from the boot of a police car and helped search for the gunman.

When Max Drake returned to Richmond Police Station and went into the men's toilets, he found a police officer crying. The door opened and another officer entered.

"You're not to say anything," Max said, "You're to keep quiet about this."

In the mess room someone brought out some beer and Max and the others there talked about what they had experienced in Hoddle Street. He went home that morning believing that everyone who had been with him at Hoddle Street no longer felt that the police force was the "be-all and end-all". He also realised that he was no longer fit enough for operational police duties. His health was not good and it was no use fooling himself or anyone else. He performed administrative duties at Richmond until he got a vacancy as an instructor at the Police Academy.

Max remembered feeling powerless at Hoddle Street, wanting to do more but unable to do anything other than remain rooted behind a tree or a car. It seemed to be how most police who had been involved felt.

Max took John Delahunty aside and told him not to let comments about his handling of Knight get him down. Some police believed John should have shot Knight, killed him. If they were not saying it to John's face, they were certainly saying it behind his back. Max told John that he had done the right thing.

In September 1991 Max had a heart/lung transplant and, in February 1993, another lung transplant. Max Drake died in 1995.

Michael Anthony

Michael Anthony was ambushed by the gunman but believed other motorists had damaged his car and wanted to fight them. He took shelter at the Mobil service station.

The radio journalist pressed his microphone to Michael Anthony and asked what was going on. "Some dude was shooting the shit out of my car," Michael said, and continued walking south along Hoddle Street.

At the Mobil Service Station a police officer had told them that they could not take their car and asked them to attend at Collingwood Police Station where their statements would be taken.

But the first priority of Michael and Colin was to be with their friends again. Just before the Eastern Freeway he and Colin Smeelie hailed a taxi and were driven to Billboard Discotheque where they met their friends. At first Michael was just happy to have survived the incident. He greeted his friends' concerns with, "It was nothing," and downed another Jack Daniels. He and Colin got a lift to the Collingwood Police Station but were then directed to Fitzroy Police Station, finally leaving at 3.00 a.m.

On Tuesday after the incident Michael retrieved his car. He covered the damaged window with a sheet of plastic and sticking tape. Across the top of the plastic he wrote, using a felt tip pen, "I survived Hoddle Street" and he stuck a bandaid over the bullet hole in the passenger door. He examined the inside panel of the door and found that the bullet had struck the cross bar to the window winder, which had been next to Colin Smeelie's left knee. It was all that saved Colin Smeelie from being shot.

To pay for the repairs on his vehicle Michael submitted an insurance claim and was advised that he would have to pay an excess penalty because of his age. His parents paid the $550 for the repairs.

Michael Anthony put on a brave front with friends and family, sneering at the suggestions that the incident at Hoddle Street could have any after-effects on him or anyone else. But any illusions he had were shattered when a car backfired outside his bedroom window. He threw himself to the floor, his heart pounding just as it did that Sunday in August. Everything that he saw that night came back to him.

For a long time Michael avoided driving down Hoddle Street. It was more than a year later when he decided to confront the area again. He was with friends and was giving the impression that he was unconcerned as they drove down the exit from Heidelberg Road. He joked, telling them to duck as he mimicked a rifle shot and feigned injury. Everyone laughed but he was relieved to turn off at the nearest side street.

He did not tell his friends that he was having trouble sleeping, and of the nightmares when he did sleep. And of the recurring dream where he was at an aunt's house when some men burst through the doors shooting everyone inside. He was behind a car, taking cover, trying to shoot back and saw his father killed. He would wake up in a sweat. Michael was given the name of a counsellor but he felt it was not for him.

For a while Michael was introduced to people as a survivor of Hoddle Street, and he would be asked about his experience. It felt good to talk about it, a thrill to recount what had happened, but he grew tired of the attention and avoided situations where the subject would arise.

Hoddle Street changed Michael Anthony's perspective on life. Before it he had seen life as one big party, living from day to day. He was a rebel and an anarchist. After Hoddle Street he felt that he had been wasting his life. He began to focus on the future.

"I used to think in scientific terms. That we live, then die and become food for the worms. After my experiences in Catholic schools, I was totally turned off God. But Hoddle Street made me realise that there is a spirit and there are other planes of existence. I feel that if there wasn't a God, then I'd be dead. I believe that anything good is a sign of a God. I believe there is something looking over me."

By 1990, Michael found that he had stopped thinking of Hoddle Street every single day.

"Prior to Hoddle Street, I did not support capital punishment, but now I do. And if there is no capital punishment, then there should be life. I'd like to do to Knight what he did to me. Sneak up behind him and wrap wire around his neck and choke him and say, 'Hey, you don't know me and this is how it feels. Remember Hoddle Street?'"

Eddy McShortall

Eddy McShortall was shot while driving his car along Hoddle Street, receiving minor injuries.

Eddy McShortall parked his Datsun station wagon a short distance from Prince Henry's Hospital and walked into the casualty area. He rang the police from a public phone, then saw a doctor who treated his wounds and allowed him to leave.

When he arrived home in Chelsea, Ian, his house mate, was still up watching news reports of Hoddle Street. He was glued to the television saying, "Look at this man. Look at this."

Eddy told him that he had been there, that he had been shot, but Ian didn't seem convinced.

"Come out and look at the car," Eddy said.

Ian reluctantly left the TV and checked the car. He ran his fingers over the gouge marks on the front bonnet where the shotgun pellets had hit before ricocheting onto the windscreen. He counted the seven holes in the toughened glass, then went back inside and resumed watching TV. He got up and went to the car again then back to the TV.

Eddy went to bed despite feeling alert and pumped up. He had a screen test at 9.30 a.m. and wanted to perform at his best. There was nothing he could do about Hoddle Street. It had happened and it was over.

It was nearly 2 a.m. when he was woken by detectives at the front door. They wanted his statement and Eddy spoke to them for about half an hour then returned to bed.

During the rehearsal for his screen test Eddy felt that he was not getting to the character as he knew he could. His mind was on Hoddle Street. He was asked by the director to throw a cup of coffee at a window and watch the contents dribble down the glass. He asked Eddy to feel that the dribble was the prison officer's view of his own life. Eddy threw the cup and felt the character come alive. He knew he would get the part.

He went to a party and had a few drinks. A small boy was playing with balloons and he burst several over a two hour period. With each bang Eddy felt himself tense and break out in sweat, and his mind flashed back to Hoddle Street. He would react in the same way when riding his motor cycle. When it backfired he would think someone was shooting at him.

With the $400 grant given to him by the State Government Eddy had his car repaired. Some three weeks later a psychologist visited him at his home and they discussed Hoddle Street. He talked of how he felt and she told him that he had a good attitude towards the incident. Eddy remembered that when his father had died some years before he had not handled his emotions correctly. He had shifted his feelings, developing a rash, which disappeared when he finally broke down and cried. This time there would be no holding back.

Not long after the psychologist had visited Eddy noticed that he did not react to explosions or loud noises anymore and his mind did not return to Hoddle Street. There was no sweat, no racing of the heart. He felt that he was making a quick recovery.

News of the Queen Street murders, however, did cause him distress. When he heard the news flash he was driving. He pulled over, his heart racing. His body was wet with sweat just as it had been in Hoddle Street.

Eddy was a member of the Melbourne International Pistol Club and each month he would go to the range and shoot his Ruger .22 rifle, his .357 magnum revolver and his M1 carbine.

After Hoddle Street he lost interest in firearms, he felt it wrong to kill and that all life was precious. After a while though, Eddy returned to the sport as he believed that hunting was part of life. So, in 1996, when firearms were being confiscated by the Government, Eddy was opposed to the move.

With the mass murders in Dunblane and in Port Arthur, Eddy felt enormous sympathy for the victims.

"I put myself in their position again and thought how lucky I was. My initial reaction with Bryant, I wanted to get him and seek revenge, I wanted to stop him.

"Since Hoddle Street, I realise the frailty of life, its fragility. One time I was scared of dying but not any more."

Eddy has no feelings of malice towards Julian Knight, however believes that Knight has received too much publicity and should never be heard from again. "He should have no voice at all, but I don't blame him. I blame the system for allowing him to have his ego massaged. It is as if he had been a nobody who became somebody by murdering and injuring many people. It is his claim to fame."

Susan Rodaughan

Susan Rodaughan's partner, Robert Mitchell, was murdered in Hoddle Street.

Susan Rodaughan lived with Robert Mitchell for three months before he was murdered in Hoddle Street. She thought that he had decided to stay overnight at their friend's house when he did not come home as expected. Then she saw the news flash and footage of the scene. She recognised Robert's rugby shirt and jeans draped over the side of the footpath and gutter. Susan wanted to go to Hoddle Street and help him. She was an intensive-care nurse and she felt that she could do something. Then, as she watched the footage repeated, she knew there was nothing she could do. Later, at the hospital where she was working, there was a patient with a similar type of head wound to Robert's. Susan was unable to attend to him.

When the Queen Street mass murders took place, Susan sought professional counselling. Her family were very supportive but she was having nightmares about being shot.

It took Susan five years to get over Robert's death, and she feels that she will never totally recover from it. She has not been in a relationship since he died.

Susan drove down Hoddle Street. It was not easy but she was glad to have confronted it. It was what Bob would have wanted her to do. It would have been a double tragedy had she let her life go down the drain because of Knight.

When Knight was sentenced she was amazed at the leniency of the penalty that he received.

"He should have no luxuries," Susan said.

Gina Papaioannou's family

Gina Papaioannou died as a result of severe injuries to her body from the M14 military rifle. Christos was her father and Rikki and Vicki were her sisters.

Christos Papaioannou was in bed when there was a knock on the front door. He looked at the clock, it was almost midnight. A police officer told him that his youngest daughter had been in an accident and was in the Alfred Hospital. When he got there, Sergeant Peter Butts of the Prahran DSG told him what had really happened. Christos wanted to see Gina but she was undergoing surgery. He drove to Thornbury to see his eldest daughter, Rikki, but she was not there.

His middle daughter, Vicki, had been watching *Risky Business* when there was a news flash. Gina had also been watching the film, but had left before it finished to spend the night at Rikki's house. Vicki rang her sister to see if Gina had arrived as she knew she would have to drive through Hoddle Street. When Rikki told her she had not arrived, Vicki became frantic. Christos had rung Rikki and she went straight to the hospital where Gina was fighting for her life.

It was the beginning of an around-the-clock vigil for members of Gina's family. There would be someone with Gina every minute of every day until she could be released from hospital. She would not be alone during her fight for survival. Gina slipped in and out of consciousness but was unable to talk. Christos wanted to stay with Gina all the time but Rikki and Vicki made him go home, shower and rest. They took it in turns to hold Gina's hand.

Christos Papaioannou

Christos felt that the ground he walked on had been taken away from beneath his feet. At first he could not believe that it was true. There must have been some mistake. He was given four weeks off from work. Gina's funeral was quite large and he remembers the police blocking the intersection and officers saluting her coffin as it went past. Then at the service he was angered to see the cameras and reporters outside. They intruded on the privacy of his family, they had no right to be there. They even knocked on his door after the funeral. Christos thought of the media as vultures.

When his wife died he and Gina nearly always did the shopping together on Friday nights. Then when Gina died he found it hard to visit the same shops. She was there, but she was not there. He lost interest in life but threw himself into his work. He wanted to come home tired each day so that he would not have to think about anything. He would just come home, eat nothing, do nothing and collapse, exhausted, onto the couch. He smoked twice as much as he used to. Every lunch time he would travel to the cemetery and visit Gina's grave. In his spare time he would write poetry. All of a sudden he felt himself become very old.

When Julian Knight was sentenced Christos was angry. Angry that Knight would one day be released. Angry with the legal system and the psychiatrists and psychologists who tried to diminish Knight's responsibility.

Christos withdrew from everyone, including his family. He has diabetes, which his doctor attributed to the shock of Gina's death. In 1990 he remarried.

Vicki

In the first two years after Gina's death Vicki found life very difficult. Drinking and drug taking became part of her daily existence. She had changed. She was more volatile and withdrawn. She felt vulnerable. She, too, could be shot, while doing the shopping. When she had children she became over-protective. Ironically, her dead sister was instrumental in helping Vicki recover from her pain. She knew that Gina would be devastated if she could see her and this thought gave her the strength to fight back.

After ten years, Vicki still mourns for her sister.

Rikki

Rikki took the song, *You're My Hero* to the hospital and played it to Gina. They saw a tear roll down her face. It was one of Gina's favourite songs. Doctors were surprised at how resilient Gina was, as her injuries were severe. The sisters were very close and believed in their hearts that Gina would live.

On 20 August 1987, Rikki was having lunch in the hospital cafeteria when she heard her name being called on the public address system. She went quickly to the intensive care unit and was told that Gina had died. Hospital security helped the family members leave the hospital through a back entrance to avoid the media pack at the front. For the next forty-eight hours the family was harassed by the media, but refused to be interviewed.

Family members, police officers, members of the public, even people from the gym where Rikki worked, had donated blood for Gina. Rikki was frustrated that her blood was not compatible. She just wanted to help her sister. When Gina died, Rikki wanted desperately for the doctors to revive her heart a third time. This was her baby sister.

Not a day passes when Rikki does not think of Gina.

Andrew Hiam

Andrew Hiam was one of the first police to arrive at the scene. He helped with the rescue of Steve Wight, John Muscat and Peter Gauci.

He was at the cafeteria when a workman started using a jackhammer outside. He jumped in fright as everything came flooding back to him.

Other students turned to look at him. Andrew Hiam found returning to his tertiary studies very difficult, eventually applying for special consideration, as he could not concentrate or focus and he was handing in assignments late.

He visited Steve Wight in hospital. He felt a bond with Steve as they had been in it together and he wanted to see him get better. Steve described how he had seen Knight, rifles firing, people being shot, and it was then that he realised how lucky he had been. If he hadn't stopped the police car where he did, if he had driven down Hoddle Street, he doubted he would be alive.

He reflected on the night and how vulnerable he had felt. He did not know the streets or many of the police. He had felt overwhelmingly helpless watching Gina Papaioannou's arm lift and then fall. He had wanted to go in and help her but had known that his own life would have been in jeopardy. He remembered the feeling of awe upon hearing of gunshot damage to the police helicopter. He wondered what type of gunfire could achieve this. As he had walked around the scene keeping bystanders and the media away, he had looked at the bullet holes in the cars realising for the first time what bullets could do to metal. It was like tissue paper against this sort of weaponry. The dead and wounded had looked as if they'd been in horrific road accidents.

In March 1988 Andrew transferred to Richmond Police Station, where in his first year, he was responsible for the investigations into two train fatalities and eight other death reports. He was nicknamed 'Doctor Death'.

He had known police not to wear revolvers when they went out. Andrew noticed changes in the police that he knew, after Hoddle Street. Everyone wore their revolvers on patrol whereas previously they had been more casual. More of them went in hard when making an arrest. The offender couldn't be given a chance to cause injury. After Hoddle Street you didn't take risks.

Shane Stanton's family

June and Bill Stanton were the parents of Shane Stanton, who was murdered while driving his motor cycle to work.

When June Stanton came home to Shepparton at 3.00 p.m. on Monday, she was happy, having won $50 on poker machines at Moama. Then she saw the faces of her husband, Bill, and her elder son, Colin.

Bill took June to the doctor. She was in shock, stamping her feet and swearing and saying things he had never imagined could possibly come from his wife's mouth. She was given sedatives but Bill refused to take any himself. They travelled to Melbourne, collecting Shane's mother-in-law from the airport on the way.

There was blood on his helmet. And on his wedding ring. They were in a cardboard box with his keys. As the box was handed to Shane's family, Colin spat on a handkerchief and started to wipe the blood from the wedding ring.

He kept wiping it and wiping it even when there was no blood left. They were thankful that they were not given Shane's clothes.

The press were waiting at Shane and his wife Debra's house. The family were subjected to constant phone calls and constant door knocking. Debra was blaming herself for Shane's death. She was the one that had wanted to move to Melbourne. Because the media would not give her time to grieve, Debra moved out of the house within days, to avoid them. Reluctantly, she gave one interview.

June and Bill returned to their home in Shepparton where they were generally left alone by the local media. Because Shane's name had been incorrectly recorded in the media as either Keith or Kenneth the media attempts to locate them led to nowhere. No one in Shepparton knew of a Keith or Kenneth Stanton who had been killed at Hoddle Street, but they knew of a Shane Stanton.

Back in Shepparton, June and Bill lived too far to be bothered by the Melbourne media. But this distance was also a disadvantage. They were ignorant of counselling available to them if they had been in Melbourne. They weren't aware of the memorial service until they read about it in the newspaper. They felt that because they lived in the country, they were considered unimportant. Out of sight, out of mind. June was thankful that she had friends that she could turn to and, "talk and talk and talk".

When Knight was sentenced at the Melbourne Supreme Court the media tried to get their views on the penalty. June spoke to television journalists for ten minutes but resisted telling what she felt for fear it would be sensationalised. She tried to be rational, despite questions that seemed obviously designed to inflame her feelings and make good television.

The Forensic Science Laboratory contacted Bill and June and asked them to collect Shane's motor cycle. Colin went to MacLeod and brought it back to Shepparton. When they were unloading the motor cycle from the trailer, something rattled. Colin checked inside the petrol tank – it, too, was blood stained – and retrieved the spent shell of an M14 bullet. This had a terrible impact on the family. The last thing they expected to see was a bullet that came from the rifle that had cut down their son.

They were holidaying in Queensland during the second anniversary of Hoddle Street, when they saw a Melbourne newspaper. Splashed across the front page was a photograph of Shane lying dead on the road, near his motor cycle. Their holiday was ruined and the trauma returned.

With the money they received from the Crimes Compensation Tribunal they redecorated Shane's room, recarpeted the house and went on a holiday. It helped them to get on with their life. The Chairman comforted them when he said he had been in Queen Street, opposite the building on 8 December 1987, and as a result of that he better understood their situation.

June went through a stage when she wanted to make contact with Knight's mother, Pamela, as she felt that she was as much a victim as they were. She felt that Pamela deserved a medal for sticking by her son.

Peter Gauci

Peter Gauci was going to the aid of Gina Papaioannou, Robert Mitchell and Vesna Markovska, when shot and wounded by the gunman. His friend, John Muscat, was murdered and Steve Wight was injured in the same sequence of events.

Peter Gauci was impressed with the ambulance officers who were with him in Hoddle Street. They went about their job in a calm and unflustered fashion despite the awareness that at any moment, they could be shot. As Peter was placed in the back of the ambulance he felt anxious that the interior lights were on. It seemed so bright. He felt safer in the darkness of the street. A drip was inserted in his arm. Relief overwhelmed him when the ambulance sped off, but it was not until he was in the shelter of the hospital that he felt confident that the gunman could harm him no more.

At the nurse's station he rang his parents. His mother became hysterical as he explained the situation.

A police officer took his statement while he waited to be seen by a doctor. Peter was concerned for his friend. "What about John Muscat?" he asked.

"He's gone," the Constable said.

Peter had mixed feelings. He was sad that John had died but aware that if he survived he would have been a vegetable for the rest of his life. His thoughts turned to John's family and how they would react.

Following surgery to his right side, Peter had to learn how to sleep on his left side or on his back. Every time he moved he felt pain and his stay in hospital stretched from his optimistic estimate of twenty-four hours, to eight days. On his twenty-third birthday nursing staff brought him a sponge cake sporting one candle.

Peter refused all interviews. He was concerned that his and everyone else's words would be trivialised and sensationalised.

He had been home only a few days when a bottle of wine and a card were delivered to him by the chauffeur of the then State Opposition Leader, Mr Jeff Kennett. Mr Kennett suggested that Peter call him if he needed any help. Being a non-drinker, Peter gave the wine to his parents. He wondered whether the gesture was a ploy to gain his vote or genuine concern.

Once a week, Peter's arms and shoulders were manipulated by a physiotherapist. The right shoulder was hanging lower than the left and he had trouble breathing from his right lung. While he had no organ or bone damage he was in constant pain. He didn't believe in taking pain killers so refused them. He didn't feel sorry for himself. Quite the contrary. He felt lucky to have got off so lightly. He had been unemployed at the time of Hoddle Street and after it went from the dole to sickness benefits. Every day for several months a district nurse visited him spending up to half-an-hour changing his dressing.

Not a day passed without Peter's thoughts turning to Hoddle Street. Yet he was determined not to let Julian Knight beat him, determined not to suffer psychologically. When he was well enough he returned to the boarding house in Ramsden Street, opposite Knight's house, and walked through the parklands trying to retrace his steps. He went to the Mobil Service Station regularly and, when he was fit enough, asked for work.

The wound in his right lower leg troubled him for many months. He was unable to walk properly and it was an effort to raise his right arm but bit by bit he worked at getting better.

Peter has completed a course in freelance journalism, and now lives in another state.

Peter Gauci's parents

Peter's mother, Carol Gauci, had a premonition that something bad was going to happen to her son.

Carol Gauci dreamed of being in the country with her son, Peter, holding his hand, while a gunman was searching for him. They hid behind a tree as the gunman, armed with a rifle, walked towards them. Carol tried to hide her son, cover him with her dress. Like a mother hen would hide her chicks from a fox. She felt herself scream as the telephone woke her. Just as she reached it, it stopped. It was 1.10 a.m. Her heart was pounding and her head throbbed.

Ten minutes later the telephone rang again. At first she did not recognise the voice, but then Peter identified himself. He told his mother that he was in hospital having just been shot in Hoddle Street.

Carol and Lewis visited Peter every day, greeting the continual queries from the media pack with no comment. When Peter came home, a district nurse visited twice a day for two weeks to change his dressing, then once a day as his wounds healed. Carol slept poorly, worrying about her son, and fearing for the family's safety.

At the time of Hoddle Street, Lewis, whose hearing was slightly impaired due to an industrial accident, woke one morning, three months after the ambush to find himself deaf in both ears. A specialist prescribed a hearing aid in the belief that shock had caused his deafness. He saw other specialists to treat mouth ulcers that were so bad he could eat nothing but soup. Five months after Hoddle Street he developed a stomach ulcer. In the twelve months after

Hoddle Street he accumulated more sick leave than in the entire twenty-two years that he had worked for Telecom.

His deafness began to create problems at work. Some supervisors were understanding and patient, while others seemed to be trying to get him to leave. Lewis became irritable and quick to anger. His relationship with Carol suffered.

Lewis wrote to the Government then headed by John Cain, seeking help for his son, Peter, who had been unable to get work for twelve months after Hoddle Street. He received no reply and was angry, particularly as the only parliamentarian to show any interest was Jeff Kennett, then the Opposition Leader.

"Knight and Hoddle Street is (sic) always on my mind. It is very hard to get them out of my head. Whenever I read about Knight in the newspapers I get very upset at how unhappy he is in prison, how unfortunate he is at not getting money to study and so on. If they say capital punishment is no good and no one would hang him, I would pull the rope. I would kill him. He has ruined my life and the lives of many others. I hope he rot (sic) in jail."

Six months after Hoddle Street, Carol sought treatment for her sleeping problems. She took the prescribed sleeping tablets a few times but then she poured them down the sink as she did not want to rely on them. During the first eighteen months after Hoddle Street she took a great deal of sick leave, primarily to cope with depression and stress.

She developed stomach ulcers and was frightened to leave her home each day for work in case she was shot or attacked in some other way. In 1994 she could cope no more and resigned from her job.

In 1991 Lewis accepted a redundancy package and lives on a disability pension

When news of the Dunblane and Port Arthur mass murders reached her she became ill for several days. She felt for "those who lost their loved ones and especially the young man who lost all three members of his family at Port Arthur".

With every tragedy her heart goes out to the families of the victims.

"We are all still suffering. We all say 'time heals', but every time I hear about another slaying, it seems to be taking forever to heal."

Carol can never forgive Julian Knight for the lives he has taken and the suffering he has caused. She feels she will make a massive leap forward in recovery when he dies, whether it is in prison or when he is released. Either way, Carol believes he should be dead.

Andrew Hack

Andrew Hack was shot while attempting to assist others who had already been shot. He fled in his car to his workplace in Fairfield, where he collapsed.

After the doctors had removed pieces of metal from his left shoulder and arm, they showed him the squashed piece of lead taken from his side. It was what was left from an M14 round. He asked to see the wound, a nurse adjusted a mirror and he vomited.

Andrew was discharged from hospital six days after Hoddle Street. The district nurse saw him daily and changed the dressing on his wounds. An apprentice chef, he was unable to return to work or attend trade school, for three months. In that time, his car was held by the Forensic Science Laboratory and then the panel beater. He relied on his girlfriend and family to get around.

The panel beater and his staff were drinking, it was the end of the week. Over a beer the panel beater told Andrew he had been in the Army, and had been shot while serving in Vietnam.

"We talked for about an hour. It felt good to talk to someone who had experienced the same. Someone who understood," he said.

When he returned to work in December 1987, no one seemed to understand why he was still affected by Hoddle Street. His hands shook so badly that he cut his finger slicing meat.

The psychiatrist he was seeing twice a week, prescribed medication to relax and sleep. Twice, within the first twelve months of being shot, he tried to take his own life.

He was working long hours, a split shift of up to twelve hours a day, and going home around midnight. He couldn't play sport and the pain in his back was not getting better. Driving to his flat worried him. He approached corners and buildings with care, worried that he would again be shot by someone hiding in the dark. He overdosed on prescribed medication and was rushed to hospital where his stomach was pumped.

When the Queen Street murders took place, Andrew had to take time off work.

He began to see his psychiatrist almost daily. He was moody and found it hard to smile. He kept bumping his wound against the benches in the kitchen. He was nineteen and nothing was working out. He quit his job before completing his apprenticeship and went into hospital for a second operation on his back.

The Crimes Compensation Tribunal awarded him the maximum – $20,000. In the County Court, a friend was awarded $97,000 for similar injuries received in a minor motor car accident.

He gets up slowly and sits on the edge of the bed. His left side cramps below the 15cm scar. He bends down slowly and pulls on his jeans. They rub against the wound so wears track suits as often as he can. It takes two to three hours for his back to loosen and he walks with a limp. A physician has told him that he may have to wear a nerve belt for the rest of his life. He had a third operation on his back in 1991 and is expecting a fourth operation in the future. Until Hoddle Street he was in good health.

For seven years he played junior football for Montmorency in the Diamond Valley League. It is his favourite sport and in 1987 he gave it up for his job. He had to work Saturdays. He always intended to go back to it, and made plans to do so in 1988. He was always making plans, but now he lives one day at a time.

He has been working for his father as a painter. The hours are better than those of a chef, and he doesn't have to drive home late at night but if he had completed his apprenticeship he would be earning considerably more as a chef. He married Kathy, a hairdresser, in 1991. He is worried about the future and is not sure how long his back will allow him to live a normal life. He cycles to keep his weight down and it helps with pain management.

Michelle Young

Michelle Young was on duty with Andrew Hiam and later provided security for the gunman's mother and sister.

Michelle Young joined the police force a week after the "Mad Max" shooting in 1986 and her father pleaded with her not to go through with her application. But working in an office was boring.

A week after Hoddle Street, the police psychologist was made available to any officer who felt it necessary. Michelle thought about seeing the psychologist but the stigma deterred her. She kept her feelings to herself, never discussing them, not even with her partner on that night, Andrew Hiam.

At Hoddle Street Michelle had felt helpless to do anything other than to take cover and prevent other people from becoming targets. In 1988 she was involved in two more shooting episodes, both within the space of twenty-four hours.

She overcame her negative feelings about the psychologist and spoke to him. He believed that she wanted to go into dangerous situations to compensate for her feelings of helplessness at Hoddle Street. It took two years for Michelle to get over that August night and she worries that when Knight is released he will repeat what he did in 1987.

Being close to death made Michelle appreciate the value of life more, and that it was there to be enjoyed while you can. She is more adventurous now whereas before she would be less inclined to do so.

Ralph Lockman

Ralph Lockman accompanied John Delahunty in the pursuit of the gunman and was ambushed in McKean Street, North Fitzroy. He and Delahunty arrested the gunman when he surrendered.

After his statement had been taken, Ralph Lockman went home to his girlfriend and his parents. He noticed that, according to the newspapers and the television, there was only one police officer responsible for Knight's arrest. He had been there too and he kept returning, in his mind, to the scene when Knight had pleaded for his life and repeatedly asked to see his girlfriend. He'd talked about his army training. Ralph thought about the army, and its emphasis on strength. Recruits were told that they are going to break them, see what they are made of. He knew from his nine years in the army that it marks you if you are considered weak.

Ralph saw the police psychologist but still thinks constantly of Hoddle Street. He tries to block it from his mind but feels that it will always be there in his life.

Ralph Lockman is a senior constable working at a police station in the northern suburbs of Melbourne.

Stephen Aylward

With his partner, Simon Black, Stephen Aylward went to the aid of the motor-cyclist Shane Stanton, and led some survivors to a safer location at the scene.

Stephen Aylward's immediate reaction to Hoddle Street was that he was going to resign from the police force. He did not get paid enough for what he was going through. He believed that he would not see his wife and family again. He felt hopeless and helpless as he listened to the cannon-like noise in the near vicinity. His .38 revolver was a toy compared with the weaponry he could hear. The M14 had even taken chunks out of the gutter. It was like a movie set.

He pulled over a car driven by Andrew Hack and they talked for half an hour. Andrew showed him his scar and Stephen found it good to talk to someone who had also been in Hoddle Street.

After Hoddle Street, Stephen had problems with memory and concentration. He forgot court dates and, on one occasion had costs of $500 awarded against him, for not appearing to give evidence in his own case. For the first time in his twelve-year career Stephen felt that he was losing his cool. He found he was doing things that were completely out of character, things that he would not have done before Hoddle Street. He was aware that he was losing his temper for trivial matters, and more often. Violent films upset him.

He believes that Hoddle Street wrecked his marriage. It took about four years.

He became over-protective of his wife, trying to dominate her. He did not like her going anywhere on her own – she could get killed. It did not occur to Stephen to seek professional help until his marriage was in disarray. It was through counselling with a psychologist that he realised that Hoddle Street was behind his problems.

He began to dislike pistol practice and he lost respect for police who carried loads of firearm clips and acted gung-ho. There seemed to be a futility in being a street police officer, and he became a district collator, work that did not require him to go out on patrol duty.

He had not been made aware of any debriefing or told of any requirement to see a psychologist. No one contacted him from the welfare office or from any other section of the police force. It was as if those involved in Hoddle Street did not exist other than for publicity about their heroic actions. There was no recognition from the police force. It was a common complaint from everyone who had been involved. There were only two police officers recognised, and they were the two police officers who had arrested Knight.

Stephen Aylward does not hate Knight. He just thinks about the devastation that he has caused. Shane Stanton still sticks in Stephen's mind, he still hears his last gasp for breath. He remembers running up the Heidelberg Road exit ramp to warn motorists, and feeling as if he was running on air, as if he was out of his body, watching himself on television. He remembers seeing Dusan Flajnik lying in his car, seemingly asleep, but dead. He remembers returning to Richmond Police Station and seeing police officers who hadn't been at the scene crying with relief that their work mates had survived.

Charlie Machen

A police officer from Fitzroy, Charlie Machen attended the Merri Creek area in North Fitzroy. He almost killed a jogger he thought was armed with a firearm.

"Police, don't move!"

The barrel end of the police revolver was pressed hard against the man's forehead and Charlie's finger was squeezing back the trigger, ready to fire.

It was at this point that Charlie Machen would wake up screaming in the middle of the night. His wife, Jenny, would try to settle him. He would get up from their bed and get a glass of water knowing that he could have killed that man running along the bike track. He was so close to pulling the trigger. Killing an innocent man was something Charlie could not live with. He was grateful that his army training had taught him to identify the target before shooting.

Seeing a psychologist was for wimps. It was the night that bothered him. During the day he was fine. But at night he dreaded going to sleep for fear of another nightmare, the same one, repeating itself. Charlie put up with the nightmares and the wet sweaty sheets for twelve months and then, with encouragement from his wife, he went to the police psychologist. It was a hard call for a man like Charlie to seek professional help. He had been critical of a policewoman who had survived the Russell Street bombing because she let the incident affect her. She took time off from work, which was particularly galling for Charlie, because she had not been injured. She should have forgotten about what had happened and got on with her life.

"It was the best thing I ever did," Charlie said of his first meeting with the police psychologist.

During counselling he explained that he blamed Julian Knight for his nearly killing the innocent jogger. He discussed his feelings of incredible nausea whenever he read about or saw Knight featured in the newspapers or on television. The psychologist explained his reactions and the nightmares stopped.

"It was the first time I'd talked about what had happened in its entirety, and then had explanations of my feelings given to me by someone who understood.

"Hoddle Street made me acutely aware of how situations can happen – instantly, and without warning. The security of 'It'll never happen to me' is gone forever. I'm still very angry, probably because of the notoriety Knight got out of it and the fact that on the night I was so powerless to help others, which is what my job is about."

Charlie Machen is a sergeant at the Ethical Standards Department.

Terry Howard

Terry Howard drove the MICA ambulance in reverse to the injured Gina Papaioannou and later joined in the search for the gunman.

Knight had been arrested but no one was really sure if it was all over. Terry Howard went with Peter Butts along the train line until they could see no further. They returned to Hoddle Street where no one had moved. People were rigid with fear, a woman was crying hysterically. Terry lifted the woman over his shoulder and carried her to the swimming pool. He then returned to the overpass and carried a man in the same way, while holding his revolver in one hand. He told the couple that they were safe. People came out of their houses and offered the survivors tea. Knowing that they were safe, Terry returned to Hoddle Street and checked the bodies in the remote chance that any were still alive.

In the mess room back at the Richmond Police Station, he shared a beer with the others who had been at Hoddle Street. Terry reassured them that they had done good work. He told them not to take the matter too seriously, that it was all over now and tomorrow they could be involved in another life-threatening incident. He said that they had seen people behave hysterically, but that they had been trained to react calmly. Unlike the civilians, they were prepared for any incident. He said that they were tough and didn't need doctors and pills. Terry was not a believer in psychiatrists or psychologists.

The first time that Terry Howard received any recognition for his actions at Hoddle Street was in 1991 when he received a Certificate of Merit from the Royal Humane Society of Australasia. He was reluctant to appear at the ceremony at Government House, but his wife urged him to go, for his children, if for no one else. Awards were not something that Terry believed police should receive. Whatever they did was part of the job that they were paid to do. The civilians were a different matter. They deserved awards for bravery. Soon after the award, he received a letter from Chief Commissioner Kel Glare, congratulating him. He treated it with contempt for, in his view, the Police Department only acted when a police officer was in trouble or there was something newsworthy. It had taken four years to receive any sort of recognition from the Police Department, and then only because of the Royal Humane Society.

Undeserved awards or recognition also bothered Terry. The media had created heroes at Hoddle Street, of people who, from his personal observations, were less than heroic. And yet there were police officers who had shown courage and were ignored by the Police Department.

Terry felt that Steve Aylward, Dennis Harnetty and Simon Black were worthy of commendation by the police force and he submitted a report recommending just that.

Terry remembers going to the City Watch-House on the night after Hoddle Street to check on the prisoners. He opened the door to the cell where Knight was being held. He felt his throat choke at the sight of "the anaemic, scrawny looking bastard" and he couldn't speak. He wanted to kill him. He slammed the cell door shut and walked away.

Some years before Hoddle Street, while in the Traffic Operations Group, Terry was seriously injured while riding a police motor cycle. The hip and spinal injuries that he sustained eventually caused him to retire on a disability pension in 1990. He lives in country Victoria.

Rick McIntosh

The Prahran detective who tried to reach the injured by crawling on his hands and knees, Rick McIntosh was later to take the gunman into custody while waiting for Homicide detectives to take charge.

This was not your normal crook, according to Rick McIntosh. This was more like a spoilt kid, who wanted his own way and, when he couldn't get it, threw a tantrum. Rick McIntosh found the interview with Knight offensive. He could not believe that these atrocious acts could have been carried out just for the experience of what it was like to kill.

Taking Kevin Farmer's statement was the hardest thing that Rick McIntosh had ever done. He had never before taken a statement from a person who had witnessed a family member being murdered. He led Kevin through the events as tactfully as he could and wished, several times, that someone else would take over from him. He felt like a bastard asking Kevin questions about what they did, where they went and what happened. When it came to the actual shooting Kevin became more emotional and Rick tried to complete that part of the statement as quickly as possible.

The police force was no longer fun for Rick McIntosh. He had been known for his dry sense of humour and his wisecracks, but overnight, things didn't seem quite so funny anymore. He realised that being a police officer is dangerous, not just in New York and in Ireland, but in Australia too.

Rick's mind still wanders back to Hoddle Street. He avoids driving along the street as much as possible. He still feels upset that some people exaggerated their role at Hoddle Street. He is now a Senior Sergeant at the Ethical Standards Department.

Graham Kent

Graham Kent was the Homicide detective who, with Senior Sergeant Brian McCarthy, interviewed the gunman and was ultimately responsible for the gathering of evidence and presentation of the police brief.

Over the few months following Hoddle Street, Graham interviewed people from Knight's past and came to the conclusion that he was never suitable for officer rank in the Army. He thought that Knight lacked the right attitude and the self-discipline necessary to make the grade.

It didn't surprise him to hear that Knight was critical of the police. Graham believed that he had been educated in prison on how to play the system. It took Graham eight months to prepare the brief, for he was also acting as a consultant to the detectives investigating the Queen Street mass murders.

During the summer, Graham took his son and a bundle of newspapers about Hoddle Street to the beach. He had not read any newspapers about the incident until then. As he read about the victims and their families, the enormity of what had happened overwhelmed him. He looked at his own son and thought of Adrian Farmer, who was the same age. He dropped the newspaper, held his son tightly, and cried.

Betty Roberts

Betty Roberts was a Northcote police officer attending Hoddle Street unaware of the ambush awaiting her and her partner, Graham Larchin. She hastened to Queens Parade and directed traffic away from the scene.

The policewoman sergeant asked her to get in. Betty looked at the police decals on the side of the car and the siren and the flashing lights on the roof. It was the last place she wanted to be. She told the sergeant no she couldn't, she felt safer out of the car. The sergeant put her arm around Betty and told her it was okay.

Betty stepped away from the police car and raised her right hand and then signalled a car to continue towards Alexandra Parade. The driver was unhappy as he wanted to turn left into Hoddle Street.

"Just do as you're told," Betty said.

The driver was about to challenge her authority but reconsidered when he saw her wipe the tears from her eyes. He put his car into gear and continued south along Queens Parade.

Betty was jumpy and hated every second standing out in the middle of the road directing traffic away from Hoddle Street.

Even though she had heard that the offender had been arrested, and it was unlikely a second person was involved, she still felt vulnerable. Some motorists complained that they could hardly see her but there was no way she was going to wear a reflectorised vest again.

Later, when other police relieved her, she went back to the police car she and Graham Larchin had abandoned. As she walked towards it there was still the feeling that she would be ambushed again. Her whole body shook even though logic told her that it was all over, that the offender was with Homicide detectives and the danger had gone.

With Graham Larchin she went to where Knight had been, searching for something that would help them to understand why he wanted to kill them. She wanted to see what he had seen, how soft a target they had been. To think that she had initially thought he was a detective or an SOG member. The thought almost made her sick. She looked at their police car and was amazed that it had no bullet holes.

They jumped the fence and walked over to the railway line, locating several empty M14 shells. Betty was amazed at the size of the shells, they seemed to be the size of cannon shells. The firepower of an M14 was enormous compared with the .38 Smith and Wesson she carried on her hip. The M14 was designed for war. Where was the war in Melbourne?

Keith, Betty's husband, contacted the police psychologist, when he realised that she wasn't coping.

Betty's medical certificate stated that she was suffering from stress. Betty felt threatened by the word, stress, there was a stigma attached to it and she felt that her career was over. Others in the police force would look at her as someone who could not cope with pressure and she would never be promoted or transferred to a CIB squad. Not that it mattered anymore. She couldn't even bear to look at her uniform.

Betty had gone sick only days before she was due to take five weeks leave. There was no way she could return to work in the state that she was in.

It was her worst ever holiday. The nightmares continued and she was continually frightened of being shot. She was filling her car with petrol when a car backfired. Betty slammed herself against the side of her car, terrified.

Betty returned to police work on night shift, earlier than she wanted to, but she had to go back. She felt other police would see her as weak, lacking in character and unreliable if she did not go back to work. Everywhere she went she felt that someone would shoot her, that she was a walking target.

Driving down Hoddle Street she clutched the dashboard anxious and sweating, hoping her partner would not notice.

When she learned that Julian Knight was not charged with the attempted murder of her or Graham Larchin, she felt worthless and cried. How could her life mean so little to the police force? She complained to the Director of Public Prosecutions and, only when Knight received the extra charges, did she feel that she could get on with her life.

Betty eventually transferred to the Moonee Ponds District Support Group as a collator. It was a position which enabled her to remain out of uniform and still work as a police officer. She and Keith have a daughter and Betty now works at Mill Park District Support Group. She hopes never to wear a police uniform again.

Darren Anderson

Darren Anderson was a police officer who worked the Northcote Police Station watch-house counter, where several survivors reported to him their experiences in Hoddle Street.

When the police helicopter was hit and went to ground Darren Anderson had felt that he was responsible. He had been guiding another operator at D24 with information that a resident had telephoned to him. His heart had sunk when he heard the pilot report Air 495 had been hit and was going to land. He had had no idea what the police force was up against and still the phones continued to ring and people kept coming to the counter with reports. Some had just wanted information. Darren had been very concerned about the safety of Graham Larchin and Betty Roberts. He felt helpless, he wanted to be out there too.

Noel McCrohan came in to the police station and needed help. For the first time in memory the Northcote Police Station, which had been open twenty-four hours a day, for decades, was locked up. Darren went on foot to help

Noel arrest Bruce Powell in McIntosh Street, still armed with a baseball bat. When he returned with Powell he saw Betty Roberts in the station and was relieved that she was still alive.

Domenic Cannizzaro

Domenic Cannizzaro was a police officer from Northcote who drove into Hoddle Street to witness the ambush near the Clifton Hill railway station. His police car was damaged when another vehicle reversed into it. He prevented other motorists from entering the ambush zone.

Domenic Cannizzaro ran over to Shane Stanton and shook him.

"Are you all right?" he asked Shane, but there was no movement, no life. Despite having a revolver in his hand, Domenic felt helpless and hopeless. He believed that if the attacker came at him he would be too scared to return fire. The gunman had greater firepower and it was pointless to shoot back. If he had the chance again, Domenic would pursue the gunman, not wait for him to attack.

When he had been a police trainee, his squad visited the morgue, where he had seen dead bodies for the first time. Some of them had undergone post-mortem examination. At night he would wake with his teeth clenched, after dreaming of seeing his family on a slab in the mortuary.

Later, he had attended a suicide in which a woman had blown her head off with a shotgun. He went to his girlfriend's house and broke down, crying, for the first time in his life. He kept seeing his girlfriend, his mother, with their heads blown off like the suicide victim. Domenic saw a psychiatrist, who helped him cope, but the images never left him until Hoddle Street. At Hoddle Street he was not repulsed by the dead bodies that he saw, that he touched. It was as if he could accept death now.

A year after Hoddle Street, Domenic was getting petrol when a car backfired. He took cover behind another car, while the garage mechanic watched, unaffected. Domenic told the mechanic that he was practising police defence procedure.

When Domenic received a cheque for $7,000 from the Crimes Compensation Tribunal he felt that he didn't deserve it, that he would have done the same thing whether on duty or not. There was no recognition from the Police Department until the end of 1991 when the Royal Humane Society awarded Domenic a Certificate of Merit. It was something that most of the police from Hoddle Street seemed to feel was missing in their lives – the lack of recognition for what they had been through. Domenic also received a letter from the Chief Commissioner of Police congratulating him on the award.

Wayne Monohan

A signalman at Clifton Hill railway station, Wayne Monohan directed the police helicopter in the direction that the gunman was thought to be heading.

The train reversed over the Urquhart Street Bridge to the Westgarth Railway Station, as a safety precaution. It was yet to be confirmed that there was only one offender. The train remained at Westgarth for more than two hours and the seven passengers were restless. One of them was a railway shunter on his way to work who didn't believe that a gunman had been randomly shooting people with military weapons. He argued with Wayne then walked along the train line towards Clifton Hill. Taxis came for the other passengers.

A police car arrived and took Wayne to the Fitzroy Police Station where a statement was taken from him. The station was packed with police and members of the public. After making his statement he was free to go home.

"How am I going to get home?" Wayne asked the police officer.

"That's your business," he was told.

It became obvious that there were many other witnesses who had no means of getting home, so the police provided transport to the Eastern Freeway – the driver would go no further. Wayne and some of the others walked up to the scene where bodies lay in situ, uncovered. Wayne offered the other witnesses with him a lift home and he was glad of their company. A police officer stopped his car and questioned everyone about where they had been. They were irritated by the questioning – they just wanted to get home and away from Hoddle Street as quickly as possible.

Initially, Wayne experienced no side-effects. His work mates he played darts with on Sundays, the Sunday Slurpers, presented him with their own medal. Then, after about two weeks, Wayne found that he could not sleep. He was angry that the media seemed to portray Knight as if he was a hero. Yet Wayne had heard from a police officer that Knight had been blubbering like a baby when he was arrested.

Wayne saw a doctor who prescribed sleeping tablets but they had little effect. About two months later, he was told, by his boss, to go home and get changed into a suit to meet the Transport Minister, Mr Tom Roper. It was the first contact he had had with anyone from the Victorian Railways, his employer, since the incident. Wayne caught the train to Parliament Railway Station and, as he entered Treasury Place, he was surrounded by railway administrators, the media and the Minister. Along with Tom Harris, Gary Stutz, Fernando Myra, Peter Harvey and Giovanni Di Vincenzo, he was presented with a brass plaque in recognition of his role in Hoddle Street. Wayne was the first called to receive his plaque and it seemed to him to be just a public relations exercise. Where were the administrators on the night of Hoddle Street? Where were they up until the day of the presentation? No one had ever asked about his health or welfare.

Wayne received $10,000 from the Crimes Compensation Tribunal. Wayne thought that people who were not really in any danger should not receive compensation. He felt that he himself didn't deserve it. Within two months he had blown the money on poker machines and alcohol. He has nothing to show for it and does not care. It was just dirty money.

Wayne used to sleep very well but now wakes in the middle of the night and watches television for hours. He applied for a transfer as a train controller because he needed to be among people. As a signalman he was always on his own. He put on 24 kilograms. Wayne used to socialise and drink a lot but he became withdrawn, preferring to stay home. He has developed a rash on both legs which comes, and goes with treatment. It's another reminder of that night in Hoddle Street.

In 1991, Wayne was awarded the Certificate of Merit by the Royal Humane Society.

Anita Adair

Anita Adair was a police officer from Northcote who, with her partner, assisted with traffic control. She resorted to showing her firearm to a motorist who would not obey her order to change direction. She also went to the gunman's home soon after he had been arrested.

At Northcote Police Station there was some merriment as Graham Larchin, Betty Roberts, Domenic Cannizzaro and Anita Adair shared a drink and discussed what had happened. They laughed as Betty reconstructed the incident where she and Graham sought cover behind their police car. Betty joked about them trying to get into the exhaust pipe, any cover was better than nothing. They teased Domenic Cannizzaro for damaging his police car.

Later, Anita was to receive an informal counselling from the Senior Sergeant for tapping on the motorist's window with her revolver. Anita learned a lot from her experience at Hoddle Street. While she believes that she was a fringe player in the incident, it taught her a lot about herself. She made mistakes that she is unlikely to repeat. She has become more aware of protecting her own safety and that of others.

Dianne Smith

Dianne Smith was working at the D24 communications centre when she heard that her husband, Colin Chambers, a traffic police officer, had been shot.

Colin was at Fitzroy Police Station when Dianne received the call. He told her that he was alright. He sounded robot-like, not like the Colin Chambers she knew, but Dianne was relieved to know that he was OK. She went to the park behind the Royal Melbourne Institute of Technology building and downed a beer with the other police, then got a lift home.

Dianne saw the police psychologist and could not return to work immediately after Hoddle Street. Everything that had been a major incident in recent years seemed to have happened while she was on duty. 'Mad Max', the Russell Street bombing and now Hoddle Street, which was the worst as she believed her husband had been one of the casualties. She saw a doctor who told her it was her personal life that was behind her problems, not her concern about Colin being shot.

Dianne was suicidal and spent a week in the police hospital before going home for another three weeks. She began to experience severe headaches and migraines. She was unable to concentrate and simple things like getting into a computer, were suddenly difficult. Her memory was poor and she became forgetful. When she returned to work she applied for a day shift position working with computers. While there she received pressure from other police officers, they thought she was a lesbian or bisexual as she was now working with a lesbian. Dianne fought the snide remarks and remained in that section for two years.

Dianne and her husband shifted house to the Mornington Peninsula and Colin transferred to Rosebud. The thought of returning to operational police duties "freaked me out". The thought of being near a police radio and being among people who carried firearms was too much, she found herself in a sweat. There was the thought that she could be shot. She had a recurring nightmare that she was driving a police car and three men suddenly started shooting at her. Colin was unable to come home wearing his police uniform – the sight of police uniforms was a poison to Dianne. Whenever she saw a police officer wearing a uniform she would break out in a sweat and want to get away. She felt that something bad would happen to her, to the police officer. For eighteen months Dianne spent her life in bed and on medication until she retired because of ill-health from the police force in 1993. Dianne is now a teacher in computers.

Daryl Jones

Daryl Jones was a member of the police helicopter crew, on board when it was shot at by the gunman and forced to land.

A late-model Ford sedan pulled up and Daryl Jones was wary. He looked out from behind the semi-trailer, where he had been taking cover.

"Good'ay," said Inspector Kieran Walsh.

Kieran checked the helicopter damage and asked if Daryl was okay. Daryl nodded even though his whole body was shaking. The next thing he remembers is being driven to the Essendon airport. There, he took out a fuel truck and returned to Hoddle Street. He heard on the police radio that there was only the one offender.

On orders, Daryl saw the police psychologist but felt that it was not a worthwhile exercise. He came out feeling worse than before. He didn't have any problems about getting back in the helicopter, but his sleep was disturbed. The Air Wing did not know of any debriefings until well after they had taken place. It seemed that, at the Air Wing, there was more concern for the damage to the helicopter than for any damage to the police officers.

Colin Chambers

Colin Chambers was a traffic police officer who was ambushed by the gunman while directing traffic. The bullet slashed his uniform and grazed his side. His wife, Dianne Smith, was working at D24 when it happened.

Was he being sent on a suicide mission? Colin wondered about this as he was sent to Rushall Crescent for traffic duty when Julian Knight had been arrested. No one was sure that Knight had acted on his own.

The full impact of having been shot did not hit him immediately. He was aware of his blistered side, the slashed tunic and shirt. He met his wife, Dianne, in the RMIT park. He was relieved to see her and felt reassured. Everyone was in a subdued mood although elated to have survived. Colin went to the Alfred Hospital where his wound was treated and he was given Valium to take at home. On his way back to the Dawson Street Police Traffic Complex he stopped the car. He could not drive any further and had to gather his composure before continuing on to complete paper work, before being driven home via the State Forensic Science Laboratory where Homicide detectives required his tunic, shirt and singlet for examination.

It was 4.30 a.m. when he got home. The phone started ringing non-stop. Police Media Liaison had mistakenly released his name and personal details to the media. Colin had been required to see the police psychologist and receive counselling. As a traffic police officer he already felt some isolation from the rest of the police force and Hoddle Street made him feel even more so. He heard nothing about a debriefing. No one contacted him, other than Sergeant Jim Cracknell, who had been at Hoddle Street too. He felt that no one, apart from his Sergeant, cared about his welfare. He saw a doctor and was given two weeks off duty. He had difficulty concentrating and remembering even the most basic of things.

Dennis Harnetty

Dennis Harnetty assisted Sergeant Terry Howard in driving the MICA ambulance to the injured beside the Clifton Hill railway station, and was later involved in a search for the gunman.

"Twenty-seven pizzas," Dennis Harnetty said. The pizza lady thought that she hadn't heard him correctly and asked him to repeat his order. The Universal Pizza shop in Lygon Street, Carlton had had large orders before but not quite like this. While he waited, the pizza lady made him a cappuccino, then a pizza for himself. He devoured it quickly. He had no money but she wrote him an invoice and wished everyone well.

Dennis drove the police car carefully back towards Hoddle Street breathing in the aroma of the steamy pizzas. It was comforting after the cold mayhem. He distributed pizzas to each police officer at the crime scene then took those left to Spensley Street, the old Clifton Hill Police Station and now District Office for the area. He distributed the remaining pizzas to those inside.

Back at Richmond Police Station he began to feel the shock. He rang Lisa, his wife, who was awake and worried, as her parents had telephoned. They had two boys and he wanted to get home to ensure that they were all right. He thought of Gina Papaioannou and hoped that she would survive her injuries. He read the D24 telexes and rang Media Liaison for news updates. He rang the hospital but was told nothing.

In the station it was quiet, there was little talk and when he grew tired of waiting for updates on Gina, he left for home.

Dennis did not tell Lisa what he had seen and she did not ask. He gave her a brief rundown. He didn't want to cause her any more distress. He went to his boys and hugged them tight. Later, with his wife, he broke down and cried.

He had continued difficulty sleeping and his restlessness disturbed Lisa. He became grumpy and moody and he and Lisa often argued.

As a former member of the Protective Security Group, and one who had been in close personal contact with such important people as the Prime Minister, he had been mentally and physically prepared for every possible situation that a police officer could expect to confront. But now he felt nervous doing his job. He was concerned when near the windows of his police station and he took anonymous threats seriously.

During January 1988 the family went to Phillip Island where they had a holiday house. Dennis had stopped running after Hoddle Street and tried to resume during his leave, but could get no further than the front door. He and Lisa sat on the beach and talked about their future. The holiday had not helped and Dennis walked to a phone box and rang the police psychologist, Simon Brown-Greaves. They talked for fifteen minutes and Dennis agreed to see him. He found himself able to go for a run down by the water's edge, where the sand was firm.

Dennis Harnetty saw Simon Brown-Greaves several times and felt things improve. He felt more comfortable telling the psychologist how he felt than Lisa. He was reassured that what he was feeling was normal, that other people, including police, felt the same way and it was to be expected. His relationship with Lisa returned to normal.

In October 1988 Dennis Harnetty worked his first night shift as a detective with Russell Street CIB. On the night of the Walsh Street murders, he had been to St Kilda investigating what appeared to be a suicide. A man had jumped from the third floor of a building. Called to Walsh Street, Prahran, he held Constable Steve Tynan in his arms and watched him die, unable to help. Dennis knew Steve Tynan and the emotions that he'd felt at Hoddle Street came flooding back.

Dennis Harnetty went into Hoddle Street treating it as just another job. But the experience changed his outlook on life. He became harder, more cynical and less tolerant. Eventually, he moved with his family to country Victoria to try and regain his old sense of self.

Graham Larchin

Graham Larchin and his partner, Betty Roberts, were ambushed as they drove their police car into Hoddle Street. Graham directed traffic in Queens Parade away from Hoddle Street. He believed he could have killed a homeless man who was fleeing from the Merri Creek and was initially thought to be the gunman.

It was 7.00 a.m. when Graham Larchin pulled into the driveway of his home. Once inside the front door he felt relieved, but didn't want to tell his wife, Ester, what had happened. It was his policy not to bring work home. He wanted to protect his wife and children. He felt that if he did speak of what happened he would break down, and he needed to remain strong and in control.

It gnawed at him that no one had contacted him, or any of the other police from Northcote, to see if they were all right.

On the Monday afternoon Graham felt too ill to go to work. The thought made him want to vomit. It was the first time he had experienced that feeling. Graham's doctor gave him a two-day medical certificate and he drove the twenty kilometres to his police station to hand it in. He did not want to claim his illness on WorkCare as he felt it would be viewed harshly by everyone in the police force, and he wanted a promotion.

As he walked from the car park to the police station he was met by his Senior Sergeant, who called him a weak mongrel, and the two clashed heatedly. Another senior sergeant came outside and restrained Graham. He saw the police psychologist who helped him understand his feelings and, in a short space of time, he felt that he could cope. With the medical certificate and a month of accumulated leave, he would manage.

He returned to duty on afternoon shift and the first job involved an offender with a sawn-off shotgun threatening to shoot on a High Street tram. A search was conducted, both on the tram and at the home of the offender, but he escaped. Two days later the offender gave himself up to Graham and it was only then that he felt that perhaps he could put the events of Hoddle Street behind him.

As a young constable in 1977, Graham had cornered a madman armed with a machete who had attacked motorists and an ambulance crew. He had flown at Graham swinging the machete, when another police officer threw a torch which struck, and momentarily distracted, the madman long enough for him to be arrested. He had not been charged with attempted murder of Graham because he was facing similar charges already.

After Hoddle Street, when Graham heard that Knight was not going to be charged with the attempted murder of Betty Roberts and himself, he was incensed. It was the first time he had felt that he was just a number; a police officer's life wasn't worth charging an assailant with attempted murder.

Graham sent correspondence containing a charge, for two counts of attempted murder, against Julian Knight, to the Director of Public Prosecutions. He was contacted by a staff member from the DPP and told that he was being ridiculous. Graham responded by saying that in the eyes of the DPP and the Police Department, he did not exist.

At the end of 1987 Graham sat for the senior sergeant exam. His mind felt like it was in a fog and, for the first time in his life, he failed an exam. He applied to repeat it, citing his experience at Hoddle Street as the reason for his poor performance. This was supported by his superior officers but rejected by the examining board. Undeterred, Graham requested an audience with an assistant commissioner but again his plea was rejected.

Graham transferred from Northcote to the Fraud Squad where he felt that he had a greater chance to recover. There would be few, if any, occasions where he would be required to confront a violent offender. He struggled to complete the Fraud Squad course. His ability to concentrate was poor and his memory felt like that of an old man. He wondered if he was in the early stages of Alzheimer's Disease; perhaps he was going insane.

The police doctor advised him to resign or transfer to Force Reserve. Graham took sick leave and, for the first time, submitted a WorkCare form claiming work-related stress which was rejected by State Insurance on the grounds that they believed his stress was not work related. He rang the Police Association for help and became abusive over the telephone. No one, not even the Police Association, seemed to care. Ester took over the phone. It was tough on her. She was still unaware of what he had experienced and what troubled him. She tried to get him to talk to her but he was reticent. Graham sat staring out of the lounge room window, drinking beer and watching television.

Eventually, with help from the Police Welfare branch, State Insurance accepted his WorkCare claim. But the fight had taken its toll.

Graham spent one month on sick leave and felt at a loose end. He was unable to sleep and was drinking alcohol every day rather than once a week. He had not touched the weights or the punching bag in his garage since Hoddle Street. He had stopped running which had been a life time habit. His only interests were watching television and drinking beer.

He began to question his self-worth, the value of being a police officer.

In early 1988 a staff member from the DPP rang to advise that, after much discussion, Knight was to be charged with the attempted murder of Betty Roberts and himself.

In 1991 the Royal Humane Society awarded Graham the Certificate of Merit for his actions in Hoddle Street.

Graham had never heard of the Rehabilitation Section of the Victoria Police until someone mentioned it to him. No one from that office had contacted him and none of his doctors or psychologists had mentioned its existence to him. Graham did not want to stay at the Fraud Squad. He rang the Rehabilitation Section and discussed his problem with a staff member. Feeling motivated, he felt that he was taking the first step towards recovery and began studying in preparation for the next senior sergeant exams.

When he again appeared before the examining board he was told he was not suitable, that he was not senior sergeant material because he could not handle stress. Graham argued with the board members and told them of his experiences at Hoddle Street. He asked whether any of them had been there, and if they were, had they been shot at? Had they been close to being murdered? The chairman apologised to Graham. He was classified A – suitable for promotion.

Graham is a Detective Senior Sergeant with the Organised Crime Squad. It has been a long road for him and it took him until 1992 to feel that he was returning to the type of life and the type of person that he had been prior to Hoddle Street. He is now the holder of a black belt in karate and has undertaken tertiary study.

John Delahunty

John Delahunty was the police officer who, with Ralph Lockman, was ambushed but returned the fire of the gunman, and effected his arrest.

John has never accepted the "military mode" explanation given by Knight. He believes that people have accepted that answer because it was one that people could handle and quickly put the case behind them. It has taken John a few years to get over Hoddle Street. He has spoken to veterans of the Vietnam War and identifies with how they feel, which is beyond the realm of most people's experience. Since Hoddle Street, John has become more serious, more cynical about the behaviour of human beings towards each other.

"It doesn't matter what people say, it's in your heart that you act."

John Delahunty quotes these words said to him by a "hardnut copper". He has been a detective for several years.

Julian Knight

Beginnings

Julian Knight was born on 4 March 1968 and was ten days old when adopted by army officer, Ralph Knight, and his wife, Pamela. He was told at an early age that he was adopted and, according to friends who knew him during this period, it was never a problem for him. He just accepted his situation and was happy with his adopted parents. His parents adopted two other children, Sarah and Matthew, who also knew that they were adopted. Knight's natural father was working as a fruit picker when he met Knight's mother, a receptionist. She left Australia soon afterwards for Durban, South Africa, where she later married and has lived since. When Knight learned of her identity, he tried to contact her but his letters went unanswered. All Knight knows of his father is that he had a degree in agriculture.

His adoptive father was a teacher in the army, and the family moved around. Julian started school in Hong Kong. When the family returned to Victoria, his father took up a position in the school of languages at the Royal Australian Air Force Base at Point Cook and they lived in Laverton. Julian continued his education at Epsom Street Primary School. It was at this school that, according to Knight, his first problems with bullies arose. When he saw other children being bullied Knight said that he would step in and, invariably, end up in a fight with the bully.

Knight adored his parents and was a happy child, always laughing and happy-go-lucky albeit mischievous, according to his cub leader. She recalled that, although he had been told not to go near sea snakes, he had thrown one into the group, causing them to scatter. This had amused him greatly. During this time his parents began to argue; his mother wanted the family to settle down. She felt that the children needed stability and a permanent home.

In 1979, aged eleven, Knight went to a private school, Westbourne Grammar in Hoppers Crossing. His parents separated in March 1980 and were divorced the following year. During this period Knight's scholastic ability declined and he struggled, failing in several subjects. For the first twelve months, he generally saw his father on alternate weekends and found it very difficult to cope. Then his father was posted to Canberra and he saw him on three extended visits each year that he was there. Mr Robert Richter, QC, commented during his plea, at Knight's trial, "As far as Mr Knight is concerned, since the time of separation, there had not been substantial and ongoing contact with his father, although, from time to time, there would be some. He does, however, have a good relationship with his father as he does with his mother."

He was not happy at Westbourne Grammar. The school was very formal; the staff wore academic gowns. Teachers saw Knight as being aggressive and volatile. He did not seem to need friends and made black-humoured comments, seemingly to shock others. He was constantly in trouble and his behaviour seemed to deteriorate the longer he was at the school.

On one occasion he locked a teacher out of her classroom. As she struggled to open the door he sat grinning. Another student let the teacher in. On another occasion he set off crackers in the classroom lockers. To some students he was the class clown, an amusing practical joker, but, it seemed to others that he was taking his dark humour too far.

On the academic front he seemed only to be interested in history. His principal at the time, Mr John Fawkner, believed that Knight had an intimidating manner particularly towards female staff, who were unhappy teaching him. There was a feeling that he would erupt into violence. Once he whispered something to a female teacher which reduced her to tears. The principal caned him and the tearful teacher predicted to her colleagues that Knight would "do something horrific in the future".

It was an opinion shared by other teachers and something that echoed in the mind of Jane Morrison, who recalled Knight saying, as he sat beside her in a school bus, "Everyone will know me. One day I will be famous and people will know me."

Knight was heard to say that he would break Jane Morrison. It seemed as if he enjoyed seeing another person crumble under his personality. On one occasion Jane saw him put his feet up on the desk in one of her classes. He had previously been disciplined by a male teacher for the same thing. When Sandra drew the attention of the class to the fact that something was bothering Knight, under the gaze of his peers, he backed down and removed his feet.

Baiting teachers was a habit that he persisted with at Westbourne. His persistent and unnecessary response of "why?" and "what for?" did not endear him to the staff or to many of his peers.

During his three years at Westbourne Grammar, his parents were sent letters advising of his behaviour, and occasionally visited the Principal's office. The school psychologist counselled him and staff went out of their way to steer him in the right direction. It seemed as if he was determined to go his own way regardless of advice or consequences.

Principal Fawkner dealt with Knight on several occasions when the heads of the junior or senior school had been unable to curtail his repeated bad behaviour. He was seen as an instigator of fights who picked on boys who were smaller and younger than himself. He was counselled for bullying behaviour and, when that did not work, he was given the strap or the cane.

In class Knight would draw cartoons and caricatures and pass them around. Generally most of them had themes of violence, bloodshed and killing people.

Around the same time as his parents separated he met Brett Piper. Both had similar interests. Brett was already in the naval cadets. They were both fascinated with war and guns and both possessed a number of air rifles. Knight also had a BB gun which his parents had given him as a present for his twelfth birthday. From his father's property in Lara, Knight would fire shots as he fantasised that he was the hero in an imaginary battle. The cars driving past his father's property were the enemy convoy and he was the one to save Australia.

He and Brett became close friends staying at each other's house on weekends and school holidays, and playing war games. In his bedroom Knight had model tanks and soldiers, which he spent hours building, painting and playing with. Already he was building up a small library of books on war and military.

Brett joined Knight, his brother, Matthew and sister, Sarah, and Knight's father and his partner, on a camping trip in the bush during the Easter holidays. Brett remembers it being in the Lake Eppalock area. They would wander off shooting at crows, cans and anything that moved. He and Knight built a fort with branches and gum leaves in the bush against a tree near the side of a gravel road. Every ten minutes, or so, a car approached and, hiding in the fort, they would shoot at the cars, aiming at the wheels as they went by. They would then go off in to the bush and stake out another area, shooting with the air gun and BB rifle at passing cars. Once they hit the side of a car and ran off in to the bush. They were French Foreign Legion soldiers, a fantasy that Knight often talked about. Sometimes he was a South African police officer. He would pretend that his sister Sarah was a kaffa, and he would pretend to beat her because she was black. Brett would join in and it was a lot of fun.

At Lake Eppalock Brett and Knight shared a two-man tent about 15 metres away from the others. When it was dark they would leave their tent and continue their French Foreign Legion fantasy. They came across a small tent, which was illuminated by a torch. There were children aged about seven or eight inside who were having trouble sleeping. Knight fired his air rifle at the tent and the children screamed out for their father and turned off the torch. Their father, who was in a tent ten metres away, came over and the children explained that someone was shooting at them. The father was annoyed. It was late and he felt that the children had been playing up long enough. He slapped one of them for making up stories and then returned to his own tent. Shortly after the torch went on again in the tent and the children started chattering. Knight fired at the tent again, sending the children into hysterics. The pellets from the BB gun should not have penetrated the tent skin but Brett and Knight did not wait to find out. They ran laughing through the bush and into their fort.

On the way home from Lake Eppalock Brett sat in the middle of the back seat with Knight on his right and Sarah on his left. As they travelled back to Melbourne through the countryside Julian nursed the BB rifle.

"I bet if I shot you in the neck it wouldn't hurt," Knight said, holding the rifle against his friend's neck.

"I bet it would," Brett said.

He had no chance to say anything else as Knight pulled back the trigger and shot Brett causing him to reel back in shock and cry out. He reached for his bruised neck just as Knight's father's partner turned around to see what had happened. She backhanded Knight, who was still holding the BB rifle to Brett's neck, and took it from him. His father was angry and told Knight he would deal with him when they got back to Melbourne. Brett remembers Knight's father taking his son into another room only to re-emerge minutes later with Knight, who was crying and sobbing. Knight apologised for what he had done and the two boys were friends again. They slept in sleeping bags on the floor of the loungeroom after watching television till late. Knight was about 13 when he told Brett that he had lost his virginity in the back of a bus on a trip from Melbourne to visit his father in Canberra. It was at about this age that he started to read *Soldier of Fortune* magazines. In 1982 he joined the Norwood High School army cadet unit in Ringwood and his father would drive him to the parades.

In November, 1982 Knight was expelled from Westbourne Grammar School. He was in Year 8 and had been playing soccer during the lunch break. The ball flew out of their area and into the arms of Archie Clarke, a Year 7 boy about eight centimetres shorter than Knight, but a bully. He, like Knight, was a misfit at the school, and had, in an incident earlier that year, broken a boy's ankle. Clarke had claimed that the other had picked on him and he responded in the way that his father had taught him. His father, a former Shrine Guard, had taught him to "finish the fight" and to "take shit from no one".

Clarke held the ball. No one can recall what happened next, but Brett Piper remembers seeing Clarke push Knight on the chest then the shoulders, again and again. The group of boys who Knight had been playing soccer with egged Knight on to hit back. Then Clarke threw the first punch, striking Knight on the right side of his face. Instinctively Knight hit back and struck Clarke several times in return, causing him to fall over, just as Jane Morrison arrived. Clarke saw her and stopped fighting – he did not want any further trouble as he had already been suspended once.

Clarke remembers pushing and shoving Knight, but not punching him, and that, as soon as the teacher arrived, he stopped, and the matter from his perspective was finished. He said that Knight then, unexpectedly, hit him, knocking him to the ground.

What is not in dispute is that Knight drew back his leg and kicked Clarke in the head. He kicked Clarke's head as if it were a football. Jane Morrison thought it was the most vicious act that she had ever witnessed and was distressed at the ferocity of the blows. She called out for Knight to stop, but he kept kicking. Other students grabbed Knight and pulled him away. Clarke saw a doctor and received treatment for cuts, grazing and slight concussion. Knight received corporal punishment from the Principal and after, boasted about getting "the cuts" on both hands. He showed the other students the red marks on his palms and laughed it off. Both boys were expelled. For the school it was an opportunity to be rid of two troublesome youths.

Clarke's father reported the matter to Altona North CIB as he felt Knight had gone too far and that his son could have been seriously hurt. Detective Constable Greg Payne, who had been in the CIB for a few months and had yet to complete the detective training school, took a statement from Archie Clarke, who seemed embarrassed about the whole matter. After making inquiries with witnesses and the Principal, Greg Payne contacted Knight's mother and arranged to interview him in her presence after she had finished work as a secretary.

At 6.30 p.m. Greg and his partner parked the unmarked police car outside their house at 6 Ramsden Street, Clifton Hill, and knocked on the door. Pamela Knight led them to the kitchen where they were surprised to see Knight wearing GP (general purpose) boots, black T-shirt and green army trousers. Pamela was defensive and annoyed that the matter now involved the police. She had sought legal advice and had been instructed to answer "no comment" to all of their questions. Knight seemed to treat the matter lightly, as if he enjoyed the attention. Greg opened his folder and recorded the questions and answers at the kitchen table. It was an easy interview as all he had to write was "no comment" to all Knight's answers. He left the house advising that he could not recommend a caution as Knight did not admit to the offence. It would have to go to the Children's Court. Greg's senior sergeant disagreed and recommended that the matter still proceed as a "caution" whereby Knight, in the presence of his parents, would be counselled at the police station. However that recommendation was overuled by an inspector who approved prosecution on one of three charges because Knight had denied the offence and his parents did not consent to the cautioning process.

On 31 March 1983 Knight appeared before the Werribee Children's Court charged with assault by kicking. Knight was now a student at Fitzroy High School and already in trouble with teachers for smoking, fighting and setting off fire crackers in the classroom. He was known there as SOF because of the *Soldier of Fortune* magazines that he liked to read. Fitzroy High School had a high percentage of migrant children and Knight found himself, unhappily, in a minority of Anglo Saxon descent.

Westbourne Grammar had a solicitor to represent the school, a solicitor represented Knight who had both parents there and Archie Clarke's father, David, was there to support his son. Witnesses to the fight had been subpoenaed and both the police and Knight's solicitor had subpoenaed the Principal, Mr Fawkner. Everyone stood around until the end of the day when the matter was called. There was discussion between the four parties: the police, Knight, Clarke, and the school, about how best to resolve the matter. Knight's parents were concerned that a conviction would prevent their son from going to Duntroon. David Clarke offered to let the matter drop if Knight apologised to Archie. Neither boy was going to benefit from the hearing, and their school reports, which were to be tabled by the school, were not complimentary.

Frank Tenni, the Children's Court Magistrate, felt an apology was appropriate and dismissed the charges. Greg Payne was annoyed. If Knight and his mother had answered questions and agreed to a caution the whole process could have been a avoided.

The next time Mr Fawkner saw Julian Knight was in the carpark of Westbourne Grammar School about three years later. It was during the summer and a north-west wind fanned a fire towards the school destroying haystacks while sweeping through two paddocks. The local CFA units attended and put out the fire as Knight, who was a passenger in a car driven by another youth, drove out of the carpark. It just seemed too much of a coincidence for Knight to be in the school grounds and for a fire to be advancing towards it.

At the beginning of 1984 Julian Knight was on his last chance as far as the education system was concerned. He was not wanted at Fitzroy High School, and was given the opportunity to leave or face expulsion. He had been disruptive and made to sit outside classes. He occasionally wore a military jacket to classes and seemed to be interested mainly in firearms and anything military.

His geography teacher remarked that he was a "capable student". In maths, he could have achieved more had he "concentrated more in class". He was considered "a very capable student who has a sound understanding of this subject" in biology. His English teacher said, "He is a clear-minded, confident and articulate student, but he should not get too complacent about his own abilities". In physics, he was "a very capable student who tends to be a little disruptive in class at times. Overall he worked very well". In history, "a capable student, but he appears to be both lazy and easily distracted". His art teacher said, "His attendance and level of commitment are poor. Julian is an intelligent and witty boy, but he needs to push himself and aim higher."

Knight was one of thirty boys who enrolled at Year 11 at Melbourne High School, a school which had produced many leaders in the community since its inception in 1854 as the National Model School. Knight transferred from Fitzroy to Melbourne on 19 March 1984. He was interested in humanities subjects and used that as the excuse for transfer from Fitzroy High. The subjects that Melbourne High had to offer were more extensive than that at Fitzroy and Knight was particularly interested in history.

During his interview with John Grigsby, the Year 12 Coordinator, Knight wore the Norwood Army Cadet uniform and presented with three references including one from Fitzroy High. It was not unusual for a school to conveniently ignore a student's past indiscretions in order to have him transfer somewhere else. John Grigsby had received a phone call from the coordinator at Fitzroy advising that Knight was not progressing satisfactorily or happily there. Often a student who did not fit in at one school would be a better student at another. Knight had to sign the School Admission Form agreeing that he would obey the school rules. His mother signed the form too as an assurance that he would comply. It was a form all students and their parents were required to sign and Knight knew that his chances of going to Duntroon were slim if he slipped up again. It was his last chance and he was determined to stay on the straight and narrow.

He started the 1984 year at Year 11 and was considered to be very quiet. He was pushed by teachers to meet deadlines and to keep up the traditional standards of excellence required of Melbourne High School students. "Honour The Work" was the school motto and was taken from a speech given by Frank Tate, a former Director of Education, who had borrowed the words of Edward Thring who said, "Honour the work and the work will honour you."

While Knight was at Melbourne High he was not once disciplined for poor behaviour. He was seen by some teachers as a loner. He seemed to exist on the sidelines of his peer group, many of whom were also from broken homes. In his first year he just managed to pass English, geography, and history. He failed politics, legal studies and economics. His marks were sufficient for him to be promoted to Year 12. His performance throughout his two years at Melbourne High was considered below average. He was often behind and lacked "depth and detail in his work," according to John Grigsby.

Of interest to Knight was the army cadet unit that had been part of the school since 1906 and was seen as important in developing character, leadership, self-discipline and self-reliance. The school pocket diary listed "unit administration, radio and signals work, map making and navigation, adventure training, medical work, elementary field engineering, bush camp siting and construction, and advanced fieldcraft" as courses available to its members. Cadets with ability were promoted to leadership ranks. It was seen as a long-range recruiting source for the army reserve, Duntroon and the regular army.

Langley Company was divided into a number of platoons. 5th Platoon contained cadets who were either not interested or showed insufficient leadership skills to be considered for promotion above the rank of corporal. Many of the boys in 5th Platoon did not want to be higher than corporal, a rank that was judged as being appropriate for Knight by his peers and those who supervised his platoon. His acceptance into Duntroon was a surprise to those who knew him during this stage in his life, as he had not advanced past corporal rank and did not display any potential for a higher rank.

In any case he seemed happier at Melbourne High and at 5th Platoon. There were fewer "wogs" at Melbourne High than at Fitzroy, and the cadets' uniform appealed to him more than the one at Norwood.

The students generally did not see each other outside of school hours and out of uniform so it surprised his peers, during a casual dress day, to see Knight wearing a T shirt, braces, tight jeans and Doc Marten boots. He looked like a skinhead standing out among his more conservative and less radical peers. Knight sometimes brought photographs to school of himself shooting rabbits and ducks.

He was seen by other boys as aggressive and sensitive about his family life and he gave the impression that he was looking for a fight. He was considered a follower rather than a leader, who liked to play practical jokes. Other cadets felt that he had a chip on his shoulder. He was contrary, a "smart arse" and an introvert.

At school Knight was the only student in his class who stood up for the white South African population. It didn't matter to him that everyone else in the class disagreed with him. Some teachers and peers felt that he enjoyed the notoriety of opposing the majority view. It made others notice him and he seemed to enjoy being the centre of attention. He spoke of joining the South African army or Afrikaaners and would joke about it by mimicking the South African accent and saying he wanted to "kill some kaffas". There was always talk from Knight about killing "blacks" or Asians, particularly the Vietnamese who he felt were "invading the country". He talked of emigrating to South Africa because he believed that national service was compulsory. During one parade, 5th Platoon was being addressed by the Sergeant Major. A Vietnamese girl was seen to take a short-cut through the hockey field towards Chapel Street. Knight yelled out "Contact!" the army expression for "being engaged visually or physically with the enemy". The girl quickened her pace as the other cadets broke into laughter. The Sergeant Major ordered Knight to do fifteen push ups as he tried to return order to the platoon.

At a camp, held in Puckapunyal during the August school holidays, the cadets were required to survive without outside help. It rained most of the time, which Knight constantly complained about. It was during exercise Blue Skin Beast that he and the other cadets pooled their money and bought slabs of beer which they buried for safe keeping while they were on a search exercise. They had to find a tree with a cross painted on the trunk, but were unsuccessful. They did find the slabs and celebrated in style by getting drunk.

When they ran out of food and water they lived on the rest of the beer and trapped "drop bears" (possums) to supplement their diet. They chased a sheep, cornered it, and carried it back to the camp where they skinned it and put it on a spit. It was quite late at night when they finally had their meal but before morning they buried the remains, which was just as well as they were reported by the farmer but nothing could be proved.

Knight was known to drop a can of cheese or vegemite into a camp fire then casually walk away to watch his mates be covered in cheese or vegemite when it exploded. It was a dangerous practice and not one that was condoned by anyone. He was censured by the others and he did it only when there were no adults about. On another occasion he dropped a magnesium battery in the fire to see what would happen. He then added powder to it to create a greater flare.

After one camp several of the boys met, in their uniforms, at a city theatre to see the film *Rambo*. They were a loud group, continually shouting "that's bullshit" and making life miserable for the rest of the audience.

Friday, 11 October 1985 was the last day at Melbourne High for Julian Knight. In the morning he took part in rehearsal for the Annual Ceremonial Parade. It was the one hundredth anniversary of cadet training at Melbourne High School and after rehearsal he and a number of other boys from 5th Platoon climbed into the station wagon of a cadet's father. They had some time on their hands and decided to go for a drive until the parade itself later that afternoon. As Jim Toomey drove along Victoria Street, Richmond – Little Vietnam – Knight complained about all the Asians. He would yell out, "Contact!" and the others would ask, "Where?"

"Every-fuckin' where," Knight would reply.

During the Annual Ceremonial Parade, Knight took part in the drill exercises with his platoon, carrying a rifle, to the music of the school band. The Parade was reviewed by the Lieutenant Governor of Victoria, Sir John Young. Apart from swatting for exams it was the end of the year for all Year 12 students. Some students went home, while others went to the Corner Hotel. If Knight passed the Higher School Certificate he would be going to university, something he didn't really want to do but would try for his parents' sake. He was one of the few cadets who wanted to be career soldiers. He had struggled in his first year at Melbourne High and with greater application had improved in his second year. At the Corner Hotel, Knight joked and unwound with the other boys, in their uniforms. He seemed to be more confident and cocky in his uniform, as if he was somebody when wearing it and nobody without it. David Heady, a former student who had left the school to take on an apprenticeship, joined the group. At about the same time, a ten-metre, converted scallop boat, Kim, motored up the Yarra River from its usual mooring at South Wharf. Part owned by Dr Richard Ward and radio broadcaster Derryn Hinch, it was carrying food and wine to help celebrate the birthday of Dr Ward's wife, Barbara. Dr Ward, the Carlton Football Club doctor, moored the Kim beside a jetty near the Morell Bridge where friends joined the boat. Canvas stanchions had been raised to give privacy to the party as many guests were well known to the public. They included Jacki Weaver, Dennis Gowing, Craig Willis and Paul Barber. It was a typical balmy October night and everyone was in good spirits. At about 8.00 p.m. Dr Ward decided to motor up to the Hawthorn area but the motor refused to start. The partygoers left the boat and continued their party on the banks of the river. At about 9.30 p.m. they moved back on board the boat. Someone saw movement among the trees.

David Heady, Andrew Ronaldson and Julian Knight approached and asked to come on board. Dr Ward politely refused them. Craig Willis told the group that it was a private party. They recognised Derryn Hinch and struck up a conversation with him. Hinch was interested in what they were doing and in their uniforms. The boys said they were going in to the city but asked again to come onboard. Rebuffed, they walked away. Soon after it was noticed that a mooring line for the Kim had been unhooked and the rear of the boat was drifting. The mooring line was replaced. Then the fore and aft lines were unhooked. Dr Ward noticed Knight and the others hiding behind trees and laughing. He replaced the lines. Derryn then saw them approach the boat 'semi-commando style". The mooring lines were again unhooked. This time Dr Ward and Craig Willis chased the youths but lost them in the shadows. Dr Ward tried to start the motor again but without success, so several of the party kept watch from the boat while others stood on the jetty. It was just after midnight when the Yarra Princess motored down the Yarra to tow the Kim back to South Wharf. Knight and the others looked on as Derryn Hinch and Peter, the sixteen-year-old son of Dr Ward and his wife, tried to push the boat away from the pier. As it drifted away Peter jumped on board while Derryn Hinch tried to do the same. He jumped from the pier but hit the side of the Kim like a champagne bottle breaking three of his ribs. When it was reported on the news the following day it was the cause of much mirth for Julian Knight and his two friends.

In the 1985 issue of *Unicorn*, the Melbourne High School year book, where each student is described in as few words as possible, Knight is described as having "inherited the role of Cadet Unit looney and chief political agitator."

When Knight met Renee Cross in September 1985 the relationship started slowly. He was her first boyfriend and he was just getting over a relationship with another girl, Helen Norman. Knight slept with Renee's best friend and it became a source of friction in the relationship over the next seventeen months. Renee could not forget. She went out with other men and informed Knight. He gave her the impression that he didn't mind but she was to discover that he did in fact mind. Knight had discussed the fact that he had been adopted and that his parents had divorced. He had broken down and cried over this. Sometimes when he got drunk he would be either very witty or become emotional and cry. He would "go on about being adopted and that he wasn't breast fed," Renee said, in a statement to the police.

Renee suggested that he see a psychiatrist. Whatever it was that troubled him seemed to have happened a long time ago. He could be affectionate one minute and the next he would be aggressive, particularly when he had been drinking alcohol. He would sit and brood and then strike out for no apparent reason and without warning. Knight talked to Renee about being a farmer but she got the impression that his family were pushing him into the Army. His bedroom walls were layered with posters of tanks, armed soldiers and photographs of dead people spread across the road. He had a montage board made up of newspaper and magazine clippings showing corpses from the conflict in South Africa and elsewhere. Renee disliked this aspect of his personality and it contributed to her feeling that there was something wrong with him.

Knight sat for his Year 12 exams and obtained passes in English (62), Australian history (69), politics (68), eighteenth century history (65) and geography (63) – enough to receive the Higher School Certificate. Before 1985 was over Knight had enlisted in the army reserve, serving at the 4/19 Prince of Wales Light Horse Regiment in Park Street, Carlton.

After he had finished school he worked for a time at McDonalds in the city, where it was noticed that he was unhappy about working with and cleaning up after Asian or southern European customers – "wogs". He would pretend to shoot them with an imaginary revolver. Renee Cross told police, in her statement, that, "He also seemed to be not only strongly anti-black, but seemed to love whites." For a month before going to La Trobe University in 1986 he sold weatherboard cladding door-to-door.

For the six weeks he was at La Trobe University he studied modern history, French, English and politics. He told others that the university was "full of wogs" and "left over hippies from the sixties" and consequently he felt out of place. He dropped out of the Bachelor of Arts course. He wanted to be in the army.

Essentially unemployed, Knight's energy went into the army reserve. He participated in a number of camps at Sale and Puckapunyal. He completed an assault troopers course where he was taught to use a variety of weapons, how to strip and clean them, the different firing positions and how to look for cover and concealment. He was taught that it was better to leave the wounded enemy alive rather than kill them as the enemy then had to attend to their wounded and would be slowed down.

He was seen by some in his regiment as a cheerful, easy-going person. Others felt he lacked maturity and was not fully committed except to anything relating to firearms. In other areas he lacked the necessary drive and was often found to be "swanning" or on "hiding patrols" while other members of his group were doing such physical work as cleaning or repairing machinery.

On the day of his eighteenth birthday, 4 March 1986, Knight walked into the Collingwood Police Station and completed an application form for a shooters licence. The twenty questions were basic and relied on the applicant's honesty and attitude. Knight was polite during the interview and said that he would have his weapons placed in a locked cupboard secured by a chain.

On 21 April, more than twenty-one days after the required cooling off period, Knight returned to the police station and received his shooters licence. It allowed him to purchase, possess, carry and use a shotgun, a pea rifle and any other rifle including military type rifle. He was not interested in purchasing an authority to hunt game licence. The fee of $30 entitled him to have the licence until 20 April 1989. He had no criminal history and nothing was known of him that would prevent him from being issued with a licence.

There was a party at his house and everyone had had a few drinks. Renee was annoyed with Knight for talking about his former girlfriend, Helen. Knight reacted in the only way he knew and that was to strike out at people. He threw some punches at the others in the small party and Renee fled to the safety of the toilet and closed the door. Knight kicked the door open dragging Renee out and, as she lay on the floor, he kicked her head with his bare feet. She fled out the back door while Knight fought with one of the guests. Then he started crying and she returned to the house to comfort him.

Around the same time Knight started a fight at Madisons Nightclub. He had been drinking beforehand and was ignoring Renee. She wanted him to take her home. He told her to go away, and in a show of frustration, started a fight and was thrown out.

On 15 May 1986 he purchased a Mossberg twelve-gauge, pump-action shotgun for $290. On 31 July 1986 he purchased, from the same dealer, Frank O'Reilly, in Thornbury, an M14 Norinco .308 calibre, automatic rifle for $550.

During the Armoured Personnel Carrier driving course at Dutson Downs, near Sale, Knight, with the other troopers, paraded early each morning and was given instruction in driving army personnel carrier vehicles in very rough terrain, at night as well as day for two weeks. The course was very intense and was essentially a five-week course crammed into two weeks to put pressure on the troopers, and expose any signs of weakness. At night the students were tested by the five instructors on what they had been taught during the day.

Knight became known as Jack (I'm alright Jack) because he was not pulling his weight. He did not like to get his hands dirty, consequently the instructors pushed him to get them dirty. While others in his squadron were servicing vehicles or cleaning up the "brew tent" (the area where refreshments were taken) Knight would be found resting in the back of an APC vehicle. One instructor openly criticised Knight for not helping his mates, who were doing all the work. Warrant Officer Kevin Hunter said that Knight stood back when given a task and let others do the work for him. He considered Knight an isolate.

In armoured crews it was necessary to have people join in and mix. Knight was seen during lunch breaks to get his meal then move away from the others, who were in groups of up to six, and eat on his own. To the instructors this was a warning signal that Knight was not relating to his peers. In conflict situations one man could not function alone despite what the movies suggested.

During this course Renee had written to him saying that she had been out with someone else. Knight rang her from Sale, screaming at her down the phone line.

During the APC course there were problems with hot water and the troopers were warned to use the showers sparingly. Everyone was to prepare the vehicles for the next day's driving but Knight was nowhere to be found. An instructor found him in the shower block making liberal use of the hot water.

After a week and a half, Knight was told that he was not going to complete the course and was given general duties to perform, which meant that he was basically a cleaner and odd jobs man. He was returned to Sale while the others in his squadron continued the course in Dutson Downs. Among his peers this was seen as a disgrace, and it was humbling for Knight to do kitchen and toilet work while they continued on the APC driving school course. Knight was aggressive and would not accept the criticism that he was an isolate and did not mix in with his peers.

During the course Knight had been counselled several times but he always responded by blaming others: "You hate me, you're down on me, trying to get me," and, "You have no right to do this."

He was told that he could appeal but nothing came of it. Knight was sullen and defensive, with a superior attitude. It was known in the army as "Dumb Insolence" When he returned to Melbourne, Knight bagged the APC course and the instructors saying that he was going to get them.

Knight did a radio operators course in August 1986 and was part of the command post which was manned twenty-four hours a day. For the duration of the two-week course no one was permitted to leave the army barracks. All the participants were on trust as there was no security. It was not as strict as the APC course where personal safety was a big issue. Knight was the only one to go AWOL and bragged to other students how he had gone to Sale to a discotheque. No one reported him but the others in his squadron felt that he had let the team down. Knight, however, topped the course and was presented with a plaque rewarding him for achieving top marks in theory and practice.

When he was accepted at Duntroon, most of those who had had any experience with him were surprised. They didn't believe he possessed either the discipline or the necessary physical fitness to get through the course, even though he had all the necessary military knowledge.

Duntroon

The Charter of the Royal Military College is to train cadets for careers in the service of the Crown as officers in the Australian Army. It aims to give each cadet the knowledge to fit him to enter upon such a career, and to foster in him the moral and mental qualities on which leadership depends. The course of instruction is designed to:

(a) Promote a sense of honour and loyalty, duty and responsibility; inculcate habits of discipline and soldierly conduct; and to give a correct understanding of the place of the armed Services in the Australian nation.

(b) Provide a balanced and liberal education in the Arts and Sciences, taking into account the special needs of the Service and the aptitude of the cadet.

(c) Develop a capacity for clear and logical thought and expression.

(d) Give a sound military education in the science and principles of war.

(e) Instruct the cadet in the military skills and techniques of modern warfare required of the junior regimental officer.

—The Charter of the Royal Military College, Duntroon.

Julian Knight first applied for officer training while still a student at Melbourne High School. He presented himself at the Melbourne Recruiting Office on 13 August 1985 for the interview phase where a psychologist noted that the seventeen-year-old "almost looked like a skinhead except he wore a school uniform. He presented well in the interview, if somewhat sensitive about his life, as if it has all been a bit mixed up. He showed determination in interview to take charge of his life and improve things."

The same psychologist noted that Knight would be lucky to pass the Higher School Certificate and "lacks the academic potential for D.A. (Defence Academy)". Further, he noted that Knight seemed to be "a bit emotionally close to his mum. Indeed he talked of deferring D.A. for a year."

Socially Knight was seen as having no difficulties but it was noted that he "could be defensive and needs some social development". The interviewer at the time noted that in order for Knight to get that development he needed to pass the Higher School Certificate, work for a year, and join the Army Reserve. It was felt that he could then present as a suitable prospect for Duntroon although he was expected to struggle academically. At the time of his interview Knight admitted to struggling at school but came away with an improved attitude. He was going to apply himself and pass.

He was found not suitable to appear before the Selection Board.

The following year, with his family backing him again in his ambition to be a soldier, he reapplied for officer training at Duntroon. Having passed the Higher School Certificate and now a member of the Army Reserve he was confident that this time he would succeed. On 1 September 1986 he was again interviewed to assess whether he was suitable to appear before a Selection Board. He had already passed the exam, and in the next stage of the screening process he was interviewed about his background.

There was then a session where candidates were evaluated for their interpersonal skills and their ability to work as a team. This involved group discussion and outdoor activities to assess coordination, physical strength and team work. Knight listed enjoyment of the military lifestyle, security, career and promotion opportunities, being part of a team and the diversity of employment as his reasons for wanting to join the Army. As it was felt that he had progressed since his first application and was motivated towards the military and interested in sport, it was recommended that he progress to the next stage.

On 2 October 1986 he appeared before the final Selection Board consisting of three majors, a lieutenant colonel, and an army psychologist. Knight met the minimum intellectual standards and a psychologist and a medical officer assessed his personality as "normal".

He was considered a "marginal" candidate – he had definite limitations but it was felt that he could develop into an adequate junior officer. It was the lowest grading for those who were successful at the Selection Board. The other categories were adequate, satisfactory and good. Those who were not successful at the Board were graded either "not yet" which meant that the candidate could present at another time as he had potential, or "not suitable" which generally meant that the candidate was not likely to be reconsidered.

Each of the four officers at the Selection Board assessed Knight as being "weak" in the category of intellectual potential. The psychologist also rated him as being "weak" in the area of academic motivation and potential. This meant that he had a weakness in that area "which is not completely damning if it is offset by other very strong qualities." Three of the four officers noted that he appeared to have been well prepared for the interview by his father.

Knight was considered "borderline" in verbal reasoning, athletic achievement, leadership experience, clarity of thought, effective group direction, military compatibility, potential to adapt to the training institution, and academic motivation and potential.

Being "borderline" meant "… a degree of uncertainty. The candidate may or may not measure up to what is expected or required in this area."

He was judged as being 'satisfactory" – "The Candidate measures up to the standard expected of a junior officer" – by one or all of the board members in academic record, team sport achievement, Head of Mission/Commanding Officer Report, written expression, verbal ability, physical performance, effective group participation, military motivation, maturity and military compatibility."

Knight was assessed as having good or strong points in peer group assessment in friendship and leadership and one board member rated him "good" in the area of group direction.

The three army officers assessed Knight as a marginal candidate. The fourth member, the army psychologist, rated him as being "adequate".

Major Strachan noted his belief that Knight was over-confident and that his abilities might not match. The psychologist, Lieutenant Colonel Robertson, had some reservations about Knight successfully performing in the academic areas at Duntroon. He wrote that Knight was "too inclined to opt out and doesn't have much intellectual leeway".

It was a view shared by other board members.

Situated on what was once 150 hectares of sheep grazing country, the Royal Military College of Australia is better known as Duntroon. Settled by the merchant, Robert Campbell, in 1825, approximately four kilometres outside of Canberra, on land given to him as compensation for the loss of his ship twenty years earlier while on charter to the government. The homestead was called Duntroon House.

After a visit to Australia in 1910 Field Marshall Lord Kitchener submitted a report upon which the Australian Government acted. It was decided to establish a military college chiefly modelled on the traditions and operation of America's West Point Academy.

Officially opened by the Governor-General on 27 June 1911, Duntroon was known among its first intake as "The Clink" because it resembled a prison farm. With a population of 1714, Canberra was more like a country town than the future capital of Australia. Seventeen of its first graduates were killed in action at Gallipoli on 25 April 1915, including its first Commandant, Major-General Sir William Throsby Bridges. His grave is in the grounds of Duntroon, on the slopes of Mount Pleasant beside the graves of commandants who succeeded him.

With anti-war and anti-military sentiment high during the 1920s, cadet intake was low and during the Depression years of 1931-36 officer training was conducted in Sydney. In 1934 allegatons of bastardisation – the stripping down and rebuilding of one's personality by humiliation and brutality – were raised officially for the first time at the College. During World War 2 the College was busy again and because of the existing circumstances of the times, the normal four-year course was halved. In 1944 a new four-year course was introduced. Mature-age cadets were introduced in 1964 and, in 1968, the College became a faculty of military studies at the University of New South Wales. The Duntroon motto is "Learning Promotes Strength".

1985 was its last year as a university and in 1986 the Australian Defence Forces

Academy (ADFA) opened on the grounds of Duntroon where trainee officers from the army, navy and air force would study for a degree in either arts, engineering or applied science. On obtaining the degree they would enter officer training for the last twelve months of the eighteen-month course.

In 1986 women were, for the first time, admitted to the College. That same year, also for the first time, entry for officer training was possible in two ways. The first was by obtaining a degree over three years at ADFA, and then commencing the fourth year as a second class cadet. The second means of entry catered for those who already had a degree, or a Higher School Certificate (Year 12), or were already in the army and under twenty-six. They could undertake an eighteen-month course, starting as third class cadets. They would go through basic training of six months, then twenty-two weeks as second class cadets, and six months as first class cadets.

Recruits came from diverse backgrounds – from jackaroo to university student – and would graduate as lieutenants in the regular army.

Officer training seeks to extract from the recruits a demonstrated ability to influence others by intellect, personality and character. It looks for the positive person with a sense of fun, which appeals to Australian soldiers, and it recognises that a motivated person has an infectious personality. The recruits train to be thinking, composed and deliberate persons. With integrity comes the ability to take and give orders, to stand up when it is unpopular to do so. The course is tough. It is physically and mentally demanding in order for the College to produce a young leader.

Within the first weeks some recruits would go AWOL and never return. Approximately one-third would not complete the course.

Recruits were placed in one of several companies, each company named after a famous battle such as Kokoda, Gallipoli, Alamein, Romani, Long Tan and Kapyong.

On 13 January 1987 Julian Knight joined 45 Section of Kokoda Company, a group of twelve cadets consisting of a mixture of third, second and first class cadets. Although happy to have been accepted he was unsure initially about taking the step required. He considered deferring as it was a wrench to leave Melbourne and his family, but after discussing it with everyone and, in particular, his father he decided to go to Canberra. First and second class cadets supervised and were responsible for the management and discipline of third class cadets when staff were not available. Each platoon had a platoon commander, a member of staff – usually an experienced officer or a warrant officer. He was seen as a mentor, one who was interested in the social and sporting activities of the cadets. He was a military adviser and a confidant to cadets.

A guidance officer was appointed to advise each cadet of their performance in sporting, field, academic and general development during their term at the

College.

A padre who represented the different denominations was attached to each platoon to counsel and help in times of need.

Each platoon had a drill sergeant. While drill might seem to the outsider, a mindless form of exercise, it creates team spirit and instinctive and absolute obedience. Traditionally drill has been seen as the way of merging individuals into a team. The drill sergeant was responsible for ensuring that cadets were managed appropriately and professionally by the more senior cadets.

Allegations of bastardisation are not new to Duntroon. In a public inquiry in 1969, Justice R W Fox, a Supreme Court Judge, reported to the Federal Parliament on allegations of initiation ceremonies involving first year cadets. These included cadets being forced to do push-ups while their heads were under water; to eat food from the floor; and to take hot and cold showers. The report found that bastardisation was ingrained in the College. As a result, seven of the nine senior staff officers were transferred and six cadets were disciplined by way of reduction in rank or reprimand.

Then again in 1983 an internal inquiry headed by Major-General Coates, the Commandant of the College, resulted in five cadets being dismissed and six receiving punishment.

On 13 January 1987 Julian Knight arrived at Duntroon for his first day as an officer cadet. In less than two months he would be nineteen. In the first seven weeks he was introduced to firearms training, and made physically fit. Each morning there was a parade, followed by lectures during the day. As a third class cadet he was under strict supervision and given such unsavoury tasks as cleaning and gardening.

During his plea to the Melbourne Supreme Court, Mr Robert Richter said, "One can accept and understand that in a place like Duntroon, as in a lot of boarding schools and various institutions, where young men are brought together, certain practices of rough play and other problems may occur, and most people take them in their stride. We do not assert that there was a deliberate program of brutalisation and bastardisation, although the nature of the institution is conducive almost by definition to some rough play. Nevertheless, as far as Julian Knight's own perception, he felt that he was being picked on, and he felt that he was being subjected to treatment that was unwarranted. He would occasionally go AWOL, but he felt that he was penalised for it more than others."

In the armed services, group unity is important. Everything is done as a group. In a crisis situation, being able to work together as a team is essential. If one person failed to act as part of the team then the whole group suffered and was punished by having to complete obstacle courses or carry out additional cleaning duties, until the group acted as a whole, a team. If the weak link affected the performance of the team then, eventually, the team would turn on that individual. Those who were accustomed to having time to themselves found this impossible. Loners were not desirable at Duntroon.

By learning how to come to terms with the heavy demands of the course and the strict discipline, the cadets learned how to face the stress of battle. In Knight's intake there were 85 cadets from more than 400 applicants. They were the elite and this was continually reinforced. Once they believed that they were the best, the most courageous, the fittest, they would not fail their mates, their country, or themselves. This ingrained attitude of greatness would inspire the cadets to remain firm in conflict and fight to the end.

The first four weeks were spent at an army camp, Majura, designed to bring the raw cadet to basic soldier level. Initially, among his intake, he was not unpopular and was known as Knightie or Niggit. But he began to show signs of arrogance. His experience in the army reserve and the cadets made some aspects of the training easier for him (26 per cent of the recruits had some former training).

Not only was he smug but he lied to impress his peers. He told them and staff that he had experience in parachuting and scuba diving, when, in fact, he had experienced neither.

Under the direct supervision of Sergeant Kim Hogan, Knight, in general discussion, revealed what was thought to be an "unusual interest towards combat and participation in combat". Sergeant Hogan said, "He spoke of operating in the trouble spots of the world. He asked me at different times about the army's attitude towards officers going to trouble spots of the world in their own time." This constant interest in combat was not a typical nor desirable attitude among the cadets or the army and he was counselled by Sergeant Hogan.

Few cadets graduated from the College without being charged and required to do extra training. Those with maturity and common sense soon realised that the army was bigger than them and that they had to conform.

Between 25 February and 20 May, Knight was charged with a total of twenty-seven offences. Eighteen of these were charges ranging from a crooked cap badge to falling asleep in class.

The charges were seemingly trifling but indicated that staff were dissatisfied with Knight's performance. Knight was seen as an average cadet who resented authority and discipline, and, in all reports, he was referred to as being immature. Knight was punished by having to do extra drill.

Then there were nine discipline offences ranging from having an insecure bayonet to being absent without leave and absent from duty, to having a female between lines. Towards the end of May, Julian Knight was moving quickly towards the Duntroon exit door.

Knight further alienated himself by showing "OR" (other rank) tendencies – non-officer behaviour. He would swear and spit and refuse to grow his hair.

Having hair, cadets were told, was a privilege. It separated the officer from the ordinary soldier. If two soldiers were seen together out of uniform and one had longer hair, then it was obvious who was the officer. When Knight arrived at Duntroon his hair was abnormally short, even for the regular army soldiers. His haircut resembled a 'skinhead" rather than a military haircut and he was cautioned to grow his hair to an acceptable length. He continued to keep his hair ridiculously short rather than maintain the appearance of an officer, at least a cadet officer. Knight, in defiance, had his hair cut even shorter. The training fostered pride in belonging to the army, the group, the platoon, the company. Julian Knight was an embarrassment.

After Majura the cadets returned to Duntroon. Those third class cadets who had survived training to this stage were then presented to the Lanyard Parade, the first step of their journey toward acceptance as officer. Each cadet was presented with a khaki lanyard cord which they would proudly wear over the right shoulder and down into the right breast pocket.

The real pressure started after the Lanyard Parade.

A typical day commenced with a 6.00 a.m. reveille, followed by exercises, breakfast, classes, PT twice daily, tactics and basic rifle instruction. Cadets were required to remember everyone's name and rank, to be in the appropriate uniform for the appropriate occasion, and there were fifteen to choose from. There was a large amount of rote learning which included learning almost all of the 72 pages of the cadet handbook. Each day there was an enormous amount of material to study and each day the pressure increased.

At 10.00 p.m. lights went out and cadets with the aid of a torch would go "fairy bogging" (cleaning their boots). There were daily tests and your room and equipment had to be maintained to a very high standard. It was under these conditions that Julian Knight really started to feel the pressure.

In the field exercises he was seen to lack the sense of urgency required of an officer. If a shot was fired during the exercise he would be the last person to react. He seemed unsure about what he was doing, and lacking in confidence. As early as February 17 reports were being made about his unreliability and lack of acceptance by his peers.

At the end of each exercise the instructors would give feedback to the cadet who was the Field Commander or the Platoon Sergeant. He would be criticised or praised in the presence of the other cadets and then asked what he could have done to improve the situation. Knight gave the appearance that he was always right. He annoyed the cadets and staff by showing no reaction to their comments. He seemed to have no need to learn and no need for approval.

Most of the field exercises were done with second class cadets who were, generally, the leaders. They taught the less-experienced third class cadets basic infantry tactics, and their task was to condition them to perform like real soldiers.

Instead of studying Knight would regularly breach regulations by leaving the College for hotels or discos in Canberra. He was ill-prepared for and sometimes fell asleep in class.

At 6.00 a.m. the third class cadets were required to rise while the first and second class cadets could sleep for another hour and a half. Knight would often sleep through his alarm clock and clock radio.

Rather than wear dress slacks, a shirt with a collar, and clean shoes – which is what the College demanded of the cadets – Knight would wear jeans with a hole in the leg, a T shirt and runners. He saw himself as a "working class hero" and spoke of Collingwood, not Clifton Hill where he had lived, as a reference point to his manliness. He seemed to be at ease with a can of beer in one hand, a cigarette dangling from the corner of his mouth and torn jeans and T shirt. The longer he remained at the College, the less attention he paid to his uniform, his room and his studies.

One of the first instances when Knight broke the code of conduct for officer cadets concerned a minor accident involving his Torana SLR. He failed to negotiate a roundabout outside the College and, in the course of mounting the roundabout, damaged the muffler and exhaust. On returning to the College he openly boasted about what he had done. No one was impressed. This was not the behaviour or attitude of an officer. His car was also not typical of an officer's car. It had stickers all over the windows, "mag" wheels and a loud exhaust. The other cadets kept their cars in a manner which did not draw attention or bring the military into disrepute. Knight had no concern for the effect that his behaviour had on the college of the military.

Christopher Whitting, a third class cadet, who was in the same 45 Squadron with Knight, had been a missionary in the Middle East and had seen people shot at and killed, and had experienced the threat of death while under attack. Knight would ask Christopher what it was like to be shot at, he wanted details. Christopher found Knight's interest unusual, if not disturbing, as he had personally found his experiences to be very frightening. In a statement to the police he said that Knight, "seemed to see it as more of a thrill and he was interested in the feelings and excitement of being in a situation where he was being fired on and where he could fire back".

It was a feeling Knight would repeat to the Homicide Squad detectives when he talked about the arrival of police and the single shot fired at him in Hoddle Street.

As part of their training cadets were required to complete a basic strip down of their rifles, re-assembling them in the dark. Knight was found by a cadet, cross-legged on the floor, deep in almost trance-like concentration. His rifle was in forty or fifty pieces – far in excess of what was required. Knight told the cadet that he knew how to make an SLR into an automatic.

During exercises in the bush it was reinforced that it was essential that soldiers could rely on their "mates". In a moment of crisis could you rely on your mate? Would he be there for you? Knight's peers were already making up their minds that he was not one that they wanted to be with in the trenches. While the other cadets had no say in whether a cadet passed or failed at Duntroon, they exerted pressure on those who they felt did not fit in.

On Exercise First Run during a "night attack", he slept while on watch duty. In times of war a sleeping soldier on watch duty could cost the lives of a whole platoon.

During Operation Tobruk the cadets were "attacked" by a larger force. The purpose of the exercise was to pull back from the area, dig in and resist the enemy. The cadets were required to dig into a rock hard surface using a small digging tool for forty-eight hours continuously. They had to dig deep enough to give troops overhead protection. Knight was observed to sit back and watch his peers dig in. When he did use the digging tool it was with very little effort.

He was found to have performed to a satisfactory level, but he was below the standard required in application and maturity. On 6 May Captain Brown noted that Knight, "did not dig with enough effort, did not take aimed shots in the live-fire exercise, did not use a correct fire position, made immature statements and was not accepted as an equal by his peers."

In a live-fire exercise truck bodies were positioned in front of the cadets. The exercise involved each cadet being given a target area, an arc, so that the Commander would know where the gunfire was going. The cadets were firing at the truck in a criss-cross manner, while Knight was seen to take shots at anything at random. He did not lie prone, as required, during the exercises. He would instead sit up or kneel which, in times of combat, would have made an easy target for the enemy.

In examinations Knight failed first-aid theory and had to be retested. In navigation theory, he failed both the original test and the retest and was counselled on 8 April. Notes were recorded about his low personal standards and poor discipline. It was observed that he started to fall behind when he had to rely on self discipline. His Commanding Officer, Lieutenant Colonel David Kibbey counselled him and advised him to, "stay out of trouble", or be recommended for a DMA's (Director of Military Arts) warning.

There were four stages of counselling before the College would wipe its hands of a troublesome cadet. The first was with a chief instructor, then the Commanding Officer, followed by the DMA and, finally, the Commandant. Knight was already at the half-way mark. He had the worst discipline record of his intake.

On 27 April he was reminded by Captain Goss that he needed to, "improve his motivation and decrease his social activities."

It was during this time that he met his former girlfriend, Renee Cross, who was in Canberra on a school excursion. He was upset that they had broken up and he told her he was not fitting in at the college. During a term break Knight returned to Melbourne and arranged to have dinner with Renee "for old times sake" but they got their arrangements mixed up and consequently met at the Royal Hotel. Renee told Knight she was going out afterwards and that he could not come with her. They were no longer an item and she had moved on in her life. Knight sat at the bar drinking pots of beer by himself when, all of a sudden, he threw his pot and punched the glass door. He started fighting with others in the bar until he was overpowered and restrained.

On 8 May, Warrant Officer Remin reported that Knight had admitted cheating in the map marking exercise. Three days later Captain Goss interviewed Knight and rebuked him for appearing before him with alcohol on his breath. Knight, the Captain reported, "did not appear to have learnt from his mistakes".

During a confidential peer-group rating conducted within Kokoda Company on 15 May, Knight was rated twenty-third out of twenty-six cadets. Several of his peers remarked that they "quite liked" him and that he was " a character." He had "no common sense" and was "too young". He was a "skinhead" in Melbourne and enjoyed that image of himself. There was the belief among his peers that he had "dug his own grave" and made things worse for himself by talking back to staff and senior cadets. It was felt that he did not attempt to fit in and he disregarded criticism.

On five separate occasions he was involved in fights with civilians while in Canberra. Each of the incidents involved a girl and excessive use of alcohol. It was rumoured that he carried an improvised "knuckle-duster" and a pocket knife.

31 May 1987

It was 3.15 a.m. on Sunday, 31 May when First Constable Shane Austin and Senior Constable Christopher Novak, of Belconnen CIB, attended at a laneway behind the ANZ bank in Ainslie Avenue, Canberra. There were two police cars already in the lane. The first was an unmarked car and the second a marked car. Leaning with his arms outstretched across the boot area of the marked police car was a denim-clad Julian Knight. His right little finger was wrapped in a handkerchief and there was dried blood on his hands. His nose was swollen with a one-centimetre laceration across the bridge. On the ground was an imitation, black-handled, stainless-steel switchblade knife, partly open and showing blood on the blade. The detectives spoke to the police who were with Knight, Inspector Hepworth and Senior Constable Weldon, then escorted Knight to the back of the unmarked police car and closed the door.

Shane Austin opened his official notebook and recorded the conversation, firstly asking Knight his personal details and then advising him of his right to refuse to answer any questions put to him.

"Mr Knight, I believe you stopped a police vehicle a short time ago and told those officers something. Is that correct?"

"Yes, it is," said Knight.

"Do you wish to tell me anything regarding the matter you informed those officers about?"

"I just had a fight with Mongo Reed, at the Bin and I went back into the Bin after the fight where I was told by one of the staff cadets that Mongo and Corporal Thorp were after me and they were giving me dirty looks and I just sat in the corner and had my drink, and then later on my girlfriend said, "Let's leave" and then, I don't know why, but I took my knife out of my back pocket and stabbed him, Mongo Reed, in the face. Then I ran out the door and kept on running and then I saw a police car near the roundabout and I ran up to the driver's side and held my hands out with the knife out (sic) and said, "I've stabbed someone at The Bin". Then at the same time I dropped the knife."

Knight was placed in the back of an ambulance and taken to the Royal Canberra Hospital, Accident and Emergency Department. While Christopher Novak kept Knight under observation, Shane Austin went to another cubicle where he spoke with a bloodied staff cadet, Sergeant Major Phillip 'Mongo' Reed. He had a deep, two-centimetre long laceration forward of his right ear, and another laceration behind the same ear, measuring one centimetre. Reed's hands and clothing were saturated in blood. The detective noted that Reed was well affected by alcohol.

At 4.20 a.m. Shane Austin returned to Knight who demonstrated how he had raised his hands up to his head and then pushed forward the knife to stab Reed. In the action of stabbing Reed to the side of the head his hand had slipped down along the blade of the knife causing his right hand to be injured. Knight read the notes that the detective had recorded in his official notebook and tentatively signed and dated each page with his left hand (he was right-handed). The detective then advised Knight that he would be charged with malicious wounding and that he would be interviewed further. A police guard was arranged as he was still in custody.

At 8.05 p.m. the detectives returned to Ward 3C of the Royal Canberra Hospital, where another police officer, Sergeant Hobart, formally charged Knight with malicious wounding. The detectives then commenced a formal record of interview, again using their official notebook to record the details. The Army had declined to offer Knight legal aid.

During the interview Knight explained that when he had arrived at the Private Bin Nightclub Reed had approached him at the bar and challenged him for being out of the College.

"... he got angry because he had told me to stay in the barracks this weekend ... he then grabbed me by the front of my jumper and started pushing me backwards. He said, 'You disobeyed me and I fucking hate that.' At this stage one of the bouncers came over and told Mongo to let go of me which he did and walked off."

Knight said that he had not expected Reed to be at the nightclub.

The previous day, Saturday, 30 May, after a parade rehearsal, staff cadet (first class) Lance Corporal Craig Thorp had approached Knight about being AWOL (absent without leave) the night before. He had been seen at the Private Bin by several first class cadets, again, wearing jeans and "scruffy shoes". Thorp had removed the bayonet from his rifle while talking to Knight.

Knight told the detective that Thorp poked the bayonet at him. Thorp, during an official investigation into the incident, claimed that he tapped Knight on the left shoulder with the bayonet while talking to him. Knight "took umbrage at the conversation and acted in an aggressive manner" by pushing Thorp, then walking away to Anzac Hall. Thorp, according to the investigation, had decided not to take the matter any further as he knew that he had improperly used the bayonet.

Staff cadet Hamburger stopped Knight and reminded him of the hierarchy chain at Duntroon and asked why he had picked on Thorp who was significantly shorter than him. Knight pushed Hamburger and walked away. Hamburger grabbed Knight by the shirt collar and pushed him against the wall. Hamburger challenged Knight to hit him. Corporal Thomson and Sergeant Stone intervened and Knight was confined to the College for the remainder of the weekend. First class cadet and Company Sergeant Major Phillip 'Mongo' Reed told him that he would consult the officer in charge of their company for advice on what further disciplinary action to take.

In a prepared statement for the Melbourne Supreme Court, Lieutenant-Colonel David Kibbey, Commanding Officer, Corps of Staff Cadets, said that the incident occurred in the presence of many witnesses and, in his view, represented "poor judgement but nothing worse".

"What happened after that?" Shane Austin asked.

"At frequent intervals throughout the night he came over to me and told me to get out. At one stage an argument developed between Mongo and my girlfriend's sister."

Knight would later explain that his girlfriend's sister was… "sticking up for me." Knight believed that Reed had no authority over him outside the confines of the College.

"At approximately 1.30 a.m. Mongo came over to me and said, 'You disobeyed me, I hate that, you're leaving right now.' Standing next to me at the bar a civilian male, who I don't know said to Mongo, 'Why don't you leave him alone?' Mongo said, 'Mind your own business,' or words to that effect. Mongo then grabbed this bloke and a fight started."

Knight then told of how staff cadet, Corporal Craig Thorp, ran with his fists clenched to help Reed. Knight stepped in and pushed Thorp back towards the door and, in retaliation, Thorp punched Knight on the nose. Knight was then held in a bear hug but he broke loose and exchanged blows with Thorp. Then Knight felt a blow to his nose. Someone had hit him from behind and his face was covered in blood. He believed that it was Reed who had hit him. A bouncer pushed Knight down the stairs and out of the main door of the nightclub into the street where he was joined by his girlfriend, her sister and her sister's husband. They discussed where they were going to go next. Knight thought about exacting revenge. Meg wanted to return to the nightclub.

They went to the public toilets near the bus terminal where Knight washed the blood away from his face and hands. He returned to the Private Bin where, in a corner, Meg was waiting. Staff cadet Entricken approached him and told him that Reed and Thorp were after him. The staff cadet suggested he leave as there were other cadets including an instructor who wanted to get him. They were going to knock him out.

"I said I wasn't going to start any trouble and that I wasn't going away. One of the drill sergeants came over to me and suggested that I leave ... he said that he couldn't 'be held responsible for anything that happened' after he left."

Knight continued by saying that Reed, Thorp and the drill sergeant, Jorgensen, and other first class cadets stared at him for the rest of the evening.

"... my girlfriend suggested we go to her sister's place. I agreed and said I was going to the toilet. On the way I saw Mongo talking with about four or five of his first class friends. I walked up to him and stopped about a face away, hesitated, then I took the knife out of my pocket, opened it and stabbed Mongo twice in the right hand side of his face."

Reed had been standing with his back against the bar talking to other cadets when he was stabbed. Knight had bought the knife two days earlier for self-defence after he had been "beaten up in the alley behind the Bin", the week before. He claimed it was an instinctive, spur-of-the-moment action and he used enough strength just to "hurt him as much as he hurt me".

"What happened then?"

"I turned and ran out of the Bin. I got about fifty metres down the street when I heard someone behind me call out, 'Come back here you cunt!' I turned and recognised it as one of the staff cadets from Duntroon. I also noticed at this stage that I had a cut in my right hand. I kept on running along the street, looking for a police car. I saw a police car near the merry-go-round and called out to it; as I went towards it they didn't hear and I kept on running after it when it turned into the alley, I was still coming out and they stopped."

"Why did you stop the police vehicle after you had left the Private Bin where you had stabbed Mongo?"

"Because I knew I had done something wrong and wanted to hand myself in."

Knight read aloud the nineteen pages of handwritten interview from the detective's notebook and signed each page as being true and correct. He was given a duplicate copy of the interview and the detectives then left. Knight was bailed to appear in court on 12 June, which was then adjourned to 10 November 1987. It has since been adjourned indefinitely pending Knight's release from prison.

Mr Robert Richter, QC, addressed the Melbourne Supreme Court concerning this incident saying, "What that incident indicated was a situation of a build-up of stress, a disinhibition of alcohol, and an explosion of temper. He recognised that what he had done was wrong and immediately surrendered himself to the authorities, asserting, as the materials indicate, that he had been pushed to the limit."

On 5 June the Military Arts Board of Studies met and discussed Knight along with the other cadets. Every three months the Board met to discuss and evaluate each cadet. Knight was considered below standard. The system was designed to give everyone an opportunity to make the grade and become an officer. Cadets were counselled if they were seen to lack leadership ability or were deficient in any areas and Knight had already been counselled; if they did not reach the standard immediately they could repeat the term and graduate, older and more mature.

The Board noted that Knight was below standard in all fifteen assessed leadership and personal qualities. He was ranked 115 out of 118 cadets. Taking into account his discipline record, that he had been charged on eight occasions with military offences, and that he had failed to pass two examinations and had cheated in a third (his academic position was 105 out of 118 cadets), the Board of Studies recommended that Knight be asked to 'show cause' why he should not be dismissed from the College. On legal advice the issue of a 'show cause' was deferred until after his criminal charges had been determined at court. Knight was interviewed by the DMA on 5, 12, and 19 June. His father visited the college and was appraised of his son's performance.

Knight was then given the option of being suspended until the court hearing or resigning from the College. He submitted his resignation and on 2 July transferred from the College to the Regimental Supernumerary List. His dreams of dying in combat and being the hero, of protecting his company against overwhelming odds, were, in the real world, over. As of Friday, 24 July 1987 he was no longer in the Australian Army.

Back home

Knight stayed in Canberra with relatives for a short time, returning to Melbourne to find that his bedroom had been made into a lounge room. He felt that he was expected not to stay long. Even his bed had been replaced by a single foam mattress which could be rolled up and tucked away somewhere out of sight. All his possessions had been placed in cardboard boxes as he had not been expected to return. He was now supposed to find employment and leave the roost, to make his own way in life. His dreams were shattered and he had to reinvent himself as someone other than a soldier.

On 17 July 1987, in response to an advertisement in *The Age* about a five-week, part-time course on the security industry, Knight attended at the offices of Dom Security in Victoria Street, Richmond. He met the director, Graeme Brown, and gave him a two-page, hand written CV. Graeme read the CV and told him that the major security companies preferred their patrolmen to be at least 25; his age was a possible barrier to working as a security officer or patrolman because of insurance problems for drivers under 25.

There was something about Knight which made Graeme Brown feel uncomfortable. Knight was very tense and soldier-like in his responses, answering "yes sir/no sir" when questioned. He seemed to lack warmth and Brown felt there was a lot of anger in him.

"What prompted you to leave Duntroon?"

Knight moved in his seat and replied that it was "one of those personality things".

He now wanted to get into the security industry. He paid a $100 deposit and was given a receipt. He was to begin the course on Tuesday, 11 August.

His other options included being a fire-fighter, a police officer or a public servant but all he could get was a job as a storeman-driver with Cuggi, a clothing company in South Yarra, which involved pricing, packing, writing dockets and making deliveries.

Barbara Murdoch, the production manager, felt that he was merely "filling in time" until something better came along. He seemed preoccupied in the two weeks he worked for the company. On his last day he walked up the stairs and wished Barbara, "Goodnight, and have a good weekend." He told seventeen-year-old Ilaio Cuteri that he was going to have a "rage of a weekend".

Knight owed an uncle $7,000 for the Torana that he had bought the previous year. His sister had dropped a coin down the gear lever and he was having trouble with it. He had advertised it for sale but knew this would be difficult if it was mechanically unsound, and he wouldn't be able to repay his uncle. Things weren't getting any better.

Knight called the RACV. Geoff Oliver, 27, arrived and tooted the horn of the yellow RACV van. Knight came out, showed Geoff the Torana, and told him that the gears were crunching. Geoff confirmed that the gear box was the problem. Knight asked him to fix the car and was told that it was a workshop job.

Something about Knight unnerved Geoff Oliver and he wanted to get away from him as quickly as possible. Knight was one of between eight and thirty customers that he would see each day. None of them had made this sort of impression on him before. Knight was trying to intimidate him and he noticed a coldness in his eyes.

Knight wanted Geoff to drive his car but it was against RACV policy. Irritated, Knight commented that as he couldn't go anywhere in his car he might as well go down to the pub, with his mates. As Geoff drove away he felt a shiver down his spine. Two days later the shiver returned when he recognised the photographs of the Hoddle Street gunman.

In custody

On the Monday following the remand hearing at the Melbourne Magistrates' Court, Knight was taken in an unmarked police car, eight kilometres to Coburg, in Melbourne's north. One of the first areas of settlement in Melbourne, it became known more for its "bluestone college". Built in 1850, as a temporary prison, it remained open for 147 years. Behind the high bluestone walls and razor ribbon wire was housed the majority of Victoria's criminal population, which was a source of complaint from the local community, particularly as the population increased and housing development replaced farmland.

Because there were fears for his safety (there had been a groundswell of public outrage) and Knight had indicated an intention to suicide, prison officials arranged for him to be taken directly to the prison hospital. He became a "celebrity prisoner" and, as such, greater precautions were taken to ensure his wellbeing. Newspapers filled their pages with reports on what he had done and journalists tried to fill the gaps in his background.

Normally prisoners were taken to the reception area of the jail in Sydney Road to be strip-searched, to have their civilian clothing exchanged for the Pentridge uniform of green tracksuit and white T shirt, and to be informed of the rules. Sniffling and crying like a child, the nineteen-year-old was walked into the hospital, at the eastern end of the prison complex, with his hands cuffed behind his back.

Inside the modern hospital wing he was taken by prison officers to the observation cell where he was strip-searched, informed of the hospital rules and given regulation pyjamas. He was then examined by the first of many doctors, psychologists and psychiatrists. Prisoners in other hospital wards yelled out for Knight to be placed with them. They were angry and wanted to see justice done, their way. Many prisoners knew that his actions would have ramifications for their future. In the months ahead, the Premier, John Cain, announced a tightening of firearm regulations and increased the penalty provisions, the criminal world winced. Even the illegal acquisition of firearms was more difficult when thousands of people handed in their weapons during amnesties.

In the observation ward, a cell encased in thick glass and bars, Knight slept on a canvas mattress on a raised slab of concrete. Knight's suicide threats warranted half-hour observation checks. At one stage Knight talked to doctors about ramming his head against the wall of his cell but decided that there was insufficient run up to give him a fractured skull. Hanging himself or slashing his wrists would take too long, he reasoned, but by the end of his second week in the prison hospital, suicide rarely entered the conversation. Towards the end of his stay, when he did mention suicide again, he said he would have more opportunity when transferred out of the hospital. At 67 kg and pencil thin, he claimed that his only vice had been to drink heavily.

In the first week of hospitalisation, Knight was tearful and frightened of the other prisoners. Being killed by one of them was his greatest fear. He lay on the bed depressed, sleeping or feigning sleep. He spoke in dull, flat tones and his face was expressionless, he made little eye contact. He would not eat or drink, and talked of preferring to die than spend what he expected would be fifteen-to-twenty years in prison. He felt a failure – he had not completed university, he had been a failure at Duntroon, he was without friends.

By the end of that week his mood changed. He asked for cigarettes and he began to put on weight. He joked that he was a "homicidal maniac, not a suicidal maniac." When told that Gina Papaioannou had died on 20 August, there was no apparent reaction. She was not important to him – he didn't know her – there had been no personal contact and he was able to remain detached.

When he was discharged from the prison hospital, two prison-security officers quick-marched him to the maximum security section of H Division. With his wrists handcuffed in front of him he was brought to the foyer of the reception area, before the Chief Prison Officer's office. A red line was painted on the floor.

Prison officers were hand-picked for H Division. They were usually tall, muscled, no-nonsense types, many with a background in the armed services. As a security measure they were identified only by nickname. It was not uncommon for the H Division prison officer to find his car had been tampered with, or to have threats made against him or his family. One had had a Molotov cocktail thrown at his house, another had a bomb left on his doorstep. Their job did not end at the completion of the shift. They had to remain on guard even while off duty.

"Toes to the line!" said Ghengis, the Reception Officer.

Ghengis felt contempt for Knight; he disliked him for what he had done in Hoddle Street, as did nearly every other prison officer. They felt that the man in front of them lacked courage; anyone could shoot without warning and slay unarmed and defenceless people.

Ghengis removed Knight's handcuffs and the security officers left. The heavy door they had entered moments earlier closed behind them and was locked. Knight stood to attention in his green tracksuit and white T shirt.

"You are now in H Division," Ghengis said. "Have you ever been in H Division before?"

"No sir."

"In H Division all officers will be addressed as sir. As part of the normal procedure you will now be strip-searched. Take off your shoes. Hold them by the heel and pass them up to me."

Ghengis spoke quietly, calmly, with the authority of an experienced prison officer. One who had been through the routine for many years. Knight removed his shoes and Ghengis examined them for contraband or weapons before putting them behind him on a table.

"Take off your windcheater."

Another prison officer, one of six, examined the windcheater. His fingers carefully ran along the stitching seams, in the pockets and all over the garment.

"Take off your T shirt and hand it to an officer."

The track pants were searched and then discarded like the T shirt.

"Take off your socks one at a time, turn it (sic) inside out, shake it out below your knees, not in my face."

When Knight did this Ghengis continued.

"Place it on the floor. Then the other sock."

Standing in only his underpants Knight began to visibly shake.

"Remove your jocks. Turn them inside out, and shake them out below the knees."

Standing naked before the prison officers Knight began to shake uncontrollably, almost on the verge of tears.

"Don't hit me boss."

To refer to a prison officer as anything other than sir was his first mistake. His second was to use the expression, "boss". In H Division it meant "bag of shit".

The punch sent Knight reeling back into the arms of the prison officers behind him. They struck him with their batons and when he tried to resist he felt the batons even harder. Subdued, Knight was told to, "Stand on your feet, toes to the line."

He was then instructed to bend forward and to vigorously run his fingers through his hair, still very short, from the back of his skull to the front. Knight did this then stopped, only to be hit with Ghengis' baton.

"Keep going. I'll tell you when to stop."

Tears streamed down his face.

"Stand up straight!"

Then, "Were you drunk Julian?"

It was a serious question from Ghengis. Knight did not have the appearance of a hardened criminal, the sort he was used to seeing in his everyday duties.

"Yes, sir."

"Not a bad shot though to kill seven and injure – how many – nineteen? And be drunk at the same time?"

"Life's hard in the fast lane," Knight said.

In less than a second he was on the ground sobbing. Ghengis held himself back though he really wanted to lay into him for his disregard for the lives of others.

Knight got to his feet and stood before the red line. As directed, he opened his mouth, lifted his tongue and tilted back his head. Ghengis looked inside his mouth, and when satisfied there were no pills or other contraband, instructed Knight to close his mouth. His hands were examined. First the fingers were spread, then the palms and along the arms for signs of track marks. His ears were examined for drugs. He was told to place his hands above his head so that his armpits could be examined. When he was directed to place his arms by his side, Ghengis noticed that Knight clenched his fists.

"If you clench your fists in H Division it will be taken as a sign of aggression and you will be dealt with accordingly. Do you understand me?"

Sobbing and trying to hold back the tears Knight said, "Can I wipe my eyes, sir?"

"No. Place your arms by your side as you have been instructed."

Knight was then told to lift his penis and testicles.

"Lift them up higher or I'll get the officer beside you to do it for you."

No prisoner had ever refused this instruction and Knight was no different.

He promptly did as he was told and Ghengis bent down to examine his groin area, and between his legs. Ghengis held his own right arm out straight.

"About turn to the right."

Knight turned in the direction of where Ghengis' outstretched right arm indicated; Knight's left.

Ghengis punched Knight to the side of the head and sent him reeling into the arms of the other prison officers, who then hit him with their batons until Ghengis intervened. His turn to the left was seen as a refusal to obey an order. It was imperative for him to realise who was in charge and what the ramifications would be if he refused to do as required.

"Stand up, toes to the line!"

When Knight stood to the red line Ghengis continued, "What was your last instruction?"

"About turn to the right, sir." Knight stood to attention and threw a salute.

"You're not a soldier's arsehole! Put your arms by your side. You were told to about turn by the right, not your left. This is your last chance."

Ghengis spoke firmly and quietly as Knight trembled and cried. It was like being on the parade ground only there was no bluff. If the prison officers did not assert their authority from the very beginning then they could lose control and being in control was what the Division was all about. It was the end of the line as far as the management of prisoners went. Told again to "about turn to the right" Knight did so, facing the other five prison officers who were in a semi-circle.

"Raise your right foot, wiggle your toes."

Knight wiggled his toes while Ghengis examined his foot. After thirty seconds Knight put down his foot.

"No one said to put your foot back on the ground."

Ghengis struck Knight across the foot with his baton.

"How long do I have to do it for, sir?"

"Keep going till I tell you to stop."

Ghengis looked at his watch and for three-and-a-half minutes watched the second hand sweep around the face of the clock.

"Place your right foot on the ground."

The procedure was repeated for the left foot. Knight raised his left foot 45 degrees from the ground. Ghengis struck Knight's foot with the baton.

"Get it up, I can't see it."

Knight raised his foot to approximately 90 degrees and wriggled his toes.

When instructed, he replaced his foot, then bent forwards, and touched his toes.

"Spread your cheeks."

When he had done this he was told to "about turn" to his right, returning to his original position and facing Ghengis, who handed him a pillow case which carried his pyjamas, a small cardboard packet of cleaning powder, a scouring pad, a bar of soap, a T shirt, a pair of jocks, a pair of socks, a prison issue tracksuit and a pair of brown prison shoes. They were emptied on to the table and he was then told to place all the articles back inside the pillow case.

He was instructed that everything had to be carried in the left hand while he was in H Division. Knight put on the pyjamas and another prison officer escorted him, holding on to the back of his pants, to his cell, number one, which measured approximately 3 metres by 2 metres and 4 metres in height. It consisted of a single bed, a mattress, blankets and a pillow, a small bookshelf, a white pin board and a stainless steel toilet. To reduce the risks of prisoners escaping they were rotated from cell to cell at random. The prison officer pushed him into the cell and locked the door.

After three weeks probation of good behaviour, Knight was issued with headphones to listen to the radio in his cell at H Division. The choice of station being at the discretion of the prison officers.

At first Knight was reluctant to leave his cell for fear the other H Division prisoners would kill him. He would hear them threaten him from their cells.

"You're fucked Knight! You won't see the year out!"

"Have a birthday party Knight because you won't see your next."

But gradually he assimilated.

He befriended Mark Read, Edwin Eastwood and Craig Minogue – all heavyweights in the prison. He was seen as a runner or go-for. He would check hand-up briefs for other prisoners and suggest questions to be asked of the police. A competent cartoonist and caricaturist, his talents were used to good effect in prisoner-reform magazines. In one cartoon, illustrating the Governor's Court where prison charges are determined, the Governor is captioned as saying, "You have been found guilty, how do you plead?"

He justified his actions at Hoddle Street to other prisoners by saying he had tried to kill the police. When the Homicide squad served the hand-up brief he showed the 354 photographs to other inmates. These photographs included graphic stills of his victims and the various crime scenes. Seeing the photographs and the cavalier manner in which he displayed them caused some disquiet among the other prisoners. He was advised by Read and Minogue to put them away. He justified showing the photographs by saying, "Only a few of my closest associates were shown the photos and only because they asked to see them. I decided that I didn't need reminders of the shootings so I returned the photos to my solicitor."

In January 1988 Knight wrote to the Premier, John Cain, and urged him to change the firearm laws in Victoria. He recommended that applicants for firearm licences be tested by a psychiatrist before being issued with a licence, and retested every year.

In an article published in *The Herald* on Friday, 4 November 1988, journalist, Keith Moor, noted, "Were it not for the fact that he had slaughtered seven innocent people and caused untold grief to so many others, he (Knight) would have been likeable. The only hint of disturbing behaviour displayed during my interviews with him was when he brought up the topic of the colour photographs police took of his victims. He asked me if I had seen them. On replying that I hadn't, he started describing them to me in graphic detail. There was a fervour in his voice not present during the rest of our conversations. I changed the subject."

Knight enrolled in a journalism correspondence course, and, as study aids, was permitted to have books and magazines on war and firearms. He referred to himself as a "soldier under sentence", an expression used in the military to describe army personnel imprisoned at Holsworthy in New South Wales.

On 19 October 1988 Knight applied to the Melbourne Supreme Court, before Justice Hampel, to have the inquest into the Hoddle Street murders declared void. He based this on the belief that a mystery shot had been discharged in his direction while he was near the railway station and that the shot may have "contributed to the deaths or injuries of any of the victims". Knight also complained that the Coroner had considered evidence which had not been tested, that the police had contributed to the deaths by being negligent in allowing motorists to drive into Hoddle Street, and that the Coroner should have made findings in relation to how the police had handled the incident.

Justice Hampel denied Knight's application and reminded him that he had been represented by barristers at both the inquest and the committal hearings and that those issues had not been raised. He said that the Coroner, Hal Hallenstein, had done as he was required: He had identified those who were deceased, the cause of their death and any person who contributed to the death.

The Melbourne Supreme Court

At the Melbourne Magistrate's Court on 19 April 1988, Chief Magistrate, Darcy Dugan, directed that Julian Knight be committed for trial on seven counts of murder and forty-six counts of attempted murder. Knight reserved his plea, meaning he had yet to decide whether to plead guilty or not guilty. For six months the families of all the deceased victims and the survivors themselves were anxious. No one wanted to appear in the same room as Knight let alone having to relive the ordeal, if he pleaded not guilty. They were revolted by the very appearance of him, revolted by the mention of his name.

Knight decided to plead guilty which meant that none of the witnesses were required to give evidence. The two investigating detectives, Graham Kent and the now retired Brian McCarthy, believed that there was no way he could avoid being found anything but guilty such was their preparation and methodical leg work. They had covered all aspects of the case involving Knight's intent and actions and it had taken Graham Kent eight months to complete the brief, ready for the committal hearing.

At the Melbourne Supreme Court on Friday, 28 October 1988 Julian Knight appeared before Justice George Hampel, who was considered to be generally lenient when it came to sentencing offenders. Knight's counsel, Robert Richter, QC, in his opening address, acknowledged that the crimes were horrendous and that the judge had an onerous task in making the appropriate sentence.

"Each life which is taken is as precious as the next, but the fact that so many lives were taken and the fact that so many other lives could have been taken is obviously something that must weigh very heavily with the court."

He continued to say that Knight had "clicked into what can only be described as a military mode. And having clicked into that military mode, the shooting would continue until he ran out of ammunition, which he did."

Knight wanted to know what it was like to kill and be killed. Robert Richter reasoned that Knight continued to act as a soldier right up to his surrender. When caught without ammunition to end his own life and without any chance of victory, he gave himself up.

Richter reminded the Judge that Knight, who had no previous criminal convictions, had been a teenager at the time. He was nineteen, a young man who was, "sanctioned by our law to possess lethal weapons in a populous place for no good reason and was trained by our society to kill, because that's what soldiers are trained to do, among other things. He was given the weapons of slaughter by our society which knew that human beings are frail, and that some may become sufficiently unhinged by the stresses and strains and influences around them to do just that, namely, to snap and to go beserk. And so, this is not merely an occasion to punish the killer, but must, in our respectful submission, be taken as an opportunity to assess our values and, in particular, the hypocrisy which, on the one hand, we profess a genuine belief and have a loathing for violence, while at the same time we glorify it and reward those who daily portray it in the cinema and on television and we make them rich and famous and we put them up for children as idols."

He went on to criticise the portrayal of gratuitous violence on film and television. He pointed out that society is concerned for the sick and yet it fails to "recognise and guard against the possibility that there are walking time-bombs among us. There are walking time-bombs who explode, not out of sheer malevolence, not out of sheer evil, but because they reach a breaking point."

He spoke of Frank Vitkovic who murdered eight people in Queen Street on 8 December 1987, and committed suicide.

"Frank Vitkovic wanted to die, was set upon dying and the notion of the ultimate deterrent (being capital punishment) obviously would not have stopped him because that's what he wanted.

"On the one hand there will be many who will argue that for a multiple killing such as this, a sentence of life imprisonment should be imposed or the community as a whole would be outraged, whether rationally or not, if a sentence of life imprisonment was not imposed. On the other hand, it might be put that the frenzied volleys of a disturbed and desperate young man are not as morally heinous as the actions of a sadistic torturer who torments his victims for the pleasure of it before extinguishing a life in cold blood and in a revolting way."

Richter went on to say that he was basing their defence on five factors:

1. That Knight was only nineteen and had no previous criminal convictions.
2. That his crimes were an accumulation of stresses he could no longer cope with.
3. That Knight was significantly affected by alcohol – he must have been at least twice the legal limit for driving a car when he fired on the public.
4. That his offences were committed on an impulse. "Something happened in the mind of Julian Knight, such that when he got up to leave the hotel, the notion that he was going to go into a combat situation had been created in his mind."
5. That Knight, while having a high IQ, had the emotional development and lack of restraint of a younger person.

Knight was pleading guilty because he recognised that he was responsible, that he wanted to spare the witnesses and victims from giving evidence, that he was remorseful, and was suicidal for some time after the incident. Richter reasoned that because of his youth, his background, and the sentencing laws of the State, that it would not be unreasonable for a minimum sentence to be imposed – a minimum which Knight would have to serve before being considered for parole.

He went on to quote the diary writings of the Queen Street mass murderer, who said, "Look for people with a history of rejection, loneliness and ill-treatment, who also have a fascination for guns and you won't go wrong."

Richter continued by saying that people snap in a variety of ways. Some would use their fists, while others will go for a knife or a firearm if it is available to them.

"The essence of it is that the background of rejection, depression, hopelessness and a fascination with firearms had predisposed Julian Knight to snap in the way that he did."

A psychiatrist, Dr David Sime, gave evidence that he had examined Knight on six occasions for twelve-and-a-half hours. He had studied literature on mass murderers and serial killers. He spoke of the "pseudo commando phenomenon", or "running amok". Knight was a gentle person who was unable to cope with his emotions. He was not a psychopath, but had a personality disorder.

Dr Sime stated that Knight was confused and wanted to know how what he had done had happened. He said that Knight's history of rejection began when he was born and his natural mother had him adopted. When, at eighteen, he sought to contact her, his letters went unanswered. His IQ was between 120 and 130, which put him into the superior range. University entrants had an average IQ of about 115. He was an adult in one sense and at the same time "very much a child and emotionally immature".

Knight had revealed that his parents' separation had been a traumatic experience for him and his siblings. Knight had given a "very dramatic description of his father revealing that he was leaving" and it was "probably the first major point of change" in his life. Even though he had not been performing well, his grades and behaviour deteriorated at school. The rejection continued when he was expelled from Westbourne Grammar and pushed to leave Fitzroy High School. His discharge from Duntroon meant that his abnormally intense interest in all things military suddenly had no place to flower.

Dr Sime compared Knight to other mass murderers. Most had training with and were preoccupied with firearms, to which they had ready access. Knight had first thought about murder while in the Royal Hotel, and from there he went home and loaded his firearms. Knight could not handle alcohol, which disinhibits the emotions, and was "rather more sensitive, definitely more sensitive, than the average individual." Alcohol, combined with five or six stress factors, contributed to Knight's actions.

Knight had started to disintegrate from the time that he entered Duntroon. He felt that he was being persecuted and he began to feel extremely stressed. The stress increased when he realised he was not going to make it as an army officer.

"I think one has to bear in mind that his whole life was orientated to becoming a soldier," Sime continued.

At the Royal Hotel he had been depressed, and rejected by Renee Cross, his former girlfriend, who did not invite him to the party to which other friends had been invited. The breakdown of his Torana, on which he owed $7,000, made his situation feel hopeless. Having his advances rejected by the barmaid was "probably the final straw".

Knight had told Dr Sime, at his first examination on 25 August 1987, that he had fantasised that Clifton Hill had been invaded. Over the years, in his fantasies, he had been a soldier in many battles throughout the ages from the fall of Rome right through to the Vietnam war. He had not mentioned any of these fantasies to the Homicide detectives because, "fantasy life is an area that is quite private to people and they don't necessarily express it".

Dr Sime said that when Knight spoke of his fantasies he was very depressed and "therefore more likely" to tell the truth. When Knight told detectives of his desire to find out what it was like to kill and be killed, "it would be more the psychopathic area."

However, Dr Sime felt that Knight was not a psychopath as he showed remorse in prison and psychopaths do not have the capacity for remorse. Knight had shown an obsession with trying to work out why Hoddle Street had occurred. He read widely about other mass murderers and expressed interest in preventing others from repeating his mistakes. Knight had the intelligence to respond to psychotherapy and to use his time in prison "usefully". Dr Sime added that the rehabilitation of Knight was likely if he "is kept occupied and interested and has purpose in life. The problem in life is if you destroy hope, then that's the end."

Clinical psychologist, Mr Kenneth Byrne, told the judge that he had examined and tested Knight on seven occasions for a total of twelve hours.

According to Mr Byrne, the tests indicated that Knight did not lose contact with reality but was very self-centred. "He has little ability to appreciate how his behaviour affects other people, or to reflect on his own role in causing people to react towards him in certain ways. He has an overall high degree of immaturity which was consistent throughout the test material. It also became clear that Mr Knight had a very deeply held personal portrait of himself as a soldier and actually as a war hero. This served to bolster what was rather poor self-esteem in which he felt quite inadequate, and this portrait of himself as a soldier, as a hero, served to make himself feel better, to feel stronger, more competent and more masculine, it is an important part of what was driving this young man."

Mr Byrne added that if Knight saw "some light at the end of the tunnel, that there is a possibility he could profit from his time in jail" and become more mature. Already Knight had enrolled in various correspondence courses including an Arts degree, which were positive indicators.

Prior to Duntroon, Knight's stress level was 85 points, which meant that he had little chance of becoming ill. During the period between Duntroon and Hoddle Street, his stress level had registered at 404 points, according to Mr Byrne.

"...There is an 89 per cent chance, roughly nine chances in ten, that this person will become either medically or psychiatrically ill because of the amount of stress that he is under."

Knight had what is known as "burnt child syndrome" which is common in children brought up in orphanages or foster homes. Persons who, early in life, had "been so hurt by their contact with other people, been so disappointed repeatedly that they give up trying to develop a relationship with others which is warm or supportive or close. They then become what is then described as a loner, as someone who is isolated interpersonally, who may, at first glance, appear to have friends but these are really more acquaintances. They are the kind of person who relates to other persons at arm's length."

Forensic psychiatrist Dr Alan Bartholomew had, in his career, interviewed and assessed approximately 180 murderers. He had interviewed Knight at the request of the police on 10 August 1987, and on two subsequent occasions, to assess whether he was medically insane. In his view Knight had a personality disorder. He is "someone who doesn't quite seem to be like the majority of us, without being ill", with some marked hysterical features.

According to Dr Bartholomew, Knight sought instant gratification, and did not learn particularly well from experience, and was indifferent to the feelings of other people. On 15 August 1987 he had examined Knight in the prison hospital and found him curled up in a corner, almost in the foetal position, with his hands over his head and screaming.

"He was hysterical and suddenly it stopped."

The first time Dr Bartholomew had heard of Knight's fantasy concerning Clifton Hill was during the evidence of Dr Sime and Mr Byrne. Knight had not mentioned it during his interviews with Dr Bartholomew. Dr Bartholomew had some reservations about what Knight had actually told him, which was that he wanted to experience a combat situation and an exchange of gunfire. He had asked Knight if he had really wanted to die, then why did he not stand up and give the police an opportunity to shoot him. Knight had replied, "We are taught to duck in the army."

Dr Bartholomew added that he had "some huge doubts" about Knight's claim to having had a fantasy during Hoddle Street.

"You can only ask him if he did have a fantasy. There is no other way of doing it, it was as though it was in a fantasy and he had a slightly modified consciousness of what was going on probably, which correlates with an hysterical-type personality and he may well have had some degree of disassociation."

During his plea, Mr Richter argued that Knight be given a minimum term to serve so that he could make some contribution to the community, "if and only if it is seen that his release would be appropriate" through the Parole Board.

The prosecutor, Mr Joe Dickson, submitted that Knight was responsible for his actions in that he chose to have the firearms and he chose to load them and go out into the streets and use them. Knight had chosen to undertake military training, it was not forced upon him and the army did not teach him or anyone else to go out and murder defenceless citizens.

"You don't need special skills to kill. Indeed, you very largely don't need special weapons to kill."

Mr Dickson questioned whether Knight had really wanted to fully experience combat as he had always sought cover by hiding behind trees and away from any form of lighting.

With respect to the sentence, the prosecution was not opposed to a minimum term being imposed.

"The important factor is to assure the community that Knight doesn't repeat his crimes, and the lack of predictability or prognosis of Knight's possible repetition of an act of this nature calls emphatically, we submit, for a sentence which would protect the community from him, rather than merely teaching him as part of specific deterrence not to do it again."

Dickson also called for the court to impose a sentence that would deter other people who had similar feelings of rejection and depression from behaving as Knight did. He also stressed that the community be aware that with a minimum sentence Knight would not be released any earlier than that sentence and there was no guarantee that he would be released at that time.

The sentence

"On 9 August 1987 you were responsible for one of the worst massacres in Australian history as a result of which seven people died and nineteen were injured. Many more were fortunate to escape death or injury as you indiscriminately fired over one hundred rounds of ammunition, from three weapons, at passing motorists and at the police as they tried to apprehend you."

These were the opening words of Justice George Hampel at the Melbourne Supreme Court on 10 November 1988. He continued, saying, "The answers to what you did lie in your background, your fragile and disordered personality, and ultimately in your inability to cope with the accumulation of pressures and stresses which operated on you."

He related the events which led to Knight being arrested in McKean Street, North Fitzroy on 9 August 1987. From the time he was adopted to the moments before he took his firearms into the street, he had felt rejected. His opportunities for employment in fields in which he was interested such as the police or the army reserve were closed. Everywhere he turned he was rebuffed, rejected.

Justice Hampel noted the differences in opinion between Dr Sime and Dr

Bartholomew and Mr Byrne. While Dr Sime believed that Knight was in an abnormal state of mind, with reality and fantasy "so mixed up that it was not possible later to determine whether at the time of the shooting you [Knight] were responding to a psychotic delusion or fantasy. The others were of the opinion that you were able to distinguish fantasy from reality and in that sense you were not acting in a state of psychotic delusion."

The Judge took into account Knight's mental condition and the improvement he had shown since incarceration, and that he was undertaking study towards a Bachelor of Arts degree. He was heartened by the fact that his condition was likely to improve as he matured and that he could cease to be a danger to the public.

"It was common ground among the doctors that in 20 to 25 years time the degree of change and therefore the degree of danger which you present can be assessed. In that sense it is thought that your prognosis is reasonable, particularly as you are bright and have a desire to better yourself."

Knight had helped the community to understand why Hoddle Street had happened by cooperating with the professionals, the experts.

"However, to understand your actions is not to excuse them."

The Judge agreed with the sentiments of Robert Richter: that the community allowed the situation to occur.

"A young man of nineteen, encouraged and trained in the use of weapons in combat situations, was permitted to own lethal weapons and have them within easy reach. All this, with the knowledge that some people, particularly some young, less mature people who may not have the make-up to cope with the stresses and influences on them, may snap and go beserk. Unfortunately, our society has not yet matured sufficiently to remove such influences and opportunities and to reorder its priorities so as to ensure, as far as possible, that the use of lethal weapons is not encouraged and their availability is strictly controlled.

"It is true that murder may be committed with other weapons, but it is also true that many killings occur because a firearm is at hand and mass killings rarely occur without the use of lethal firearms. The availability of, and easy access to, firearms were important factors in these killings. General deterrence, and to a greater extent, personal deterrence, are not as significant in this case as they may be in others, although I am mindful of the well-recognised "copycat" phenomenon in mass killings.

"There are, in your case, a number of significant mitigatory factors, such as your age, the absence of prior convictions, your abnormal mental state, your cooperation and plea of guilty and the fact that, from one point of view, the killing and attempted killing of so many people can be seen as part of one continuous course of conduct. It is also significant that these killings were not motivated by gain or revenge and were not accompanied by acts of torture or cruelty.

"However, as Mr Dickson pointed out, they were random and particularly 'public' crimes which caused not only deaths and injury, but also a great amount of suffering to so many people. The only appropriate overall sentence which must be imposed, despite the mitigatory factors I have mentioned, is one of life imprisonment. The sentences must be proportionate to the crimes.

"Accordingly, you are sentenced to be imprisoned for life in respect of each of the seven counts of murder. For each of the 46 counts of attempted murder, you are sentenced to be imprisoned for ten years. These terms will be served concurrently with each other and concurrently with the life sentences."

The Judge then sentenced Knight to serve a minimum of 27 years before being eligible for parole. He considered his age and rehabilitation prospects as well as the matters he had already mentioned which were mitigating factors in passing sentence. The minimum sentence was not only in Knight's interest but also in the interest of the community. He stressed that Knight could not be released until he had served a minimum of 27 years.

Knight, who stood before the judge in his prison greens with his arms folded, made no comment and was led away to the cells. His mother sat in a corner of the court, expressionless.

In September 1992 Knight ordered from prison authorities, along with sporting and gymnasium equipment, five Sega games for use in K division where he was then being held. The games were called *Double Hawk*, *Aerial Assault*, *Alex Kidd in Shinobi World*, *Poseidon Wars 3D* and *Bomber Raid*. All were based on combat and killing. The games were not issued.

In August 1992 Knight appealed to the Federal Administrative Appeals Tribunal because he was forbidden by law from receiving Austudy assistance, a monetary payment to students to help them complete their studies. Knight requested that he and other prisoners be granted an education supplement of $30 a week to enable them to pay for fees, charges, and the costs of books and materials. His appeal was rejected.

Knight became a model prisoner, although he tried to manipulate various prison officers, as he had tried, throughout his life, to manipulate teachers, army officers and friends. He served a short period in another division and he was able to convince prison officers that he should be allowed to make unlimited phone calls. The Governor of the division heard this rumour, disguised his voice and rang the prison requesting to speak to Knight. He was duly put through to him. The prison officers were disciplined and Knight was transferred back to H division.

Knight complained about prison officers who he suspected were stealing his mail. He ordered books accusing prison officers of stealing them when they did not arrive. An investigation by the Prison Squad revealed that Knight had not paid for the books when ordering them so the bookshop had not sent them.

Knight has completed a number of TAFE courses, and in 1995, obtained a Bachelor of Arts degree from Deakin University, majoring in strategic and defence studies, and journalism.

The discipline and conditions in prison suit him as in some ways it is like the army. The constant routine, the decisions all made for him, never a concern about where the next meal is coming from. The only thing missing is his freedom. He spit polishes his shoes, his foot drill is excellent and his bed is made without any creases to be seen. The other prisoners, most of whom have had no military experience, do enough to get by. Knight was the only prisoner in H Division to salute prison officers and is often asked facetiously by them, where his cap was. Some prison officers in H Division called him "Captain" while the inmates knew him as Hoddle.

Postscript

In 1996 Knight developed Chrohns Disease.

At the time of publication, Knight was an inmate at the Port Phillip Prison. He is not eligible for parole until 8 August 2014.